CW00972701

PACIFIC BASIN BOOKS

Editor: Kaori O'Connor

OTHER BOOKS IN THIS SERIES

ABOUT THE AUTHOR

JUKICHI INOUYE

Home Life in Tokyo is a charming and beautifully written account of life in Japan's capital during the 1910's. A remarkable man from a remarkable family, Jukichi Inouye (1862–1929) was sent to England at the age of 11 to study the country and its people. This strategy was to become part of a policy whereby high-ranking Japanese were despatched all over the world, to discover what it was like and to bring back skills useful to their homeland. Inouye was inspired by his own experiences to introduce Japan to the world, and affectionately lays out his countrymen before us, their manners, customs and foibles, in this fascinating memoir. Not only of great historical interest, *Home Life in Tokyo* makes compelling reading for anyone visiting or having an interest in Japan.

HOME LIFE IN
TOKYO

BY JUKICHI INOUYE

KPI
LONDON, BOSTON, SYDNEY AND HENLEY

First published in 1910
This edition published in 1985 by KPI Limited
14 Leicester Square, London WC2H 7PH, England,

Distributed by
Routledge & Kegan Paul plc
14 Leicester Square, London WC2H 7PH, England,

Routledge & Kegan Paul Inc
9 Park Street, Boston, Mass., 02108, USA,

Routledge & Kegan Paul
c/o Methuen Law Book Company
44 Waterloo Road,
North Ryde, NSW 2113, Australia

Routledge & Kegan Paul plc
Broadway House, Newtown Road,
Henley-on-Thames, Oxon RG9 1EN, England

Printed in Great Britain by
St Edmundsbury Press, Bury St Edmunds, Suffolk

ISBN 0-7103-0131-6

PREFACE.

———◦━✦━◦———

THE object of the present work is to give a concise
account of the life we lead at home in Tokyo. I am aware
that there are already many excellent works on Japan
which may be read with great profit; but as their authors
are most of them Europeans or Americans, and naturally
look at Japanese life and civilisation from an occidental
point of view, it occurred to me that notwithstanding the
superabundance of books on Japan, a description of
Japanese life by a native of the country might not be
without interest. I believe it is the first time that such a
task has been undertaken by a Japanese, for works in
English which I have so far seen written by my countrymen treat of abstruse subjects and do not deign to touch
upon such homely matters as are here dealt with.

The information I have endeavoured to convey in
these pages is open, I fear, to the charge of scrappiness.
It is unavoidable from the very nature of the work, the
purpose of which is to select from the wealth of material
in hand such matters as are likely to interest the general
reader. I make no pretension to completeness or com-
prehensiveness of treatment.

I may also explain that I have confined myself in these
pages to the depiction of life in Tokyo. To attempt to

include the various customs that prevail in other parts of the country would be difficult and tedious. I felt that it would add materially to clearness and simplicity if I localised my observations; and it was only natural that Tokyo the capital should be selected for the purpose.

Finally, I would point out that I have made no distinction in the grammatical number of the Japanese words used in this book. It may at times puzzle the reader to find the same words occur, as in Japanese, in both the singular and the plural; but to the Japanese ear the addition of the English plural suffix seems to impair the euphony of Japanese speech.

JUKICHI INOUYE.

Tokyo, Japan,
    September, 1910.

TABLE OF CONTENTS.

ix

ILLUSTRATIONS.

xiii

HOME LIFE IN TOKYO.

CHAPTER I.

TOKYO THE CAPITAL.

The youngest of the capitals—Yedo—The feudal government—Prosperity of Yedo—Its population—The military class—The Restoration—The new government— National reorganisation—Centralisation—Local government—Tokyo the leader of other cities—Struggle between Old and New Japan—The last stronghold of Old Japan.

TOKYO is the youngest of the great capitals of the world, for it was only in 1868 that the present Emperor of Japan left the old city where his ancestors had for centuries lived in seclusion and made the Shogun's stronghold his new home and seat of government. It was a politic move ; because though the Shogun had already resigned his office and surrendered the absolute authority he had exercised in the government of the country, there were still many among his followers who were unwilling to give up their hereditary offices. Had the Emperor then remained in Kyoto and there established his government, it would have been comparatively easy for these discontented partisans of the Shogun to foment an insurrection in the largest city of the Empire, which might assume serious proportions before it could be quelled, especially in those days when the means of communication and transportation were yet very primitive. Hence, it was decided to remove the central government to the possible hot-bed of disaffection and, by the strong arm of the newly-constituted administration, to nip in the bud all signs of rebellion. And so the Emperor and his Court forsook the city which had been the nominal capital for a thousand years and took up their abode in the great military centre which was known as Yedo ; but when the Emperor arrived at the old castle of the Shogun, he gave it the name of Tokyo, or the Eastern Capital, to distinguish it from the late capital, Kyoto, which is on that account also spoken of by the people as Saikyo, or the Western Capital.

But Yedo itself was not very old. Towards the close of the fifteenth century, a renowned warrior, Ota Dokan by name, built a little castle in the village of Yedo. Not long after his death, his family became extinct and others succeeded to the lordship of the little castle. A century later, Tokugawa Iyeyasu, one of the most powerful daimyo, or territorial lords, at the time, became master of the Eight Provinces east of the Hakone Mountains and was on the point of establishing his government at Kamakura, the capital of the first line of Shogun, when he was persuaded by his suzerain, the Taiko Hideyoshi, who is best known to history for his invasion of Korea, to set up his headquarters at Dokan's castle-town which possessed great strategic advantages over Kamakura. Accordingly, in 1590, Iyeyasu came to the village of Yedo and saw that the castle could be developed into a formidable fortress. At once he set to work rebuilding it on a gigantic scale. Bounded on the north and west by a low line of hills, on the south by the Bay of Yedo, and on the east by marshes, it was in those days of bows and arrows and hand-to-hand fights almost impregnable. Behind the hills lay the wide plain of Musashino, across which no enemy could approach unobserved, while it was equally difficult to make a sudden attack upon the castle from the sea or over the marshes. The castle covered upwards of five hundred acres within its inner walls. The swamp was reclaimed, and merchants, artisans, priests, and men of other crafts and professions were induced by liberal offers to settle in the new city. The reclaimed land soon became the principal merchant quarter.

In 1603, Iyeyasu became Shogun, or military suzerain of the country. The Shogun was appointed by the Emperor, who delegated to him the civil and military government of the land. The Emperor made the appointment nominally of his own will; but in reality he was compelled to confer the title on the most powerful of his subjects. It was to Iyeyasu but a confirmation of the influence he already wielded as the most formidable of all the territorial barons. And thus fortified by the Imperial nomination, he began at once to take measures for the general pacification of the country which had for years been plunged in a terrible civil war. His first step was to consolidate his power; and it was done with such success that the Shogunate remained in his family for two hundred and sixty-five years. This predominance of his family was in a great measure due to his skill in providing against those evils which had wrecked former lines of Shogun. All these dynasties had fallen through coalitions of powerful daimyo in different parts of the country and the consequent inability to cope with insurrections which broke out simultaneously in various quarters. To prevent such coalitions Iyeyasu created small fiefs around the territories of great daimyo and gave them to his own adherents, who acted as spies upon these daimyo and frustrated any attempts they might make at conspiracy. The territories along the great highway between Yedo and Kyoto he also apportioned among his followers, so that he had always a ready access to the Emperor's city and could without difficulty control every movement of the Imperial Court. Another plan he formed towards the same end, though it was not actually carried out until the time of his grandson. This was the compulsory residence of the daimyo in Yedo for a certain term every other year; the time for reaching and leaving the city was fixed for each daimyo by the Shogun's government. Their wives, with rare exceptions, remained permanently in Yedo and were practically hostages at the Shogun's court.

The effect of this last measure was the increased prosperity of Yedo. All the daimyo were compelled to keep a house in the city. They built most of their palaces around the castle, and in the same enclosures were erected numerous houses for their retainers. Many daimyo had one or more mansions in the suburbs, not a few of which were noted for their size and their beautiful grounds. The most celebrated of these mansions is now the Imperial Arsenal, the garden of which is one of the sights of Tokyo; and another forms a part of the Palace of the Crown Prince and is also the place where the Imperial chrysanthemum party is given every autumn. The building of the daimyo's mansions, the number of these lords being at the time about two hundred and fifty, naturally attracted merchants, artisans, and other classes of people from all parts of the country. And Yedo rose before long to be the most flourishing city in Japan. It set the example to all the other cities of the Empire, for the daimyo copied in their own castle-towns all that they found to their taste during their forced sojourn in Yedo. This leading position which the Shogun's city held in the feudal days has been retained even in an increased measure by the capital of New Japan.

Some idea of the prosperity of Yedo may be formed from the fabulous accounts of its wealth current among the country-people, who believed that in the main streets of the city land was worth its weight in gold. But a more definite proof is to be found in the computations which were made from time to time with respect to its population. Estimates based upon official records in the early years of the Shogunate are very incomplete. Thus, we are told that there were in 1634, 35,419 citizen householders and twenty-three years later, as many as 68,051, which would give a citizen population, at the rate of 4.2 persons per household, of 148,719 and 285,814 respectively, an increase which is obviously too great for so short an interval. The first trustworthy computation is probably that for the year 1721, when the citizens and their families were said to aggregate about half a million and the military class, with their servants, were put at a little over a quarter of a million. Priests, street-vendors, and beggars with whom the city swarmed did not most likely fall much below fifty thousand, so that we may without any great error take the total population at eight hundred thousand. More than a century later, in 1843, that is, a few years before the outbreak of the dissensions which finally broke up the feudal government, the total population was calculated from similar sources at 1,300,000, of which 300,000 or nearly one quarter, belonged to the military class. Old European travellers put the population of Yedo at various figures ranging from a million and a half to three millions, but the above computation is probably as near the truth as we can hope to get ; and in view of the fact that

Yedo was a dozen years later torn by factions and was practically in a state of civil war, we may safely conclude that its population never exceeded that calculated for the year 1843.

In the above-mentioned estimate the military population of Yedo is put at 300,000. It was computed in the following manner :—There were in the country two hundred and sixty-seven daimyo, every one of whom had two or more mansions in Yedo. The total number of their retainers and servants, with their families, in fact, of all who depended for their subsistence upon these barons, was calculated at over 137,000. The immediate feudatories of the Shogun who all lived in Yedo, numbered 22,000 ; and they, with their families and servants, made up 160,000 From these figures the great influence wielded by the samurai in Yedo may be readily inferred.

Though Yedo thus prospered and the Shogun's rule there seemed firmly established while thousands of samurai were ready to lay down their lives for his welfare, contentment was far from universal in the country. Some of the great daimyo whose ancestors had submitted to Iyeyasu only because of his overwhelming power, would have gladly raised the standard against his descendants if they had seen any chance of success; they knew that two centuries and a half of peace had enervated the Shogun's court and luxurious habits corrupted his government and that it would not be a difficult task to crush him if they could form a coalition against him. But as yet they did not know whom to trust among their fellow-daimyo, and discontent smouldered ready to burst out at the first opportunity.

And that opportunity came in good time. The arrival of Commodore Perry's squadron and the subsequent conclusion of treaties by the Shogun with the foreign powers are matters of history. Centuries of isolation had lured the nation into the belief that it could for ever remain free from all contact with the outside world ; the treaties, therefore, came upon it as a rude awakening from its long-cherished dream, and the possible consequences of the opening of the country to foreign trade and intercourse naturally aroused all its fears. A strong agitation arose in denunciation of the

Shogun's act to which the Emperor's sanction had not yet been given; and when orders came from Kyoto to abrogate the new treaties, the enemies of the Yedo government saw their opportunity; they turned to the sovereign who lived hidden from public gaze in his palace and knew that the salvation of their country could be brought only by the Emperor coming to his own again and assuming the direct government of his people. Leaders among these loyalists were the clans of Satsuma and Choshu, two of the most powerful in Japan, which were later joined by those of Hizen and Tosa, and many others. The Shogun did his utmost to suppress these risings; but being at length convinced, by his utter failure, of his own powerlessness, he resigned his office in 1867 and restored the reins of government into the hands of his sovereign.

The Emperor thereupon made Yedo his capital and to it flocked the men who had helped to overthrow the Shogun's government. The small bands of the latter's adherents who still offered resistance were soon overcome. The national government was reorganised by men from the loyal clans. Though the Shogun had been denounced for his friendly attitude towards foreigners, the new government was even more cordially disposed towards them. The truth is that though the Shogun's enemies were at first all for the expulsion of foreigners out of the country, wiser heads among them soon came to understand that it would not be possible to get rid of these unwelcome visitors and return to the old state of isolation. This conviction was especially brought home to the great clans of Satsuma and Choshu when Kagoshima, the chief town of the former, and Shimonoseki, the seaport of the latter, were bombarded for outrages upon Europeans, one by a British fleet in 1863 and the other by combined squadrons of Great Britain, France, Holland, and the United States in the following year; and they saw that the only way for their country to preserve her independence and secure a footing in the comity of nations was to be as strong as those powers and advance in that path of civilisation which had given them such a commanding position in the world. But so long as the Shogunate stood, they let the anti-foreign agitation take its course; when, however, it fell and the way was cleared for a reorganised government, they set to remodelling it on western lines. Then commenced that process of national renovation which has astonished the world.

With the fall of the Shogunate and the reorganisation of the national government the feudal system was doomed; for such a programme as Japan had already sketched out for herself was incompatible with that medieval form of government. This fact was soon recognised by the daimyo of Satsuma and Choshu, who offered in 1868 to surrender their fiefs; the generous offer was gladly accepted and their example was followed by all the other daimyo. But for the time the ex-daimyo were all appointed governors of their respective fiefs so that they might aid in bringing their former subjects to a full sense of the new condition of things. Three years later, in 1871, the clans were abolished and the whole country was divided into prefectures. The daimyo and their retainers received government bonds in commutation of the incomes they had thitherto derived from their fiefs. The substitution of prefectures for clans was made with the object of breaking up the clan bias which was prejudicial to national unity and of giving the central government a more complete control over the provinces by the appointment to prefectural offices of high officials from Tokyo. For to prevent disaffection or crush open revolt in the provinces, it was necessary to centralise as much as possible the government of the country; and with all its precautions, the new government had to cope with several little uprisings, culminating in the Satsuma rebellion which spread over a greater part of the island of Kyushu and taxed its resources to the utmost. But when this was quelled, the country enjoyed absolute peace; no internal disorder has since taken place with the sole exception of a small local trouble in 1884.

The result of this centralisation was that Tokyo became the centre of the whole national life. Men seeking office hurried to it; students entered its schools; the trades and professions seemed to thrive only in the capital. The measures which the government took at the time tended still further to make Tokyo attractive. For the Restoration and the consequent national reorganisation were for the most part the work of the military class, or rather of the samurai of a few clans under the guidance of a small group of leaders. The country bowed to the inevitable ; but the people had little or no voice in the matter. Whatever drastic measures the government might take, the nation at large could not at a word of command throw off the immemorial traditions in which it had been brought up ; it failed to realise the drift of the new policy its leaders were entering upon. Consequently, the first and most important duty of the government was to guide its people in the path it had taken. New laws were published with minute instructions ; schools of all kinds were established on the western plan, the higher colleges being located in Tokyo ; model government factories were built in the environs of the city ; in short, nothing that a paternal government could do was omitted to take the people by the leading-strings. The higher schools were soon filled ; their graduates found ready employment. The country was ruled by a huge army of officials, who, taking as they did the place of the old samurai in the popular estimation, commanded respect and deference often out of proportion to the importance of their posts, which, with the comparatively high salaries they enjoyed in those days, made government service the most attractive of all occupations. In fact, in the early days, Tokyo may be said to have derived its enhanced prosperity from the superabundance of officials Then too, men of the legal, medical, and other professions all opened practice in Tokyo ; only in recent years when every rank has been overcrowded in the city, have they sought fresh fields in the provinces.

It was not long, however, before the evils of excessive centralisation began to make themselves felt ; and when the task of national reorganisation was fairly complete, steps were taken towards decentralisation. Prefectural assemblies were opened in 1881 as a preliminary measure to the establishment of the national assembly. In 1888, local self-government was granted to provincial cities, towns, and villages, and everything was done to promote local prosperity. The close of the year 1890 saw the opening of the national diet. The war with China in 1894-5 and that with Russia ten years later brought on in either case a sudden activity in all departments of commerce and industry and gave a great impetus to railway enterprise. Many bogus companies, it is true, were formed at the same time, and their collapse was a serious set-back to the national economy. But the undoubted increase of commercial and industrial enterprises has served to relieve the pressure of population upon Tokyo. Osaka, for instance, which has for centuries been a great commercial centre, has within the last few years become as great a centre of industry, with a population exceeding a million. Kyoto, the old capital, remains somnolent ; but Nagoya and the trade-ports of Kobe and Yokohama are forging ahead. In short, though Tokyo, as the capital, will probably remain the the largest city in the Empire, it cannot be denied that it is not now so far in advance of the rest as it was a few years ago. This rise of great provincial cities is a necessary result of the growth of manufacturing industries which are bound, if the country is to prosper, to take the place of agriculture, which is too limited in its scope in a country of such a moderate extent as Japan. It is indeed but a repetition of the rise of the great provincial towns like Birmingham, Sheffield, and Manchester in England in the last century.

Still Tokyo must take the lead in all that pertains to the adoption of western civilisation. Osaka and other manufacturing cities will develop the inevitable but unwelcome phases of western industrialism. Already the labour problem looms before us, and the government must before long legislate on the question. There are also signs of socialistic agitation. But these questions do not affect Tokyo so seriously as other cities, for the factories on its outskirts are comparatively few and the land is too valuable for residential purposes to be occupied by manufactories.

Tokyo will remain what it has always been, the home of the best classes in every department of national life. It will always indicate the high-water mark of oriental culture and occidental influence. Here, as nowhere else, will be seen that antagonism of the two, the pressure of western customs and ways of life following on the heels of the sciences and practical knowledge we are eagerly imbibing from the West and the resistance of oriental traditions and

usages, which refuse to admit a tittle more than is absolutely
necessary to bring the country to a material and intellectual equality
with the foremost nations of the world.   To those who look below
the surface nothing is more interesting in viewing the progress of
Japan than this combination of radicalism and conservatism.   The
Japanese, for all his apparent love of innovation, still retains that
stolid self-satisfaction usually associated with the oriental mind,
though it is no rarer in the West.   He has long recognised that
his country must advance along the lines taken at the Restoration,
but he would have the development take place without the sacrifice
of the national characteristics which have marked his countrymen
from time immemorial.   The agitation which was set up some
twenty years ago for the preservation of these characteristics by
those who feared the mania for everything European which was
then at its height would result in the obliteration of the qualities
which have kept Japan in full vitality through the centuries, still
finds an echo in his heart.   The threatened sudden metamorphosis
of those days was but a passing whim ; the change is now slower
and more subtle, and it is hard to mark the exact line at which
the encroaching tide of European civilisation shall be made to stop.
But the Japanese feels that the line must be drawn somewhere.
The problem is certainly difficult to solve.   It appears hardly
possible to reap the fruits of the material and intellectual progress
of the West and yet to shut out the moral and religious sources of
that progress ; but for all that, it would be premature to pronounce
it impossible.   For we have already done what seemed at first
beyond the verge of possibility.   Who, for instance, of the thousands who nightly thronged to the Savoy Theatre to laugh over
the famous Gilbert and Sullivan opera, would have thought at the
time that a few years thence their country would form a treaty of
alliance with the land of Koko, Yum-yum, and Nankipoo ?   They
would have flouted the very idea ; but that alliance is generally
regarded as a natural outcome of the recent course of events in the
Far East.   Would it be, we wonder, a much harder task to
discriminate the elements of European civilisation?

There are of course people who find their account in advocating the rapid adoption of everything European; but their utmost efforts notwithstanding, there is one citadel which will long resist their attacks and remain almost as purely Japanese as in the days of their forefathers. That impregnable citadel is the home; woman is in Japan as elsewhere the greatest conservative element of national life, and within her sphere of influence tradition reigns as supreme as ever. Globe-trotters who advise their friends to visit this country with as little delay as possible for fear that in a few years Old Japan would cease to be, do not reckon with our domestic life. Japanese women are as a class gentle, pliant, and docile; and these qualities stand them in good stead at home. Whether it be that they manage with all their demureness to twist their lords round their little fingers or that the latter are afraid that any change in home life would develop a new revolting woman who would refuse to be as submissive as they are at present, the fact remains that with the mass of the nation there has been little change in the conditions of domestic life. And what these conditions are and how little the influx of new ideas has affected the home of Old Japan, it is the object of the following chapters to relate.

CHAPTER II.

THE STREETS OF TOKYO.

The area and population of Tokyo—Impression of greater populousness—Street improvements—Narrow streets—Shops and sidewalks—Road-making—Dusty roads—Lamps and street-repairs—Drainage—Street-names—House-numbers—Incongruities.

THE area of Tokyo is not so great as is generally supposed. The people of Yedo used to say that their city was ten miles square; but the extreme length, from north-east to south-west, of Tokyo which does not differ materially in its limits from the old city, is no more than eight miles. The actual area is only 18,482 acres, or nearly twenty-nine square miles. The population fell with the decline of the feudal government and was under a million in the early days of the new regime. The registered population returned to one million in 1884. The municipal census which was taken for the first time on the first of October, 1908, gave the settled population as 1,622,856, composed of 872,550 males and 750,306 females, and the number of families as 377,493. This took no account of the floating population which probably exceeds a hundred thousand; there is also a large population, not less than a quarter of a million, which the rise of rents and the facilities of electric-tramway communication have sent outside the administrative limits of the municipality; it forms, properly-speaking, a part of the population of the city.

Tokyo is therefore a great city; but the stranger who visits its streets for the first time usually gets an impression of an even greater populousness. For the streets are always in the evening teeming with young children; they are not gutter-snipes, but children of respectable parents, small tradesmen or private persons of slender means, who let them run about on the public road rather than romp in their narrow dwellings. But it is not the children alone

A STREET IN YEDO.

(FROM A PICTURE BY SETTAN, 1778-1843).

who think they have a greater right of way over the roads than the public ; for on summer evenings especially, men and women turn out of doors and walk about or sit on benches outside their houses. Shops are completely open and reveal the rooms within, so that whole families may be seen from the streets ; and as most houses are of only one or two stories, people live for the most part on the ground-floor. Even in private residences of some pretensions, the thin wooden walls allow voices to be easily heard on warm days when the rooms are kept open. So that from the people he sees crowding the houses and the noises he hears on all sides, the stranger is often deceived into giving the city credit for a larger population than it actually possesses.

The streets themselves are worth notice. If the foreigner who comes to Japan expects to see in such a great capital the asphalt carriageway and paved sidewalk of his native country, he will be sadly disappointed, for Tokyo, with all its multitudinous thoroughfares, cannot boast even the boulevards and avenues of a European provincial town. In spite of the efforts of the Tokyo municipality, the streets are still narrow. Their total length is about six hundred miles, with a width ranging from one yard to fifty, the average being nine yards. It was decided twenty years ago to widen some three hundred miles of these roads, giving the largest a width of forty yards for carriageway with a footway on either side of six yards, and the smallest a carriageway of twelve yards and a footway one yard wide. The work is to be accomplished in ninety years. Improvements to this end are slowly going on. The fact is that the City Fathers missed a great opportunity in the early years of the new regime when, upon the desertion of the residences of the daimyo and other feudatories after the fall of the Shogunate, land could have been purchased for a song, for it went begging in the heart of the city at less than thirty yen an acre. Those who were wise 'enough to buy it have made big fortunes, for the same land now sells for a hundred thousand yen or more per acre. Now, however, the municipality cannot command sufficient funds to purchase the land needed for improvements along the streets proposed, but buys it up only when it is absolutely necessary to relieve the congestion of traffic ; and elsewhere it waits patiently until a fire burns down the streets and clears the required space for it as, in that case, it will not have to give any compensation for the removal of the houses.

In the old days, the narrowness of the streets did not interfere with such traffic as was then carried on. The daimyo and others of high rank rode in palanquins, and officials went about on horseback ; but the rest of the world walked. The citizens were not allowed to make use of other legs than their own. Those who had to go about much put on cheap straw-sandals, which were thrown away at the end of their journey, so that they did not give a thought to the width or the state of the road as they had in any case to wash their feet afterwards ; while others, of the common people, were, if they met a daimyo's procession, thrust to the wall or oftener into the ditch, and they too cared as little for the width of the thoroughfare. And when a samurai met another in a narrow lane, it was by no means rare, if their sword-scabbards touched in passing, for an altercation to arise and be followed by bloodshed ; but as brawls were in their way, they did not trouble themselves about the widening of the road. Pedestrians, moreover, could always pick their way in any street, and if they saw coming towards them a daimyo's retinue or a company of swash-bucklers, they usually turned into a side-street. To the happy horsemen and palanquin-riders the size of a street was a matter of absolute indifference, for if those on shanks' mare got in their way, it was their lookout. But luckily for these walkers there was little else for them to dodge, for vehicles were comparatively few. The only objects on wheels were handcarts and waggons drawn by horses or oxen. These waggons came from the country with bags of rice, fuel, and other necessaries, and were used, not for their speed which was a snail's pace, but for their carrying power.

In these latter days, however, things have materially changed. Men to-day would be put to the blush by the hale old survivors of those pedestrian times, for they have gone to the other extreme. The conveniences of the jinrikisha, or two-wheeled vehicles drawn by men, and latterly of electric tramways have sapped all energy out of them, and we hear little nowadays of walking feats. There were in 1900 forty-six thousand jinrikisha in Tokyo; but the electric cars, which began to run a few years later, are driving them out of the city, for they are now less than one-half of that number. Still, the pedestrian has need to keep a good lookout on the road, for where, in the absence of footways, men, women, children, vehicles, and horses move about in an inextricable jumble, it is a matter for wonder that accidents are not more frequent. Besides the jinrikisha and electric cars, there are thousands of handcarts, some drawn by coolies and carrying objects of every description from household articles to stones for road-making and trees for gardens, and others drawn by milkmen with their milk-cans, by apprentices with their masters' wares, by pedlars with various assortments to attract the housewife's eye, or by farm-boys with vegetables fresh from the field. There are but a thousand waggons drawn by horses or oxen in Tokyo; but as there are twice as many more in the surrounding country, they are very much in evidence in the city since they make their presence unpleasantly obtrusive in narrow streets. These waggons, however, move slowly and give one time to get out of their way. In this respect they are better to meet than the carriages which drive on indifferent to the width of the road; in narrow streets the latter are preceded by grooms who hustle all loiterers out of the way. They are only less eagerly shunned than the motor-cars and the files of handcarts which move leisurely along with pink flags marked " ammunition" from the Imperial arsenal.

But the Ishmael of the streets of Tokyo was until lately the bicycle. A few years ago there were six thousand of these machines in the city; they were patronised by shop-apprentices who, with large bundles on their backs, scorched through crowded streets careless of accidents to themselves or others. These apprentices were therefore in the policeman's black books; nor did the jinrikisha-man look upon them with any favour, for he regarded bicycling as an innovation intended to defraud him of his fares. But his hostility against the bicycle melted away when he was confronted by the electric car which has proved itself the most formidable of his foes. The bicycle, too, has suffered an eclipse;

for apprentices and others of its patrons find it more expensive to keep it in repair than to travel by the car at the cost of a penny per trip. The motor-car also made its début a few years back and the dust it raises and the smell of petrol it leaves in its track have brought upon it the anathema of all pedestrians ; and though the police regulations prohibit a motor-car from traversing streets less than twelve yards wide, it runs merrily through lanes and small side-streets. It sometimes charges into shops and makes havoc among their merchandise. The pranks it plays in the hands of unskilful chauffeurs are not likely to lessen its unpopularity.

What with carriages, jinrikisha, waggons, handcarts, and bicycles jostling one another and men, women, and children threading their way through the labyrinth or fleeing before motor or electric cars, the more frequented streets of Tokyo present a confused mass of traffic ; but in respect of actual numbers they are really less crowded than western streets of similar importance. The busy appearance is mostly due to the absence of sidewalks, and the bustle is increased by the wayfarers having to run to and fro to get out of the way of the vehicles. In streets provided with sidewalks one would expect less confusion ; but as a matter of fact, people are so used to walking among vehicles of all sorts that they prefer sauntering on the carriageway to quietly pacing the sidewalks ; and it is no uncommon experience to meet a company walking abreast in the middle of the road and dodging carriages while the sidewalks are almost deserted.

Sidewalks are not likely to gain in popularity until improvements are made in the arrangements of shops. There are no streets in Tokyo which are known as fashionable afternoon resorts, because the shops are so constructed that one cannot stop before them without being accosted by the squatting salesmen. Only in a few main streets are there regular rows of shops with show-windows against which one could press one's nose to look at the wares exhibited or peer beyond at the shop-girls at the counter ; but then business is not done in Japan over the counter, nor do shop-girls hide their charms behind a window, for the shops are open to the street and the show-girls, or "signboard-girls" as we call them, squat

A SHOP IN TOKYO.

at the edge visible to all passers-by and are as distinctive a feature of the shop as the signboard itself. The goods are exhibited on the floor in glass cases or in piles, a custom which is not commendable when pastry or confectionery is on sale, for standing as it does on the south-eastern end of the great plain of Musashino, Tokyo is a very windy city, and the thick clouds of fine dust raised by the wind on fair days cover every article exposed and penetrate through the joints of glass cases, so that in Tokyo a man who is fond of confectionery must expect to eat his pound of dirt not within a lifetime, but often in a few weeks. If one stops for a moment to look at the wares, he is bidden at once to sit on the floor and examine other articles which would be brought out for his inspection, whereupon he has either to accept the invitation or move on. One seldom cares therefore to loiter in the street. The only shops that are often crowded by loiterers are the booksellers' and cheap-picture dealers'.

But even more unpleasant than the narrowness of the streets is the state in which many of them are to be found. In a few streets the roadway has been dug up and pyramidal stones have been laid on the bed with the points up; they are then covered with earth and broken stone and finished with a top-dressing of gravel. They are not, however, rolled as steam-rollers have only lately made their appearance in Tokyo; sometimes small stone-rollers, about two feet in diameter, are drawn over the metal by a dozen coolies, but the work is inefficient as the pressure of such toy rollers is too slight to make any sensible impression. For the most part, therefore, newly-made roads are left to be levelled with the beetle-crushers of the long-suffering public. The municipality finds it the cheapest way. This is bad enough on the gravelled road, but the tortures it inflicts on men and beasts of burden, to say nothing of the rapid wear and tear of vehicles, are indescribable when the thoroughfare is repaired in the orthodox style. Whenever the road wants mending, cartloads of pebbles are, according to this method, brought from the beds of the rivers in the neighbourhood of Tokyo and scattered over the highway. They are laid evenly, but not levelled or rolled. The public press them down as they walk with their clogs, sandals, or boots; immediately any part is embedded in the soil, that path alone is used till it is beaten flat, so that one often sees a narrow path meandering in a wide stone-covered road, along which all traffic is carried on and the rest of the road is practically unused. When this path is beaten in and becomes hollow, more cartloads of pebbles are thrown upon it and the public recommence their patient task of road-levelling. But fortunately for them, they are materially aided in this benevolent work by the solstitial rains, which when they come down in torrents, soon bury the stones in the clayey soil, and for the nonce the people walk over it rejoicing until the municipality sets them a new task; or the rains have done their work but too well and the poor pedestrians find themselves wading through quagmire.

Indeed, quagmire is what we find in many streets after rain; for the supply of rubble is necessarily limited as it comes mostly from the rivers in and about the city, and consequently a majority of roads are left uncared for. These, after a heavy rain, are covered with a thick coating of mud, which when the sun has dried it, leaves behind deep ruts, making the roads more unpleasant to walk on than when covered with pebbles. In midsummer when the ridges of these ruts have been pulverised and blown in all directions so that one appears to be walking on sand, the roads are watered twice or more every day. The watering is done on high roads by coolies with small hand-drays out of which water is sprinkled spasmodically, and as the men stop from time to time to take breath, there are on many spots pools of water in which one can soil one's footgear as effectually as on the rainiest day. But worse still is the watering done by private persons on the part of the road facing their dwellings. These merely ladle the water from their pails and sprinkle it in splashes, leaving in the middle of the street puddles for children to make mud-cakes in. In short, the great objection to the way in which the streets are watered in Tokyo is that it is too much for laying the dust, but not enough for flushing the roadway.

The pedestrian has therefore to be very careful in selecting the part of the road to walk on in both wet and fine weather. This is not very difficult in the daytime; but at night, especially when there is no moon, the task is hard to accomplish with success;

for rarely are street lamps set up at the public expense, and in most streets the inhabitants have lamps for their own convenience over their front doors or gates ; but the light of these lamps is very meagre as they are naturally not intended to guide the stray wayfarer over the road. But even these are of some service in streets of shops where the front doors are ranged pretty closely together ; in roads, however, where there are only private houses, the gates being far apart, the lights are also at some distance from each other and the passenger has mostly to trust to his luck to keep himself clean. That luck, however, deserts him at times, for the repairs which the roads seem to undergo in every part of the city are astonishingly frequent. It is not the mere mending that is the cause of the trouble, but the constant pulling up of the roads for laying or repairing gas-pipes, water-pipes, and what not that so often brings one to an *impasse*. As, moreover, the authorities work independently of one another, a road which has been dug up for one purpose and filled in again, may be pulled up for another. Matters are not likely to improve in the near future, for before long the telegraph and telephone authorities must have a hand in digging up the road; at present the wires are overhead, but the poles are already overweighted and cannot be loaded much more without serious danger to traffic. Electric-light wires are equally menacing ; and the situation is only aggravated where the electric cars run through crowded streets of the business quarters.

The wretched state of the roads after rain is undoubtedly due to imperfect drainage. The cross-section of the roads has little or no curvature or gradient, and the gutters, where they have been made, do not drain off and are only receptacles for muddy stagnant water. They are occasionally cleaned by heaping the mire on the road-side. And yet, curious to state, in spite of these insanitary methods, the rate of mortality in Tokyo is not so high as might be expected. It varies from twenty to twenty-five per thousand on the registered population and therefore must be less when the floating population is taken into account. It shows that Tokyo is not an unhealthy city, and when the municipality has carried out the plan it has made for a drainage system, the Japanese capital will probably compare favourably with most other great cities of the world.

There is one peculiarity about the streets of Tokyo which deserves mention, that is, the way they are named. Of course every thoroughfare has a name given to it; but it differs from streets in other countries in that name being the designation, not of the thoroughfare itself, but of the section or piece of land through which it runs. Thus, two or more thoroughfares which run through the same section are known by the same name; in a large section there may be a dozen streets running in all directions and bearing the same name. When a road runs on the boundary of two sections, the opposite sides would be known by different names, and a man walking in the middle of such a road would be perambulating two streets at one and the same time. Some of the larger sections, if regularly built, are divided on the main road into subsections by streets crossing them; but irregular streets are arbitrarily subdivided so that it is often very hard to find one's way through them. As many sections are full of tortuous streets with turnings and alleys, the numbering of houses in a section is often complicated, and one seldom knows where the numbers begin or end. Frequently consecutive numbers are to be found in entirely different directions and in hunting up a number, one has to traverse the length and breadth of the section before one comes upon it.

The numbering of houses is further complicated by the fact that the same number is given often to dozens, and sometimes to hundreds, of houses. The explanation is that the numbering first took place while the great daimyo's mansions were still standing; and when they were pulled down and cut up into smaller lots, these lots retained the same numbers. There are in Tokyo at least two of these great estates which have been divided into nearly a thousand house-lots. It is indeed hard to see how these houses could be renumbered, because in that case every division of an estate would necessitate the renumbering of the whole street, which, in a city like Tokyo where the sizes of houses are constantly changing, would be simply intolerable. Besides these divisions of mansions, we must take into account the frequency of fires.

Changes take place not seldom after a fire in the number of houses in a street, and it would of course be impracticable to renumber the whole street whenever, a portion of it is burnt down. Sometimes an additional designation, usually a second set of numbers, is given to a group of houses with the same street-number; but fancy names, such as are common in the suburbs of London, are hardly ever given to dwelling-houses. It may therefore be imagined that it is no light task to look up a friend in an unfamiliar quarter.

The stranger, then, who visits the streets of Tokyo will find much to arouse his curiosity in the open, windowless shops, the jinrikisha, the native dresses of men and women, the throngs of hawkers, and the ceaseless din of traffic ; and at the same time, as he comes to Japan usually in search of the quaint and *bizarre*, he will perhaps be disappointed when he sees the countless overhead wires, the electric trams, omnibuses, and bicycles, European clothes of all shades and descriptions, and other encroachments of western civilisation, which he had hoped to leave behind him and which somewhat shock his artistic sense in their new surroundings. But these inæsthetic innovations he must put up with, for they are typical of the present stage of Japanese civilisation, and nowhere else are they more marked than in Tokyo. The herculean task Japan has set herself leaves her little leisure to consider its artistic effects ; she is too much in earnest to waste a thought on the awkward cut of the habiliments she is donning ; and only when she has so adapted herself as to fit them exactly, will she turn her attention to their frills and trimmings.

CHAPTER III.

HOUSES : EXTERIOR.

Name-plates—Block-buildings—Gates—The exposure of houses—Fires—House-breaking—Japanese houses in summer and winter—Storms and earthquakes—House-building—The carpenter—The garden.

WE have already said that the complicated way of numbering streets and the inclusion of a large group of buildings in one number make it hard to find any particular house. They necessitate a dreary going to and fro through a series of thoroughfares, which is very trying to one's temper and would in most cases oblige one after a long search to give it up altogether, were it not for the circumstance that not only shops and private offices, but also nearly every private house, has a name-plate nailed over the front-door or on the gate-post. If, therefore, we can, in the course of our wanderings through a street, alight upon the right number, we can generally find the house, provided there are not too many with the same number. The name-plate has usually inscribed on it the number of the house and the name of its occupant, and his title if he is a peer. Besides the name-plate, there is on the gate-post the brass-badge of the insurance company if the house has been insured, to enable the company's private firemen to identify the house and give necessary assistance in case of a fire in the neighbourhood. The gate-post has also the telephone-number placarded in large figures for the telephone-rate collector's convenience.

Shops and most mercantile offices open directly upon the street; but with respect to private houses there is no definite rule. Cheap houses are built in long blocks; of these the worst description is to be found in back courts; they are of one story, or if of two stories, the second has a very low ceiling. They are usually in a dilapidated condition and propped up on all sides; they are in fact our slums. The smallest of these houses is only twelve feet by nine. A block may be made up of a dozen such houses, six

IN THE SLUMS.

on either side with a wall running through the middle from end to end. It is a peculiarity of our tenement houses which have to be low on account of the frequency of earthquakes that they are thus divided vertically into narrow compartments and differ in this respect from the many-storied houses in the West, which are divided horizontally and occupied in flats. While the ground-rent is still comparatively low, this habitation in transverse sections, so to speak, is feasible for the poor ; but even now, as the rent is steadily rising in all quarters, the tendency is to drive these humble dwellers outside the city limits. As it is, only in the poorer districts are these miserable houses to be seen ; for in the busier quarters the ground-rent is already too high for them. But buildings in blocks are not all of the poorest kind, though it must be admitted that dwelling in a "long building," as a block of this description is called, implies on the face of it life on a humble scale. In the old times well-to-do retainers, who had large houses of their own in the country, lived when in Yedo in the "long buildings" surrounding their lord's mansion. Small shops are also built in blocks.

Though many private houses in the business quarters have no gates, those of any pretensions in the residential districts where land is naturally cheaper, are mostly provided with them. It is not usual for professionals in humbler walks of life and for artisans to live within a gate ; but officials and others of some social standing prefer to have one to their houses. Sometimes there is a single gate to a large compound with a number of small houses in it ; in such a case the gate-post is studded with name-plates. Gates, too, vary in size and form. The most modest are no more than low wicker-gates which can be jumped over and offer no bar to intrusion. Others are of the same make, but stand higher so that the interior can be seen only through cracks. But the most common consist of two square posts with hinged doors which meet in the middle and are kept shut by a cross-bar passing through clamps on them. These gates may be of the cheapest kind of wood, such as cryptomeria, or may be massive and of hard wood. Another common kind has a roof over it with a single door which is hinged on one post and fastened on to the other and provided with a small sliding-door for daily use. The larger pair gates have also small side-doors for use at night when they are themselves shut.

After entering by the gate, we come to the porch ; the distance

between them varies with the size and exposure of the house. It
is not true, as has been said by some writers on Japan, that in our

A HOUSE AND A GATE.

houses the parlour and the garden invariably occupy the rear while
the kitchen is in front. Their position depends upon the exposure
of the house. No people short of savages probably lead a more

open-air life than we do in our wooden houses. Our paper sliding-doors, which are our only protection against wind and cold in winter, admit both light and air ; and we provide personally against the cold by wearing wadded clothing and huddling over braziers, while in summer all the sliding-doors are often removed to let the cool breeze blow through the house. It becomes, then, an important matter in building or selecting a house to see that its principal rooms are so arranged as to get the warm rays of the sun in winter and the cool breezes in summer. As both these are to be obtained from the south, the principal rooms are made to expose their open side to that direction. In winter the exposure of these rooms makes a vast difference in the consumption of charcoal as the sun shining through the open side warms the rooms more thoroughly than the braziers can do. Next to the south, the east is the favourite direction, as the east wind coming over the Pacific Ocean is milder than the north or west. The west wind, crossing as it does the snowy ridges of Central Japan, is cold in winter while the piercing rays of the westering sun make the rooms intolerably hot in summer ; and the north wind is cold in winter and in summer breezes seldom come from that direction. In short, then, the principal rooms face the south, if possible, or south-east, or sometimes the east. As the garden is naturally in front of the principal rooms, its position depends upon theirs, and it is made to lie, if possible, on the south side of the house. If the gate is on the north side of the premises, it is close to the house ; but if it is on the south side, the garden intervenes. It should, however, be stated that some people purposely make their principal room face north ; their reason is that if the garden lay south of the house, the trees and plants in it would display their north or rear side to those within, and they are therefore willing to put up with the cold blasts from the north for the pleasure of looking at the front and sunny side of their plants.

Most houses in Japan are made of wood. In Tokyo only a little over one-eighth of the houses are made of other materials, that is, of brick, stone, or plaster, so that the capital may be said to be a city of wooden houses. It is therefore, needless to add,

often ravaged by fire. In old Yedo fires were known as the
" Flowers of Yedo," being as much among the great sights of the

A ROOFED AND A PAIR GATE.

city as the cherry blossoms on the south-east bank of the River
Sumida, the morning-glories of Iriya, or the chrysanthemums of
Dangozaka, for which Tokyo is still noted. Under the feudal

government occurred several fires which burnt down tens of thousands of houses, and even under the new regime disastrous fires are not unknown. On two occasions, in 1879 and 1881, over ten thousand houses were destroyed ; but the last great conflagration took place in 1892 when four thousand buildings were devoured by the flames. Since then, though fires have been frequent enough, their ravages have been more limited, thanks to a more efficient system of fire-brigades and plentiful supply of water. During the last few years the average number of houses annually destroyed has been about seven hundred, which cover an area of seven and a half acres ; and as the total area of buildings in Tokyo is three thousand seven hundred acres, the fires destroy every year one five-hundredth part of the city. The actual loss of property is not so great as might at first sight be supposed ; for it is a notorious fact that houses in Tokyo are not so carefully constructed as in Kyoto and other cities, and the greater risks from fire incurred in the capital discourage the building of costly houses unless they are to stand on extensive grounds. Formerly it was calculated that the average life of a house was about thirty years ; but now the lesser frequency of fires would give them a much longer lease. This is comforting to house-owners ; but it must be confessed that wooden houses more than thirty years old are not pleasant to live in. The timber, unless extremely well-seasoned, becomes warped and the pillars of the house get out of the perpendicular, with the result that the sliding-doors refuse to close flat upon them but leave a space at the top or bottom through which the cold wind whistles at will in winter. This is the case even with carefully-built houses, while in others the defects are still more glaring. The jerry-builder's hand is conspicuous in most houses to let, and the rent is high compared with the cost of construction. The landlords protest that they have to charge a high rent as whole blocks may be swept away in one night through malice or stupidity. And there is something to be said for their argument, especially as fire insurance is still far from universal, for it is strange when one comes to think of it that there are not more destructive fires. It is so easy to burn down a wooden house. A rag soaked with kerosene is enough to destroy any number of houses and is the favourite means with incendiaries who hope to steal household goods which are brought out in confusion into the street whenever there is a fire in the neighbourhood. Besides, a slight act of carelessness or neglect may lead to a terrible conflagration ; a candle left too near a paper sliding-door was the origin of the great fire of 1892 already-mentioned. Similarly, a kerosene lamp or a brazier overturned, a pinch of lighted tobacco or an unextinguished cigar-end, an over-heated stove or a piece of red-hot charcoal dropped on the floor, these are among the commonest causes of fires ; and even the cheap Japanese matches, of which as the splints are not dipped in paraffin, at least half a dozen are needed to light a cigarette in the open air, are responsible for as many fires every year. Since such slight accidents may at any time lead to great disasters, the inhabitants, as they go to bed, are never sure, especially in crowded quarters, of still having a roof over their heads next morning. They may be aroused from their slumbers by the dreaded triple peal of the alarm-bell and find the neighbouring street or next door wrapped in flames, and just manage to run out of their houses with nothing but the clothes on their backs. We are, however, so used to the fire-alarm that if the peals are double to indicate that the fire is in the next district, we only get out of bed to look at it from idle curiosity and turn in again unless our house is leeward of the burning district or we have to run to the assistance of a friend there ; and if the bell gives only single peals, which signify that at least one district intervenes between the burning street and the fire-lookout, we turn in our beds and perhaps picture to ourselves the lively time they must be having in that street. A fire is, on account of its uncertainty and suddenness, only less feared than an earthquake, and the general feeling among the citizens is that of insecurity.

There is, however, still another element of insecurity in wooden houses. House-breaking is by no means difficult in Tokyo. In the daytime the front entrance is generally closed with sliding-doors which can, however, be gently opened and entered without attracting notice unless some one happens to be in an adjoining room. The kitchen door is usually kept open, and it is quite easy to sneak into the kitchen and make away with food or utensils. Tradesmen, rag-merchants, and hawkers come into the kitchen to ask for orders, to buy waste-paper or broken crockery, or to sell their wares, so that there is nothing unusual in finding strange men on the premises. Sometimes these hawkers are really burglars in disguise come to reconnoitre the house with a view to paying it a nocturnal visit. At night, of course, the house is shut and the doors are bolted or fastened with a ring and staple, but very seldom locked or chained. As the doors are nothing more than wooden

DOOR-FASTENINGS.

frames with horizontal cross-bars, on which boards less than a quarter of an inch thick are nailed, it would not be difficult to cut a hole with a chisel large enough for the hand to reach the bolt or the staple or to clear the whole space between the cross-bars for the body to pass through. But quieter methods are generally preferred. Single burglars usually come in by the skylight, closed at night by a small sliding-door, which does duty as chimney in the kitchen, or crawl under the floor which is some two feet from the ground, by tearing away the boarding under the verandah and come up by carefully removing the loose plank of the floor, under which fuel is kept in the kitchen. If the burglars are in a gang, they naturally come in more boldly than these kitchen sneaks. Once inside, the thief has the run of the house as all the rooms communicate by sliding-doors and are never locked, and the whole household is at his mercy. Since, then, houses are so easy of entry, it might be supposed that burglaries are very frequent in Tokyo ; that such is not the case is probably due to the somewhat primitive methods pursued by these gentry and to the effective detective system of the police authorities. The strict police registration of every inhabitant and the easy access of all the rooms in a house make concealment very difficult, and the criminal is readily shadowed as he wanders from place to place throughout the Empire.

To this general insecurity from fire and burglary all wooden houses are subject ; but if we take into consideration the actual number of homes which fall victims to them, we are compelled to conclude that though the feeling of insecurity may always be present, the chances of its being realised are somewhat remote, so that it is not so bad as it looks in these respects to live in the wooden houses of Tokyo. Fires are most frequent in winter from braziers being then in use and kerosene lamps being in requisition for longer hours every evening, and burglaries, too, increase in the same season from the sufferings of the poor being intensified. But in the summer heat the Japanese house is extremely pleasant. The whole house is open and lets the cool breeze blow from end to end ; bamboo screens are hung in front of the verandah where it is exposed to the burning rays of the sun. On the second story we sit in thin cotton garments and feel the breeze all over the ,body, and look down upon the landscape garden before us or beyond at the peerless Mount Fuji on the south-west or at Mount Tsukuba on the northern edge of the Musashino plain. It is especially enjoyable when fresh from a hot bath, we squat or loll on the mats, fan in hand, and engage in desultory talk or in a quiet game until the sun sinks and wine and fish are brought before us. The Japanese house is an ideal summer villa when we can rest ourselves from the heat and dust of the busy city. But in the city itself it is far otherwise. The dust blows in with every gust, and the house, to be properly kept, must be swept several times a day. The narrowness of the streets and lowness of the ceilings give the shops in crowded quarters insufficient light, though more than enough of dusty air. But in winter we feel the inadequacy of wooden houses; it is next to impossible to keep out the cold effectually; a room never gets thoroughly warmed. The wind blows in through the crevices of the sliding-doors, for the edges on which these doors meet are flat and never dovetailed. The paper of the doors is porous, and through its pores the air gets in; there is certainly this to be said for it that in a Japanese room one need never fear asphyxiation, however much charcoal may be burning in the braziers. These braziers are for warming the hands and the face if one crouches over them; but for the body, we get the warmth from the abundance of wadded clothing. We can therefore keep fairly warm if we merely sit on the mats; but directly we move or stand up, the cold attacks us. Most Japanese are, however, used from childhood to these cold rooms and do not feel the chill. Many of them think nothing of sitting for hours in a cold draught.

A Japanese wooden house looks pretty when new; but after some years when the outside is weather-beaten, the pillars begin to warp and the walls to crumble, its charms, too, are on the wane. A well-built house may be comfortable for twenty or at most thirty years, after which it is uninhabitable without considerable repairs. The few private houses which still remain that were built before the Restoration are at best rain-proof, and afford little protection against wind. There are certainly public buildings, such as shrines and temples, which have survived many centuries and are not unfrequently picturesque as they peer through their groves; but a close inspection would soon reveal the repairs they have undergone, pillars repainted, roofs retiled, gable-ends regilt, and the interior generally renovated. There is wanting in Japanese dwelling-houses that poetical charm which age lends to brick and stone buildings in the West with their dark-stained casements and ivy-mantled walls; and time which mellows and imparts a deeper hue to stone dry-rots wood and saps it of its strength, and long before storms make any impression upon brick, the frame-house falls to the ground. But in Japan it is not merely wind and rain that houses have to contend against; the earthquake is the foe that makes them to totter. Every earthquake, by shaking them up, tends to loosen the joints and disturb the equilibrium of the building; and as a good many such shocks, about a hundred and fifty, occur in the course of a year, their combined effect is by no means negligible. Houses have therefore to be built with the possible effects of earthquakes in view.

The most obvious of the provisions against earthquake effects is the small height of the houses. Most dwelling-houses in Tokyo have only one or two stories; there are far more of the former than of the latter; and even of the latter kind, the upper story is usually much smaller than the lower. The floor stands about two feet from the ground; the ceiling is eight or nine feet in height on the lower floor and often less than eight feet on the upper. The outer walls sometimes rest on a low stone course; but the verandah is supported by short wooden pillars resting on stone slabs. The house, in fact, merely stands on a few stone slabs and courses and can, as is indeed sometimes done, be lifted bodily and removed to another site. Over the verandah, if there is a story above, a small roof projects to prevent the rain from blowing into the rooms behind it. The housetop is never flat, but has a great rough-hewn beam for roof-tree with rafters on either side, which are covered with lath. Semicircular tiles are laid over the roof-tree with a thick substratum of mortar, while the slanting sides are covered with pantiles. The gutter is sometimes made of copper, but more commonly of bamboo or tinplate. The roof is built before the walls or the floor. First, the ground is levelled and the stone foundation made for the pillars. Meanwhile the pillars, joists, beams, and ties have been made, and are now set up and fitted. As soon as the frame is built, the roof is put on and covered for the while with matting so as to enable the workmen to work inside irrespectively of the weather. The verandahs, floors, ceilings, and grooves for sliding-doors are made. The carpenter's work is then done; and the tiler is called in for the roof-tiles, the plasterer for the walls, and the joiner for the sliding-doors. The tiles are of a uniform size and generally of the same shape. The

A HOUSE WITHOUT A GATE.

walls are made with a lathing or frame of slender bamboo, which is covered with clay and over it one or more coatings of plaster. In some buildings the coatings of the outer walls are replaced by clapboards, which are painted black if the wood is of an inferior quality or too weather-beaten. The paper-hanger is called in to paper the sliding-doors and the mat-maker comes to cover the floor with mats. The house is then complete.

In Japan there was neither an architect nor a builder as a distinct calling. Even now, ordinary dwelling-houses are not built by either of them; it is the carpenter who has charge of their construction. The carpenter's is a dignified craft; he is called in Japanese the "great artificer," and stands at the head of all artisans. In the building of a house, a master carpenter is called in; he prepares the plans, and if they are approved, he sets to work with his apprentices and journeymen. The other artisans, the tiler, the plasterer, and the joiner, work under him. He is not as a rule an educated man and knows his trade from having worked at it from apprenticeship; and for his diligence or intelligence he has been set up by his master, or it may be that he has found a wealthy patron, or more probably, he comes of a carpenter's family and has succeeded his father. Making use only of the knowledge acquired during his term of apprenticeship or service as journey-man, the master carpenter has little occasion to display his inventiveness or originality, for he need only follow the time-honoured conventions which hold sway in his craft as in all other arts and crafts of the country. Hence, monotony is a distinctive mark of Japanese domestic architecture; there is a sameness of style in all our dwelling-houses. The chief and perhaps the only point upon which the carpenter has to bring his ingenuity to bear is the arrangement of the rooms. If he has a large site to build on, he will spread out the building so as to secure as much southerly or south-easterly exposure as possible without counteracting inconveniences; but if the site is confined, he has to change his plans accordingly. Much depends upon the lie of the land. His object is to have no rooms that are useless or inconvenient. This is not such an easy task as may appear at first sight in a house in which, with one or two exceptions, the rooms may be turned into any use; for the very indefiniteness of their disposal makes the problem more difficult to solve than in the case of a house in which a definite use is assigned to each room at the time of erection.

Convention also makes itself felt in the laying out of a Japanese garden, though a greater latitude is allowed to the gardener's ingenuity. Still the principles remain unchanged. In a large

A GARDEN.

garden we usually find a pond, dry if no water is available, and surrounded with rocks of various shapes, and a knoll or two behind the pond with pines, maples, and other trees, and stone lanterns here and there. A few flowering shrubs are in sight, but these are planted for a season; thus, peonies, morning-glories, and chrysanthemums are removed as soon as they fade, while corchoruses and hydrangeas are cut down leaving only the roots behind. The chief features of the garden are the evergreens like the pine, trees whose leaves crimson in autumn like the maple, and above all, the flowering trees like the plum, the cherry, and the peach. A landscape garden presents, when the trees are not in blossom, a somewhat severe or solemn aspect; we do not expect from it the gaiety which beds of flowers impart. Indeed, many European flowering plants have of late been introduced, such as anemones, cosmoses, geraniums, nasturtiums, tulips, crocuses, and begonias; but they still look out of place in a Japanese garden. Roses are sometimes planted, but they are almost scentless. The humidity of the climate appears to militate against the perfume of flowers.

CHAPTER IV.

HOUSES: INTERIOR.

A Japanese room is measured, not by feet and inches, but by the number of mats it contains. A mat consists of a straw mattress, about an inch and a half thick, with a covering of fine matting which is sewn on at the edges of the mattress either by itself or with a border, usually dark-blue and an inch wide, of coarse hempen cloth. It is six feet long by three wide; this measure is not always exact, but may vary by an inch or more in either direction. When a house is newly built, the mat-maker comes to make mats to fit the rooms in it. But in spite of the variation, the size of a room is always given in the number of mats it holds, so that we never know the exact dimensions of a room. The smallest room has two mats, that is, is about six feet square; the next smallest is three-matted, or three yards by two. Four-matted rooms are sometimes to be found; but such rooms are unshapely, being four yards long by two wide. A room with four and a half mats is three yards square and has the half mat, which is a yard square, in the centre. The next size is six-matted, or four yards by three and is followed by the eight-matted, or four yards square. The ten-matted room is five yards by four and the twelve-matted is six yards by four. It is only in large houses that there are rooms with fifteen or more mats. In some restaurants and story-tellers' halls we come upon rooms with a hundred mats. Some rooms have five or seven mats; but they are really of six or eight mats with the space of one mat occupied by a closet or an alcove. It will thus be seen that in most rooms the length is either equal to the breadth or at most only half as much again. This tends to make the proportion between the two somewhat monotonous.

The commonest rooms are those with four and a half, six, or eight mats, that is to say, rooms which are three or four yards square or four yards by three. Such rooms would be very small

A SIX-MATTED ROOM AND VERANDAH.

in a house built in European style ; there would hardly be elbow-room and one could not move an inch without knocking down some piece of furniture. But in a Japanese room there is but little furniture, and certainly none that one could bring down by knocking against it with the exception, perhaps, of the screen. Our rooms look very bare to foreigners and appear to lack comfort to those who have lived in European apartments ; but from the Japaneses point of view, rooms furnished in the approved European style suffer from excess of furniture and partake too much of the nature of a curiosity shop or a museum.   This may be going too far ; but there is undoubtedly something repugnant to the Japanese canons of taste to find all the art treasures of the house exhibited from day to day on the walls or in the corners of the rooms to which guests have access.   The absence of movable furniture in a Japanese room, by allowing more free space, makes it look larger than a European room of the same size.   We squat on the mats, and our line of vision, being consequently much lower than if we sat in a chair, gives the room a further appearance of greater size.   The illusion is kept up by the lowness of the ceiling, which though seldom more than eight or nine feet high, seems to be loftier as we squat under it.

The size of a mat being, as already stated, roughly six feet by three, the yard has naturally become the unit by which other parts of a room or a house are measured.   Thus, the sliding-doors are usually a yard wide.   As these doors are always in pairs and move in two grooves each at top and bottom, there are a pair in grooves six feet long and two pairs in those of twelve feet ; but in grooves nine feet in length there are either a pair or two, commonly the latter, in which case the sliding-doors are each three-quarters of a yard wide.   The sliding-doors are of two kinds : the *shoji*, or paper sliding-doors, which are partitions admitting light, and the *fusuma* (also called *karakami*), or screen sliding-doors, which merely serve as partitions.   The *shoji* consists of a wooden frame, an inch or more in thickness, with thinner cross and vertical pieces forming lattices about nine inches wide by five high.   It is covered on the outside with thin rice-paper, which admits light but is not transparent.   It is of use when there is light on one side as at the verandah or window or where a room or a passage would be too dark if *fusuma* were put up.   The *fusuma* consists of a wooden frame with a few pieces within, which is pasted over on both sides with thick paper and covered with ornamental paper.   It is quite opaque.   The frame and lattices of the *shoji* are of plain white wood ; but the frame of the *fusuma* is often varnished, though it may also be left plain. The *fusuma* has a small hollow handle, a few feet from the floor, which is sometimes highly ornamented.

The verandah is also usually three feet wide. It consists generally of long narrow planks ranged parallel to the grooves of the sliding-doors, though it is sometimes made up of wider pieces set at right angles to them. In the former case the planks, as they age, shrink and leave cracks between, which admit light when the outer doors or shutters are closed in the daytime. Bamboos are sometimes laid between the pieces to cover the shrinkage. The shutters run in grooves on the outer edge of the verandah. They are also three feet wide and kept in a receptable at the end of the groove. The last one only is usually bolted. There are similar shutters at all the windows, which are also provided with paper sliding-doors and lattices or bars as precautions against house-breaking. When a verandah runs along more than one room, there are pillars on its outer edge just inside the groove of the shutters and opposite the pillars dividing the rooms. All sets of sliding-doors need a pillar to close against at either end.

The smallest houses are those in the slums which have only three yards' frontage and a depth of four yards. The entrance, the space for kitchen utensils and the sink, and perhaps a closet or cupboard would leave room for little more than three mats, on which the whole family live ; but as children spend all their playtime outside and come in only for meals, it is at night that the house is crowded, and even then as they sleep higgledy-piggledy, a couple or so of children do not inconvenience their parents to any appreciable extent. A two-roomed house is common enough and is not confined to the slums. A childless old couple, when the wife has to do the household work, find such a house large enough for them. Artisans also live in them. Three-roomed houses, too, are very common. Houses built in blocks are oftenest of this size. They are made up of the porch, the sitting-room, and the parlour or drawing-room. These three rooms are the essential portions of a house ; and larger houses merely add to them. A visitor calls at the porch, the paper sliding-door is opened, he is invited to come in, he leaves his hat and greatcoat in the porch, and enters the parlour. The master, or in his absence his wife, entertains him there, while the rest of the family remain in the sitting-room. In cold weather the sliding-doors between the two rooms are closed; but in summer they are kept open, or frequently doors with reed screens within the frames are used. These admit the breeze and let the people in the other room be seen; but the fiction of their invisibility is kept up and those in the inner room are not obliged to greet the visitor.

In a four-roomed house the fourth room may be the servant's room, if one is kept, a toilet-room, or a reserve room without any definite purpose. A five-roomed house may be taken as the smallest in which a man of the middle class would live. One living in a smaller house may be reckoned among that class; but five rooms are perhaps the fewest in which one can live with comfort if there are not too many children or dependants. A servant would be kept and a room assigned to her, though it would not be exclusively her own as much household work would be done there. The fifth room would be the anteroom or a private room where the family effects, especially the wardrobe, would be kept. Houses with more rooms are pretty numerous; but probably ten rooms may be put as the limit for the middle class proper, if they do not indeed exceed its means. The average size for that class may be given as seven or eight rooms. In such a house there would be, in addition to the three rooms first mentioned, the anteroom, the servant's room, the room for the wardrobe, and one between the sitting-room and the kitchen or back-entrance where inferior callers, such as tradesmen, artisans, servants' relatives, or former dependants would be received. The eighth room, if there is one, may be reserved for the father or mother of the master or his wife, who may be staying with them, the master's private room, the children's study, or the student's room. As the rooms, with the exception of the porch, parlour, and perhaps the servant's room, are not built with a definite object in view, they can be used in any way. This is in a sense convenient; but it has also this disadvantage that the very indefiniteness of their object often makes them inconvenient for any purpose, for in many houses there are rooms which cannot

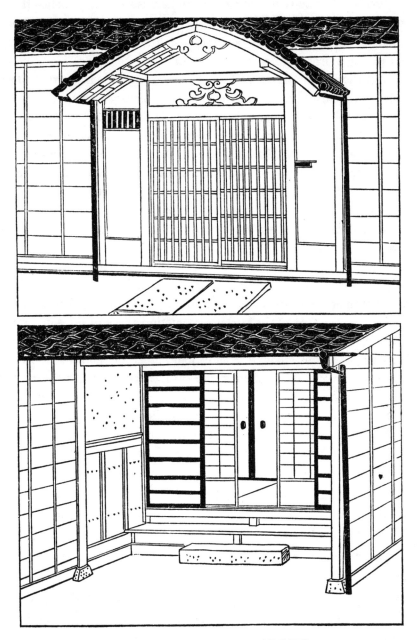

THE PORCH, OPEN AND LATTICED.

be utilised, sometimes owing to their exposure which makes them too cold or too hot for comfort or too dark to work in, and sometimes by reason of their position which renders them good only for passages from one room to another.

Although, as has already been stated, there is no hard and fast rule for the disposition of the rooms, the commonest is perhaps the following:—At the front entrance there is the porch; the ground in front of it may be open with only a roof projecting over it, or it may be enclosed by latticed doors. In the open porch there is a stone step where the foot-gear are taken off before entering, while in the closed one there is a wooden ledge for stepping from the ground on to the mats. The porch itself, which would correspond to the hall in a European-built house, is of two or three mats; here the visitor leaves his hat, greatcoat, and other articles which he would not take into the parlour. On one side of the porch may be the student's room if there is one at all and on the opposite side the porch opens upon the anteroom. The size of this room depends upon that of the parlour; sometimes it is of the same size, but more frequently smaller by two or more mats. Thus, if the parlour is of ten mats, the anteroom has eight; and if the former has eight mats as is oftenest the case, there are six in the other. The anteroom opens upon the same verandah as the parlour; and the two rooms are separated only by sliding-doors, so that these doors may, when necessary, be removed and the two rooms run into one. Such a room, which would have from fourteen to eighteen mats, would be large enough for most purposes. The anteroom thus opens upon the porch on one side, upon the verandah on another, and upon the parlour on the third, and on the fourth it usually communicates directly or indirectly with the servant's room. In large houses, however, there is a separate passage from the kitchen to the porch. Thus, the room is open on all sides though there may sometimes be a bit of a wall by the doors from the porch and the kitchen. The room has little furniture, except, perhaps, one or two framed pictures or writings over the lintels of the doors; and in rare cases there is an alcove

AN EIGHT-MATTED PARLOUR.

by the wall.   Cushions for callers are usually kept in a corner of the anteroom.

The parlour, the principal room of the house, is always kept tidy.   It has an alcove, six feet long by three deep, consisting of a dais, a few inches high, of plain hard wood, which will bear polishing, though a thin matting is sometimes put over it.   Not unfrequently, another piece of wood, generally square, forms the outer edge so that the thickness of the floor of the alcove can be concealed.   The dais has a special ceiling of its own, or a bit of a wall, of plaster or wood, coming down over it a foot or more from the ceiling.   On the dais is set a vase of porcelain or metal, bottle-shaped or flat, in which branches of a tree or shrubs in flower are put in, and on the wall is hung a *kakemono*, or scroll of picture or writing.   These two constitute the main ornament of the room. New flowers are put in every few days and the *kakemono* is changed from time to time.   This is the peculiarity of the *kakemono* as a piece of house decoration.   We do not exhibit all our treasures in *kakemono* at the same time, but hang them one, two, or three at a time according to the size of the alcove and the *kakemono* themselves, so that the visitor calling at different seasons may delight his eyes with the sight of fresh pictures or writings each time he calls.   The inmates, too, do not grow weary with gazing at the same pictures day after day, but enjoy the variety the seasons offer.   To the Japanese it is a more artistic and pleasurable method of displaying his treasures than keeping them all, as it were, on permanent exhibition.   The flowers, too, in the vases are arranged in an artistic style ; their arrangement is an art which boasts many schools and professors and is considered an indispensable branch of a girl's education.   They are not thrown haphazard in a bundle into a vase and expected to give pleasure merely by the profusion of colours and forms.   It may be a single stem or half a dozen with the flowers ranged in relation to one another after fixed canons of the art.

There are in the parlour as in the anteroom pictures or writings in frames over the lintels of the sliding-doors.   On a line with the alcove and usually of the same length is another recess, with a small closet at the top or bottom where the *kakemono* and their cases are generally kept. In this recess there are, also, a pair of shelves at different heights and coming out from opposite walls, the free ends of which overlap each other a few inches. On these shelves some ornaments, usually curios, are placed. When unoccupied, the room is kept clear of any other object. When a visitor calls, even the cushion is brought from the anteroom for him

A VISITOR.

to sit on, and then a small cup of tea set before him and a brazier if it is cold and if warm, a *tabako-bon*. The cushion is round or square ; that for summer is made of matting, hide, or a thin wadding of cotton in a cover of hempen cloth, while for winter use the wadding is much thicker and the cover is silk or cotton. It is about sixteen inches at the side if square. The brazier is of various shapes and makes. It may be a wooden box with an earthenware case inside or with a false bottom of copper, or it may be a glazed earthenware case alone ; the wooden box may be plain with two

holes for handles, or it may be elaborately latticed ; and sometimes
a brazier is made of the trunk of a tree cut with the outside rough-
hewn or only barked and highly polished.   The *tabako-bon*, or
"tobacco-tray," is a small open square or oblong box of sandal-wood
or other hard wood, which holds a small china or metal pan, three-
quarters full of ashes, with a few tiny pieces of live charcoal in the
middle to light a pipe with, and beside it a small bamboo tube with
a knot at the bottom for receiving tobacco-ashes.

The sitting-room has little furniture.   An indispensable article
in it is the brazier, usually oblong, with a set of three small drawers
one under another at the side and two others side by side under the

A SITTING-ROOM.

copper tray filled with ashes, on which charcoal is burnt inside an iron or clay trivet. On this trivet is set a kettle of iron or copper. The iron kettle is made of thick cast-iron and kept on the trivet so as always to have hot-water ready for tea-making : and the copper kettle is used when we wish to boil water quickly. Beside the brazier is a small shelf or cabinet for tea-things. Behind the brazier is a cushion where the wife sits ; this is her usual post. There is also a cushion on the other side of the brazier, where the husband or other members of the house may sit.

As for the other rooms of the house, there is no fixed article of furniture as much depends upon the uses to which they are put. The general absence of furniture in the rooms, however, does not imply that we are absolutely without necessary articles of daily use. The principle on which we proceed is to keep in a room only such articles as are in constant use, the rest being put away as soon as they are done with and brought out again when they are needed. Hence, one of the most striking features of a Japanese house is the number of closets and cupboards in it. Indeed, next to the arrangement of the rooms, the most important consideration in selecting a house is the number of closets it contains. These closets are three feet deep and a yard or two in width. Considering the quantity of household goods that are put away in these closets, there is no inconvenience we feel so much as their scarcity.

There are no rooms specially set apart for sleeping. This absence of bed-rooms enables us to put up with fewer rooms than would be required in a European house for a family of the same size. There are no bedsteads. A bed consists of one or two mattresses, and one or two quilts according to the season, and a pillow. These beds are spread in any room that is handy and put away in the closets in the morning. The parents and the children, especially if young, sleep in the same room ; and unless there is an out-of-the-way chamber where they can sleep in peace, their beds are made in the parlour. For if the beds are made in that room, the others can be swept and made ready for use while the family are still in bed. In the sitting-room breakfast can be got ready, while the anteroom can be used at once if a visitor calls, as he sometimes does very early in the morning or very late at night when the children have been put to bed. In a two-storied house an upstair room is often used as a reserve parlour, so that the anteroom need not be got ready for receiving callers at unseasonable hours. If the family is a large one, the rest shake down where they are least in the way. The rooms to sleep in every night are of course assigned to permanent members of the household; but country-cousins on a prolonged visit can be put to bed anywhere without much inconvenience. For the belated guest the bed is spread in the parlour and its usual occupants are driven into other rooms.

There is no special dining-room. The family take their meals in the sitting-room. If there is a visitor, a dinner-tray is set before him as well as before the host in the parlour; thus, there is no need to have a room set apart for dining. A Japanese at home, then, may remain all day in one room; he can sleep, take his meals, receive his friends, or study without once standing up, for the room changes its character with the articles that are brought into it.

A CHEST OF DRAWERS AND A TRUNK.

Articles of clothing are put into chests of drawers or wicker-trunks. Chests of drawers are commonly made in halves with two drawers each, put one upon the other and fastened by iron clamps. This is to facilitate their removal, a provision which is of importance where fires are frequent. The wicker-trunk has a lid which is as deep as the trunk itself and encloses it, and thus any amount of clothing may be put into it up to the joint depth of the two. The trunks are hidden away in the closets; but the chests of drawers, if they cannot be put into a closet without inconvenience as they are over three feet wide, are set in a corner or against a wall. Indeed, they are purposely put sometimes where they can be seen and become part of the furniture of the room. In large houses where there are godowns, or fireproof plaster storehouses, the chests are put in them, and only such as contain articles of daily wear for the season are kept in the house itself.

If the house is large enough, a special room is set apart for toilet ; but even then, as the toilet-case and its appurtenances can be readily moved to any other room, the toilet-room is more useful for keeping the necessary articles than for the toilet itself. And from the way in which Japanese dresses are worn, that is, as nothing is put on over the head like a jersey or the feet foremost like the European nether garments, a Japanese woman can change her clothes without exposing her body, and it is possible for her to dress or undress in any part of the house. When she is going out with her children, she often manages to turn the house inside out by calling upon its inmates to help her and the children to dress. Tables or desks are set for children in a spare room or in a corner of one that is occupied ; but there is no nursery, and the children pervade the whole house. They play wherever they please, and peace prevails only when they are out or asleep.

Nor is there a special room for books, for the library does not find a place as an important feature in a Japanese house. We Japanese are not a nation of readers. A man of ordinary education has studied the Chinese classics and read the legendary histories and quasi-romances of his country recounting the exploits of the favourite national heroes ; he also reads the papers and some of the current literature ; but his knowledge of books cannot be said to be wide or sympathetic. What books he has, if they are in the usual Japanese style of binding, are piled up in small wooden cases with lids in front. If he has a godown, he keeps the more valuable of his books in it and only brings out such as he may require at the moment ; but there are not many, besides those with whom literature is a hereditary calling, with so many books as to need storing in godowns. Far more Japanese take to the composition of Chinese poems or Japanese odes as a refined pastime, while a still larger number lose their heads over games of *go* and chess. For these they use their private rooms more frequently than for reading and study.

Public baths are, on account of their great convenience, largely patronised in Tokyo ; but in many private houses bath-rooms are also built. A bath-room of the ordinary size is three yards by two. The bath of the commonest kind is made of wooden staves bound together with metal hoops. It is oval in shape and inside the bath near the edge a thin iron cylinder with a grating at its lower end passes through its bottom. Into this cylinder live charcoal is put in to heat the water of the bath ; and a small plank partitions the cylinder to protect the bather from being burnt by contact with it. Oblong baths are now made with thick wooden sides and a furnace at one end which is fed with coke or faggot. The ground of the bath-room is paved with stone or beaten down with concrete ; and on it stands a movable flooring, a foot or more high, of narrow planks with open spaces between to allow the water to run down. The bath holds one person or at most two spare persons, and the water in it is deep enough to cover the crouching body. The bather always washes himself on the flooring and gets into the bath only to warm himself.

Sometimes a small square hearth is cut in the sitting-room or some other convenient room ; and in cold season a wooden frame supported by four pillars is put over the hearth and covered with a large quilt. Live charcoal is put into the hearth and the family sit around it with their knees under the quilt or lie down with their feet stretched out to the hearth. At other seasons the wooden frame is removed and a small mat of the same size as the hearth is put over it. As the hearth cannot be moved about, most people

FOOT-WARMERS.

prefer a portable foot-warmer, which is usually a square wooden box with openings at the top and sides ; one of the sides slides open and through it an earthen pan of live charcoal is placed inside. A quilt is laid over it as in the case of the hearth. Another, made specially for putting in bed, is of earthenware with a rounded top, which takes some time to heat. As the ordinary cut charcoal is consumed too quickly, balls of charcoal dust are used in these foot-warmers.

CHAPTER V.

MEALS.

Rice—*Sake*—Wheat and barley—Soy sauce—*Mirin*—Rice-cooking—Soup—Pickled vegetables—Meal trays—Chopsticks—Breakfast—Clearing and washing—The kitchen—The little hearth—Pots and pans—Other utensils—Boxes and casks—Shelves—The sink and water-supply—The midday meal—The evening meal—*Sake*-drinking.

RICE is the staple food of the Japanese; and no other food-stuff stands so high in popular esteem, or has a tutelary deity of its own. This rice-god has more shrines than any other deity, for he is worshipped everywhere, in town and village, and often a small shrine, no bigger than a hut, peeps amid a lonely cluster of trees surrounded on all sides by rice-paddies, its latticed door covered from top to bottom with the *ex-votos* of the simple peasant folk. Under the feudal government the incomes of the territorial lords and their retainers were assessed, not in money, but in the quantity of rice that was annually brought into their granaries; and rice naturally became the standard for the valuation of all other commodities. The rice so garnered was subsequently converted into currency by exchange-brokers. Under the new regime, however, rice no longer holds the same pre-eminent position, but it still rules to a great extent the market for other goods. The fluctuations of its prices on the rice exchanges are eagerly watched by the whole nation; and references to the weather, especially in summer, invariably end in speculations as to its effect on the rice-crop, and the people put up unmurmuringly with the heavy solstitial rains because most rice-fields are paddies to which a plentiful supply of water is essential. Japan, in fact, is still an agricultural country, and the progress she has of late made in her manufacturing industry is not yet great enough to shake off the domination of agriculture, for no industrial problem agitates the nation so much as the annual question whether

the country can produce its normal harvest of rice, which amounts
to about two hundred and twenty million bushels.

A SHRINE OF THE RICE-GOD.

Rice, however, certainly deserves the solicitude the whole
nation feels for it; for it is not only the principal food-stuff, but it
is also the grain from which the national drink is made. *Sake* is
produced by the fermentation of rice, and contains about fourteen
per cent. of alcohol. Though foreign wines are now imported into
the country and beer is also brewed in large quantities, *sake* is still
the principal alcoholic beverage in Japan; almost all other drinks
which were in use in the old times were either varieties of *sake* or
contained it as their chief ingredient.

Among other cereals that are largely used are barley and
wheat. The former is now much in request for brewing beer; and
as it is more digestible than rice, a mixture of the two is eaten by

many families in Tokyo. Wheat is mostly used as flour ; it enters into many dishes as well as cakes. It is a popular favourite when it is made into maccaroni, though in this respect it is eclipsed by buckwheat.

But in point of utility the soy bean comes next to rice, for our soy sauce which enters into almost all dishes is made from the bean, wheat, and salt. So extensively is this sauce employed that table salt is comparatively little needed. The bean is also the principal ingredient in *miso*, which is a mixture of the soy bean, steamed and pounded, with rice-yeast and salt. This *miso* is largely used in making soup ; and soups into which it does not enter are usually flavoured by boiling shavings of sun-dried bonito and straining them off.

Mirin is a sweet variety of spirit, made by straining a mixture of *sake*, steamed rice, and a spirit distilled from *sake* lees. It is largely used in boiling fish and other food. Vinegar is made in various ways from rice, barley, potato, or *sake* lees.

The cooking of rice is a delicate process. It is first well washed overnight by rinsing it again and again until the water is quite clear, and emptied into a basket to strain. In the morning it is put into a deep iron pot which rests on a round earthen hearth or range by a flange around it ; then, water is poured in, the actual amount requiring nice adjustment so as not to make the rice too soft or too hard, and next a thick wooden lid is put on. A few faggots are lit under the pot ; but as soon as the rice begins to spurt, the fire is withdrawn, and the pot is allowed to cool slowly and equably ; it is next lifted off the hearth and set on a straw-stand. When the rice has stood long enough to be of the same temperature and consistency throughout, the lid is removed and the rice transferred into a cylindrical wooden tub. Well-boiled rice is soft, but its grains have a lustre and are distinct from one another so that any single grain can be picked up with chopsticks. Excessive heat would have burnt the parts nearest the sides of the pot, while sudden heat would have produced rice of unequal consistency.

After the rice-pot is removed, another pot is put over the hearth for making *miso*-soup; if the kitchen range is double-hearthed, the remainder of the faggots lit for the rice is transferred to the neighbouring hearth over which the soup-pot is hung before the rice-pot is removed from the other. *Miso*-soup contains strips of garden radish, edible seaweed (*alopteryx pinnatifida*), bean-curd, egg-plant, or other vegetables according to the season. These two, the rice and the soup, are all the cookery required in the morning. There must of course be hot water for tea.

An invariable accompaniment at Japanese meals is the pickled vegetables. The commonest of these is the garden radish which has been pickled in a paste of powdered rice-bran and salt until it assumes a rich golden hue. Greens are also treated in the same way until their colour is dulled. But garden radishes, greens, small turnips, and egg-plants are also sprinkled over with salt and pressed for a few days. A few slices of these vegetables, after being thoroughly washed to get rid of the bran or salt, are always served at a meal. Most foreigners consider their smell nauseous; but to a Japanese a meal, however rich or dainty, would appear incomplete without these vegetables, pickled or salted. *Kōkō* or *kōnomono*, which is the common name for them, means " fragrant article," and it is believed by many foreigners that the name was given them on the *lucus a non lucendo* principle; but the Japanese has no such aversion to their smell. The repugnance of strangers to these pickles is similar to the attitude of most Japanese towards cheese, the taste for which would require as much cultivation as that for *kōkō* on the part of one to whom both articles are foreign.

The breakfast is, then, very simple. Sometimes the family take their meals together at a large low table which is set before them at each repast; but often a small tray, about a foot square and standing six inches or more high, is placed before each member. In the left corner of the tray near the person before whom it is set, is a small china bowl of rice, while on the right is a wooden bowl of *miso*-soup. A tiny plate of pickled vegetables occupies the middle or the farther left corner, while any extra plate would fill the remaining corner. This plate also holds something very simple, such as plums preserved in red perilla leaves, boiled kidney bean, pickled scallions, minute fish or shrimps boiled down dry in soy sauce, a pat of baked *miso*, or shavings of dried bonito boiled in a mixture of soy and *mirin*.

A MEAL-TRAY.

The chopsticks are laid between the rim of the tray and the bowls of rice and soup. They vary in length, those for women being shorter than those for men but longer than children's; their length may, however, be put at between eight and ten inches. Some are square in section, while others are round; but most of them taper towards the tip which is either rounded or pointed. The commonest kind is of cryptomeria wood, others are of lacquered wood or of bone, and the best are of ivory. Many of them are also tipped with German silver. Chopsticks may appear at first hard to manage; but their manipulation is not really difficult when one comes to see the way in which they should be handled. They are held near the upper or thicker end in the right hand. One chopstick is laid between the thumb and the forefinger and on the first joint of the ring finger which is slightly bent, and held in position by the basal phalanx of the thumb; this chopstick is almost stationary. The other is laid near the third joint of the forefinger and between the tips of that and the middle finger which are kept together, and is held down by the tip of the thumb; it is, in short, held somewhat like a pen, only the pressure of the thumb is much lighter, for if it were heavy, the force put into it as the chopstick is

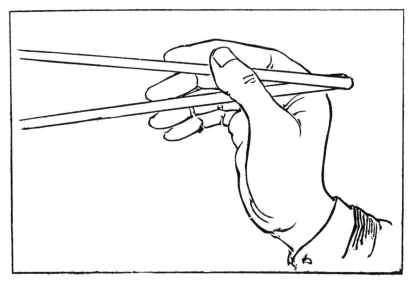

HOW TO HOLD CHOPSTICKS.

moved would relax the pressure on the other stick and cause it to drop. The tip of the thumb serves, therefore, only as a loose fulcrum for moving the stick with tips of the fore and middle fingers, while the upper half resting on the last joint of the forefinger is allowed free play. The most difficult part is the use of the thumb; beginners press the stationary chopstick too hard and make the tip of the thumb so stiff that the other chopstick cannot be freely moved. It is quite easy, when one gets used to the thing, even to move the stationary chopstick a little at the same time as the other. The tips of the chopsticks must always meet. In the hand of a skilled user a needle may be picked up with them; but it is quite enough for ordinary purposes if we can pick a fish or take up a grain of boiled rice.

When the breakfast trays are brought, cups of tea are poured. The tea drunk at meals is common tea, which as it consists of old leaves, may be taken in any quantity without affecting the nerves. A handful of the leaves is thrown into an earthen tea-pot and hot water poured into it; and the pot is set over a fire to keep it hot. The infusion is of a reddish-yellow hue and is almost tasteless. The cups used are generally cylindrical, like mugs without the handles, and are assigned one to each member of the family. The china rice-bowls are also permanently given to the members. When the tea has been sipped, the bowl of rice is taken up and brought near the mouth, and a small quantity is separated with the chopsticks and eaten. In eating rice, the chopsticks scoop it up and bring it to the mouth as it would take too much time to pick it up grain by grain. Alternately with rice, the soup is sipped, and the condiments are also picked a little at a time with the chopsticks. Two or more helpings of rice are taken; as it is considered unlucky to eat only one bowlful, at least two are eaten even though the second may be a small dose consumed for form's sake. One or two helpings of the soup are also taken; but it is not good form to ask for a second helping of the vegetables and other condiments on the tray. Rice is brought in the cylindrical tub into the room and served out there; but the soup is kept over a fire in the kitchen and the wooden bowls are taken there for the second helping. The last bowl of rice is often eaten with tea poured into it, and the bowl is brought to the mouth and the rice pushed into it with the chopsticks. It is, we may mention in passing, only the rice-bowl, besides those containing soup, tea, and other liquid or semi-liquid food which cannot be picked up with chopsticks, that is brought to the mouth; all other dishes are kept on the tray and the food is taken up with the chopsticks. Finally, the rice-bowl is filled with tea only to wash down any grains of rice that may be left in it.

This finishes the breakfast. It does not take more than ten or fifteen minutes; indeed, people pride themselves upon their quickness at meals, especially at breakfast, as it implies that they have no time to dawdle over their food, which is taken solely to ward off hunger and maintain their health and strength. But it must be

A MEAL.

admitted that indigestion not unfrequently follows these hurried meals, to which children are early taught to habituate themselves by parental instruction and by a proverb which puts quickness at meals as an accomplishment on a level with swiftness of foot. When the breakfast is over, the trays, plates, and other utensils are taken back into the kitchen, washed, and put away until they are needed for the next meal. The wooden tub of rice is put into a straw casing in winter to prevent its getting cold and hard and on a stand in a cool, breezy place in summer to keep it from sweating.

Let us next turn to the kitchen and see how it is arranged. The kitchen varies very much in size ; but the commonest range from six to sixteen square yards, that is, it would, if it were matted, hold from three to eight mats. But the floor is usually entirely boarded, though in a large kitchen a mat or two are laid for the servants to sit on. There is a space of ground at the entrance for leaving clogs in, and another on which the sink is set. The most prominent feature of the kitchen is the hearth for cooking rice. It is made of a shallow wooden box, on which a square plaster casing is built with a round hole at the top and an aperture at a side. On the hole the rice-pot is put ; and the side-opening is used for feeding the hearth with small faggots which are kept in a cavity under the wooden box. The hearth is as often as not double, and over the other hole the soup-pot is set. The plaster between the two holes is often replaced by a copper boiler for boiling water with the heat of the faggots under the two pots. Over the hearth is a skylight in the roof, for the part of the house where the kitchen is situated is always one-storied ; and a sliding shutter is moved up and down along the incline of the roof and fastened by a cord. The skylight is useful on a fine calm day as an outlet for the smoke of the hearth ; but when a wind blows against the roof or the rain comes pouring in, it has to be closed at the time when it is most needed, for if the skylight is closed, the windows are also shut, with the result that the smoke spreads over the whole house. In some houses, therefore, chimney-flues have taken the place of

THE KITCHEN.

skylights, which are, moreover, as has already been observed, among the burglar's favourite means of ingress.

For ordinary cooking purposes a small hearth of plaster, stone, or iron is used. It is round or square, and larger at top than at bottom. The top is open with an earthen grating at a few inches' depth from the edge, and an ash-box underneath, which has an outlet at the side for raking out the ashes and fanning the fire. But little charcoal is needed as the space between the grating and the bottom of the pot is very limited. Near the larger hearth is a black earthen pot with a lid, into which half-burnt charcoal is put and extinguished with water ; and when they are dry, these half-burnt pieces are used for lighting fresh charcoal with as they catch fire much more readily. For stirring and clearing the hearth, we use a shovel with a long wooden handle and a pair of long iron rods which are held like chopsticks to pick up pieces of charcoal or cinders. The tongs which are used for braziers are much shorter and made of iron, copper, or brass ; they are also used like chopsticks and are indeed called in Japanese " fire-chopsticks." A hollow bamboo tube with a knot at one end which has a little hole in the centre takes the place of bellows.

Besides the iron pots for making soup and other food on a large scale, which are set on the great hearth, we have small pots and pans for the little hearth. The pots have semicircular handles of metal, the ends of which are hooked into holes on opposite sides of the pots, while the pans have wooden handles fitting into sheaths at the side. They all have wooden lids. Fish and other food are roasted on an iron netting, about a foot square, which is put over the little hearth. When a fish is roasted, the fat melts and drops into the fire, raising large volumes of oily smoke and emitting a smell which fills the whole house. One can always tell, when a mackerel pike, for instance, is being roasted, long before one enters the house.

For transferring rice into a tub or a bowl a wooden spatula is used, while soup and other food which cannot be picked up with chopsticks are put with a wooden spoon into bowls or on plates. For gravy a small earthen spoon is used. Kitchen knives are of three kinds : the square for common use, the triangular for dressing fish, and the long narrow-edged one for cutting thin slices of fish.

A SKYLIGHT AND THE KITCHEN GOD.

The dresser is a thick, two-legged board, at which one has to kneel or squat. There are also bamboo baskets for carrying vegetables and other food which require to be washed ; but those things which are eaten without first washing and must therefore be kept free from dust are brought home in a round wooden box with a lid and a handle. For pounding soft objects there is an earthen mortar shaped like an inverted cone, with rough ribbed sides, against which the objects are rubbed with a wooden pestle.

Uncooked rice is kept in a large box in a corner of the kitchen and is measured out whenever needed with a square wooden measure. Charcoal is brought in straw bags and emptied into a box under the floor of the kitchen or kept in an outhouse, and is in either case brought out for use in a bamboo or cane basket lined with paper. Soy is usually sold in wooden kegs as it does not change with time ; but the poor buy it in half-pint bottles. *Sake*, on the other hand, is apt to grow sour, especially in hot season, and is bought in long-necked bottles holding a few pints ; but if there are heavy drinkers in the family or many guests to entertain, casks are laid in. Pickled vegetables are made in old *sake*-casks which are put in a corner of the kitchen, often on the ground.

Around the kitchen are shelves, open or with doors, on which the services and utensils are kept. The sets for use when there are guests are carefully wrapped in paper or cotton and stored in special boxes in the kitchen or some other room. There is no pantry ; but as every preparation is served separately in a bowl or on a plate, the quantity of crockery in a Japanese kitchen is very great. There is a shelf high upon the wall near the large hearth, dedicated to the kitchen deity, to whom offerings of rice and flowers are daily brought.

The sink, which is of wood, usually lies level with the kitchen floor, and one either squats on the floor or stands on the ground before it. Here all kitchen utensils and services are washed, everything in fact, except the kettles of copper, bronze, or iron, which are never washed but grow mellow by being patted with pieces of cloth steeped in hot water. Beside the sink are an earthen jar to hold water for washing and a wooden pail for drinking water, but there is really no difference in the quality of the liquid in the two receptacles as it has in either case been drawn from the well. The wells are either private or public ; in the latter case, they are used by the whole neighbourhood, a small tax being levied for their maintenance, and are the favourite resorts for the exchange of scandals. As these wells have all wooden sides and a square wooden flooring where washing is done, they present a far from cleanly appearance, and the water is as often as not contaminated, especially in the crowded quarters of the city. The Tokyo municipality undertook some years ago to supply pure water, and as water-pipes have been laid throughout the city, the wells are rapidly disappearing in Tokyo.

A WELL.

As we have described the general appearance of the kitchen, we will now return to the sitting-room. The breakfast things have been removed; but preparations have before long to be made for the midday meal. If the master of the house is not at home, or indeed even if he is, unless he has a visitor, the meal is very simple. It may consist of some vegetable soup, boiled vegetables, such as carrots, burdocks, turnips, or pumpkins, or dried or cured fish, like salmon, sardines, herrings, or mackerel, or perhaps fresh fish boiled, basted, or roasted. There may be the same condiments as at breakfast.

The evening meal is the principal repast of the day. It may not differ materially from the midday meal, though fresh fish is more frequently served then than at noon. The fish may be boiled in a mixture of *mirin* and soy, be put into a soup made with an infusion of dried bonito shavings, be roasted on the iron netting with a sprinkling of salt or repeated coatings of soy, or be taken raw in thin slices. This raw fish is a peculiarly Japanese dish. A side of a fish, after removing the bones, is cut into thin slices and served with grated garden radish and eutrema, the latter in its hot taste being something between ginger and mustard, and also with a boiled yellow chrysanthemum. The fish is soaked in a little plat of soy in which the radish and eutrema have been mixed. The raw fish, especially if it is the sea-bream, is a delicacy which is highly appreciated in Japan, though many Europeans who relish raw oysters recoil from the very idea of eating any fish uncooked.

People who take *sake* have it usually with their evening meal, though some, of course, drink it at every repast and between meals as well. It is, however, the custom to take it in the evening when the day's work is done. It is brought in a little china bottle which has been put into a boiling kettle and warmed. It is taken hot, and its effects are naturally more rapid than when it is taken cold, and pass off as rapidly. It is poured into a tiny cup ; and as one sips it cup after cup, it warms one up quickly, but when its effects pass off, it is apt to give one a chill ; hence, a man who goes to sleep immediately after drinking *sake*, needs more bedding than usual to avoid a cold on awaking. Another peculiarity in *sake*-drinking is that we take it with fish or other dishes at the beginning of a meal, and when we have done with it, we take rice. This drinking on a empty stomach helps to make it effective ; and the Japanese way of drinking produces a quick but brief state of exhilaration.

CHAPTER VI.

FOOD.

Japanese diet—Vegetables—Sea-weeds and flowers—Fish—Shell-fish—Crabs and other molluscs—Fowl—Meat—Prepared food—Peculiarities of Japanese food—Fruits— The bever—Baked potatoes and cracknel—Confectionery—Reasons for its abundance— Sponge-cake—Glutinous rice and red bean—Kinds of confectionery—Sugar in Japanese confectionery.

IT will be seen from the foregoing chapter that the Japanese diet consists almost entirely of fish and vegetables. It is true that we also eat domestic and other fowls, and in Tokyo and other large towns a quantity of beef and pork, and horseflesh as well, is consumed; but their consumption is insignificant compared with the part fish and vegetables play in the Japanese culinary art.

We have a great variety of vegetables. The commonest and most useful of them is the garden radish, which is pickled or salted, boiled almost dry with *mirin*, sugar, and bonito shavings, put into soup, or grated to flavour raw or fried fish. Carrots and turnips, the burdock and the arrowhead are also boiled and served by themselves or together on a plate. We boil or put into soup the potato, the yam, and the taro, of which we have several varieties. Cucumbers are either pickled or served raw with pepper and vinegar. The egg-plant and the melon are also pickled or put into soup. We pickle or boil the onion, scallion, spinach, and lettuce. The kidney, horse, and other beans are in great favour and dressed in various ways. Mushrooms and several other fungi growing on trees or on rocks are served with fish or vegetables. The bulb of the tiger-lily and the rhizome of the lotus are boiled; the former is very soft, but the latter is hard and indigestible. The bamboo-shoots, when very young, become soft on boiling and are much in demand in April; but they grow fast and soon become too hard. Rice boiled with bits of bamboo-shoot is a favourite food in that month.   The water-shield is held by some people to be a delicacy, while others esteem as highly the common bracken, snake-gourd, and water-pepper.

Sea-weeds are also in great demand.   Of these the principal are the *konbu (laminaria japonica)*, which is largely exported into China, and the laver, which is obtained in thin sheets and taken with soy alone or with rice rolled in it.   The cherry-flowers and the chrysanthemums are also articles of food ; the former are salted, put into hot water, and served in place of tea, while the latter, always the yellow variety, are either fried with a coating of *kuzu (pueraria Thunbergiana)* or boiled in brine and pressed.

Japan is especially rich in fish, as is to be expected from her extensive coast-line and great length from north to south.   There are said to be about six hundred varieties of fish in the waters surrounding the country.   Of these the one which is held in

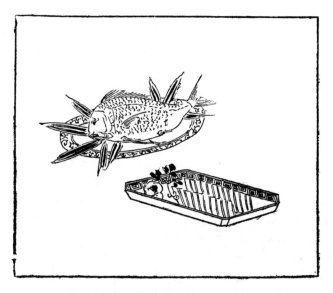

RAW FISH, WHOLE AND SLICED.

highest esteem is the *tai*, a species of the sea-bream *(pagrus cardinalis)*.   It is served in various ways ; indeed, so numerous are these ways that there is extant an old Japanese book entitled " The Hundred Excellent Methods of dressing the *Tai*."   It may be boiled, roasted, basted, salted, or taken raw. Most other fish may be similarly treated, though they may not be considered so delicate. For being taken raw in thin slices, the fishes esteemed next to the *tai* are the plaice, gilthead, tunny, and bonito. Others are mostly preferred boiled. Among the commonest of these fishes are the gurnard, Prussian carp, common carp, wels, flying-fish, mackerel, frigate mackerel, horse-mackerel, mackerel pike, trout, rock-trout, white-bait, sand-fish, goby, sting-ray, sword-fish, sardine, salmon, sole, hair-tail, goose-fish, cod, half-beak, yellow-tail, grey mullet, shark, and sea-eel. The salmon comes to Tokyo salted, while the herring is sun-dried. The sardine and mackerel pike are usually roasted. The eel is treated only in one way; it is split from gill to tail, the back-bone is extracted, and the head cut off; the two sides are laid out flat and bamboo skewers are passed through them, and they are roasted over a fire, being from time to time dipped in a gravy of *mirin* and soy. Tokyo is especially noted for eels served in this way. The loach is also split and the bones are extracted; it is served in a pan over a hot-water bath, with eggs and chips of burdock.

There are also many kinds of shell-fish in Japan. Of the univalves the principal are the sea-ear and top-shell, while among the bivalves are the oyster, clam, sea-mussel, razor-shell, cockle, swan-mussel, otter-shell, and rapana. They are mostly boiled; the clam and sea-mussel, and others with comparatively thin shells are served in a bowl of slightly-flavoured hot water, which can hardly be called soup. The oyster is always shelled and served by itself or with eggs.

Crabs, squills, lobsters, shrimps, and prawns are abundant. The cuttle-fish and octopus are very common articles of food, and the pond-snail is appreciated by some people. Sun-dried cuttle-fish are also very common; they are flat and hard, and are cut into slices which are roasted and dipped in soy.

Of fowls the variety is somewhat limited. We have of course the domestic fowl. The most esteemed of all fowls is the crane, after which come Bewick's swan, the heron, wild goose, wild duck, common duck, pheasant, quail, pigeon, woodcock, and water-rail,

while among the smaller birds are the sparrow, lark, and siskin. As
we do not use a knife and fork at table, all fowls have to be cut up
before they are served. A favourite way is to serve them in small
slices in soup ; but they may also be brought in with vegetables on
a plate. The commonest method with the domestic fowl and duck
is to boil them in small slices in a shallow pan with bits of onion in
a gravy of soy, *mirin*, and sugar. The pan has a small hollow
at a side, into which the gravy runs so as not to saturate the meat
too much. The small birds are served whole, and when chopsticks
fail, the hands and teeth are brought into requisition.

It is only of recent years that we have begun to eat beef and
pork ; but we have in Tokyo a large number of shops where
they are sold. There are two kinds of such shops ; one is the
regular butcher's, while the other is a sort of restaurant where beef
is served in the same manner as the domestic fowl and duck above
mentioned. Here *sake* and rice are also obtainable, There are
many restaurants in European style ; but the cuisine in most of
them is non-descript and the dishes are confined to the simplest
kind. The absence of mutton, moreover, sadly limits the range of
plats.

Though cooking is mostly done at home, no small quantity of
prepared food is bought for the meals. The most important of
such food is the bean-curd. For this the soy bean is soaked in
water, ground, steamed, and strained ; and the liquid is allowed to
coagulate by the addition of brine and then pressed in a square box
with a cotton-cloth bottom until the water has been drawn off,
leaving behind a soft white curd. This curd is cut into small slices
and put into soup in the morning ; it is sometimes thrown into hot
water, and as soon as it is warmed, dipped into a mixture of soy
and *mirin* and eaten. It is also fried. Indeed, the bean-curd
shares with the *tai* the distinction of having a special treatise
dealing with a hundred ways of dressing it. Another favourite
breakfast food is the steamed peas, which are eaten with mustard.
Plums which have softened and reddened by being preserved in
perilla leaves are often, after extracting the stones, boiled with sugar
until they become gelatinous. Boiled beans, the egg-plant pre-

served in mustard, and ginger in perilla leaves are common breakfast condiments. Fish and vegetables coated with flour and fried in rape-oil are favourite articles of diet. Commonest among fried vegetables are sweet potatoes, leek, and lotus rhizomes, while lobsters similarly served are highly esteemed. Another favourite is the flesh of sturgeon minced very fine, seasoned with *sake* and salt, and baked. It is made into a roll with a hole through the centre or is semi-cylindrical with a flat side.

It will thus be seen how completely our diet differs from the European ; and it is no matter for wonder that the other conditions of life should be as dissimilar. Many Europeans in Japan find our meals unsatisfying ; but at the same time there are not a few Japanese who do not feel that they have had a full meal unless they finish up a European dinner with rice and pickled vegetables. There is certainly far greater sustaining power in European food, and our medical authorities urge a more extensive use of animal food besides fish. Rice and vegetables, it is true, fill the stomach ; indeed, one may even feel surfeited, and yet in a short time the strain disappears and hunger returns. For this reason coolies and others engaged in severe physical labour take four or more meals a day. Pickled vegetables are indigestible ; but as they are indispensable at every meal, the natural result is that dyspepsia is one of the commonest ailments that a Japanese is subject to. It should, however, be added that it is not pickled vegetables alone that are responsible for this prevalence of dyspepsia ; for the Japanese, and more especially the citizens of Tōkyo, probably take more food between meals than any other people, and that too at irregular intervals.

As there is no dessert at a Japanese meal, fruits are commonly eaten at odd hours, especially by children. In the early months of the year we have the apple and the orange. The former is mostly cultivated in Yezo, the most northerly of the larger islands, while the latter comes mainly from the southern section of the main island. Oranges are all mandarins with or almost without pips ; of these there are many varieties, and some of them are very sweet. The shaddock is also very common. There are different kinds of citrons ; but they are seldom eaten by themselves, being like the lemon mostly used to flavour dishes. Strawberries there are in plenty ; but they are mostly watery and lack sweetness owing to the great humidity of the Japanese climate, which spoils both fruit and flower, depriving one of taste and the other of fragrance. Cherries have recently been introduced and cultivated in many localities; for the Japanese cherry-tree is grown solely for its beautiful flowers and its fruit is too small to be eaten. The Japanese plum-tree is also reared for its flowers, but produces fruit in large quantity ; it is hard, and is eaten raw with a little salt to counteract indigestion, pickled in vinegar, or preserved in perilla leaves. The Japanese apricot is inferior to the English apricot and nectarine ; and so is the peach which is pointed at the top and hard-druped. Figs are always eaten raw. The loquat tastes fairly good, but its large stones leave but little to eat ; and the pomegranate is open to a similar objection that it is too full of seed for enjoyment. The Japanese pear is different to the European species ; it has not the peculiar shape of the latter, but looks like a large pippin in shape and colour, only that it is speckled all over with minute greenish-white spots ; it is juicy but comparatively hard. Acorns of different kinds of oak are parched and shelled. Our chestnuts do not differ from the European. They are roasted or boiled unshelled ; but when they are shelled and boiled soft, they form part of an important dish at Japanese dinners. Grapes, too, are plentiful ; they are fair, though of course inferior to European hot-house grapes. Bananas we get from the Bonin Islands and pine-apples from Formosa. But the best of all Japanese fruits is the persimmon ; it is a peculiarly Japanese fruit. There are many varieties, some of which are delicious. Some of the larger sort are thrown into empty *sake*-casks and left to mellow, while others are peeled, dried, and preserved in sugar.

As the second meal of the day is taken at noon and the last at sundown, it is not unusual, especially in summer, to have something at three or four o'clock. When there are artisans or labourers at work in the house, they are always given tea with some food about that hour ; and if there is a visitor, a lady or a friend of the family,

its women folk generally manage to have this bever. It may be
no more than confectionery ; but the most common food taken on
such an occasion is *sushi*, which is a lump of rice which has been
pressed with the hand into a roundish form with a slight mixture of
vinegar and covered on the top with a slice of fish or lobster, or a

SUSHI AND *SOBA*.

strip of fried egg, or rolled in a piece of laver. As the lumps are
small, being seldom more than two or three inches long, several of
them are set before each person. The favourite fish for the purpose
is the tunny, though others are also largely used. Another
common dish for the bever is the *soba*, which is a sort of macaroni
made of buckwheat ; in its simplest form it is brought on a small
bamboo screen laid on a wooden stand ; it is dipped, before eating,
in an infusion of bonito shavings flavoured with a little soy and
mirin, to which small bits of onion and Cayenne pepper have been
added. The macaroni is also boiled with fried lobsters, fowl, or
eggs and served in bowls. Wheaten macaroni is also dressed in
the same manner ; it is much thicker than that of buckwheat.

But it is in winter evenings that there is a great deal of eating to while away the dreary hours after the early supper. Children, students, and others to whom inexpensiveness is a consideration, take to sweet potatoes which are boiled in slices or baked whole or in pieces. Another article, equally in favour for its cheapness, is a kind of cracknel made by baking and dipping small disks of rice or wheaten flour in soy. Parched peas rolled in salt or sugar and roasted acorns and chestnuts are also much in demand.

The variety of confectionery is very great. This is due to two causes. First, it is the custom to take a present with us when we go to visit a friend whom we have not seen for some time or to pay our respects to a superior. It may be some fruit in season, or a box of eggs, a brace of wild ducks or geese, or a case of beer, handkerchiefs, or, indeed, any article conceivable ; but the commonest is confectionery. If one goes to ask a favour or express thanks for a service rendered, or to keep oneself in the other's good books if he is a superior, where, in short, some personal advantage is sought immediately or prospectively or has been gained, one naturally makes presents of some value ; but if it is only to pay the compliments of the season and merely to remind the other of one's existence, articles of slighter value, such as confectionery, are given. In the latter case the recipient makes to the other a similar present when he returns the call. This exchange of presents takes place among friends, especially at the end of the year. So general is the custom that on a man with a wide circle of acquaintances these gifts about the New Year's tide entail serious expenses. He may of course send to a friend a present he has received from another ; but he has to be very circumspect how he disposes of such presents, for it sometimes happens that this repeated passing on of a gift from one person to another ends in its reverting to the original donor in a condition by no means improved by its frequent journeys. Similar presents are made in midsummer, though the custom is not so general as at the other season.

The second reason for the variety of confectionery lies in the custom of setting some cake before a visitor. When any one calls and is shown in, tea is brought before him together with a plate of confections. The tea is of course drunk, but the cake is more frequently left untouched ; it ought in that case to be wrapped in paper and given to the visitor to take home, but the rule is not always observed and the cake is often left to do duty before successive callers until it becomes too stale for presentation. In a family with children, they generally manage to make away with it as soon as the visitor is gone. When, however, a doctor is called in, the cake is always wrapped in paper and given to him ; and the doctor takes it as a matter of course.

These two customs, then, naturally create a large demand for confectionery of all kinds. The most common cake for making a present of is a sort of sponge-cake. It is not of Japanese origin, but appears to have been introduced by the Spaniards in the early

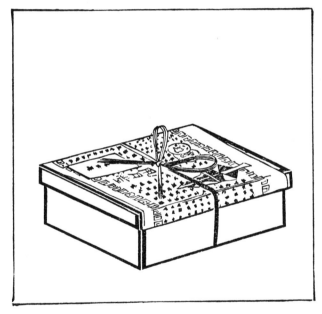

A BOX OF SPONGE-CAKE.

days of foreign intercourse more than three centuries ago. It is put in a card-board or wooden box ; and, in view of the custom above referred to of passing a present on from one to another until it grows stale, the best confectioners in Tokyo now put on the box the date of its sale so that their reputation may not suffer through the deterioration of their confection by its repeated travels. The precaution, however, is hardly necessary as the custom is too widely known for any one who receives musty sweetmeats to accuse their maker of dishonesty.

The bulk of confectionery is made of rice, red beans, millet, or sugar. Glutinous rice is steamed, pounded in a wooden mortar into a pasty consistency, and left to cool. This is made into little cakes, which are boiled and eaten with greens in soup at the beginning of the year and are at other times baked and dipped in soy and sugar. But for making confectionery, the pounded rice is not allowed to cool as it is, while hot, soft enough to take any shape. It usually forms the outer cover of dumplings filled with a sugary mixture. The red bean is boiled, pounded, and strained through a coarse cotton bag to get rid of the skin, though the latter is sometimes retained, in which case the straining is unnecessary, and finally mixed with sugar. This red bean jam is the most important ingredient of Japanese sweetmeats as there is in our confectionery no other equivalent of the fruit jam. Sometimes, however, other beans are substituted for it, especially when a white jam is needed. The red bean jam is also used in making red soup into which small rice dumplings are thrown ; this soup is much in demand, especially in winter, to while away the tedium of long evenings. The red bean is also boiled with rice to give it a colour ; the red-bean rice is eaten in old-fashioned families three times a month, on the first, fifteenth, and twenty-eighth. A kind of white candy is made from a mixture of glutinous rice and rice-yeast. Agar-agar, or the Bengal isinglass, which is obtained from a sea-weed, is used for making jellies. Starch extracted from the root of the *kuzu (pueraria Thunbergiana)* is also much employed in confectionery.

Numerous as are the confections made, the more common among them are the following, which may of course be varied by the addition of other ingredients. A kind of Turkish delight is made from a mixture of glutinous rice, syrup, and white candy, boiled and brought into proper consistency by throwing in a little *kuzu* starch. By steaming a mixture of red beans, sugar, wheat, and *kuzu,* we get a sweet dark-red cake, which is almost as popular as the sponge-cake. A mixture of glutinous rice steeped in water and rice-yeast left overnight in a hot-water bath is, after being strained and steamed with a small quantity of wheat, made into little balls around a lump of red bean jam. This is also a very common confection. Caramels are made with long beans or peanuts inside. By boiling a mixture of agar-agar and sugar for some time over a slow fire, we get a soft, translucent jelly which is put into a mould and afterwards cut up.

There are many others of a similar composition, often coloured, flavoured, or peculiarly shaped ; but their principal ingredients are the articles already mentioned. Japanese confectionery is noticeable for the large quantity of saccharine matter it contains, which varies, except in rare cases, from one to three fourths of the whole composition. It is not, therefore, to be wondered at that indigestion is a frequent result of a too free indulgence in Japanese confections.

CHAPTER VII.

MALE DRESS.

Japanese and foreign dress—Progress in the latter—Japanese clothes indispensable— *Kimono* —Cutting out—Making of an unlined dress—Short measure—Extra-sized dresses — *Yukata*—The lined *kimono*—The wadded *kimono*—Under-dress—Underwear— *Obi*—*Haori*—The crest—The uncrested *haori*—*Hakama*—Socks—How to dress— Wearing of stocks.

stranger in the streets of Tokyo cannot but be struck by the number of Japanese, especially men and boys, who are dressed in European clothes. The western costume, if less picturesque, is certainly more handy than the Japanese ; it allows a greater freedom to the limbs, whereas in the latter the long sleeves are apt to be caught by knobs and corners and the skirt is always in the way when we wish to run or walk fast. For this reason the European male dress is largely worn in schools, government offices, and private places of business, which are built in a style more or less foreign and furnished with chairs, benches, and tables ; for squatting is uncomfortable with foreign clothes and, whatever the dress may be, is a more complicated way of resting ourselves than sitting in a chair, besides requiring a greater effort when we wish to rise. But there are further reasons for the favour which European clothes enjoy in Japan. They last much longer than Japanese, for silks wear out pretty quickly if they are constantly in use and are, moreover, torn more readily. If they are soiled, they have to be taken to pieces, washed, perhaps redyed, and remade. Besides, a Japanese outfit of fair quality is more costly than a European suit. And as the custom stands in Japan, we have to provide ourselves with several Japanese suits ; whereas so many changes are not needed of European clothes, in respect of which the Japanese people, as a whole, have not yet learned to discriminate so rigidly as when their national costume is concerned. A man may, in fact, wear the same frock-coat all the year round and make it last long by taking as great care of it as he does of his Japanese clothes. All things considered, then, European clothes are both more handy and economical, and on that account preferred to Japanese on business and ceremonial occasions.

In the early days of the new regime when European clothes were comparatively rare and not unfrequently worn rather as a sign of their wearers' progressive spirit than for their convenience, it was considered sufficient if they were simply European, no account being taken of their cut or style. A man in a tweed cutaway or serge lounge suit found ready access to an evening party or a semi-official gathering. But as time went on, the frock-coat became the usual dress on such occasions ; still, silk hats were not yet generally worn, and bowlers remained the common wear. The evening dress was the official suit and was worn at one time even in the morning, if there was an official ceremony at such early hours. It is only within the last decade that silk hats have come into vogue ; and they are now worn with the frock-coat or evening dress at all parties and social gatherings. But as they are still only worn at social functions, they last a long time, and at garden parties silk hats of all ages and styles may be seen.

The rapid encroachment of European clothes into Japanese society is undeniable ; and if we may judge from the steady increase of tailoring establishments in Tokyo and elsewhere, they seem destined to command a still greater popularity. But there appears to be little ground for the prediction often made by European writers that the national dress is doomed. For so long as Japanese houses remain radically unchanged and we are forced to squat on the mat, Japanese clothes cannot be dispensed with. European clothes are not comfortable to squat in ; as the body cannot be kept quite straight, the collar presses on the throat, the waistcoat gets creasy, the trousers soon become baggy about the knees, and the socks are but a poor protection against the cold since they cannot be hidden as under the skirt of the Japanese dress. In a room warmed only by a small brazier, we feel the winter chill more severely in European clothes than in Japanese   In summer no one who has once worn the Japanese *yukata* would willingly take it off, for it is the slightest possible consistent with decency as it is nothing more than a single unlined dress. It is the coolest imaginable. Other Japanese summer clothes are only less cool than the *yukata*. Hence, a Japanese of the upper or middle class has usually to provide himself with both European and Japanese suits, that is, if he wears European clothes at all, and is put to double expenses in the matter of clothing. And to be completely equipped in both requires no light purse.

The ordinary Japanese dress is shaped like a gown with hanging sleeves. As the exact shape of the *kimono*, as it is called, appears unknown to those who have never seen it, we will here explain how a *kimono* is made.

The *kimono* is made out of a piece of silk, cotton, or hemp cloth, usually eleven inches wide and about thirty-five feet long. Cloths are always made of nearly the same measure or of double the length just mentioned, that is, if they are for making *kimono*. The length and width may vary slightly, cotton cloths being for instance smaller than silk. The cloth is cut out into two pieces each for the body, the sleeves, and the gores, and one for the band and sometimes another for the upper band, or into seven or eight pieces in all. The body pieces are each ten feet long and the sleeve pieces three feet and a half, so that the two pairs take up twenty-seven feet; they are of the same width as the original piece. The remainder is cut into two strips, usually six and five inches wide, of which the former is cut in two lengths of four feet three inches each, if possible, for the gores and the latter into a strip, five feet eight inches long, for the main band, the remainder being used, if needed, for the upper band.

We now pass on to the making of the male unlined *kimono*, as naturally it is of the simplest form. In the first place, the length of a *kimono* varies with the size of the wearer; it is not only his height, but his condition as well, that has to be taken into consideration, for broad shoulders, a thick chest, and rounded hips require more cloth, longitudinally and laterally, than a body of the same height but with less flesh. The usual length is about four feet six inches for the average Japanese whose height is five feet three or four inches. The two body pieces are first placed side by side and sewn together half the length, the edge sewn in being about half an inch ; and then at the end of the seam the pieces are cut two inches and a half and folded down at that width all along to the free ends, so that when they are spread out, there is a channel five inches wide along half their length. They are then folded in two so that the free halves are exactly over the sewn halves. The outer edges are then sewn from the end up to a point a foot and five inches below the fold. The sewn halves form the hind part and the free halves the front of the *kimono*. Next, the pieces for the gores are sewn on from the end along the free edges of the body pieces. The skirt is stitched, and the *kimono*, which is now an inch or so less than five feet, is tucked in to the required length at the hips where the tucking would be concealed under the *obi*, or sash. The edge of each gore is stitched to a certain height which depends upon the length of the *kimono*, and from this point to the top of its juncture with the body piece the gore is turned, and the triangle thus formed is folded again and again so as to be enclosed in the band which is next sewn on over the folded edges of the gores and round the breast and neck of the body pieces. The band itself is made by folding the band piece lengthwise into two and turning in the edges. The upper band which serves as an anti-macassar is then sewn over the main band around the neck. The sleeves have in the meantime been sewn into oblong pieces a foot and seven or eight inches long by ten inches wide. The outer edge has been sewn together for nine and a quarter inches from the bottom, the remainder being hemmed round to allow the hand to pass through ; and the inner edge, of which two and a half inches have been stitched at the lower extremity, is now sewn on to the body piece.

The dress is now complete. Sometimes when the cloth is slightly short of measure, it cannot be made in the way just de-scribed. The body pieces are taken at lengths which admit of but little tucking at the hips ; and the gores are cut slantwise, leaving no triangular pieces to be folded in. But in that case, when the dress

is remade, the same parts of the gores will be exposed, whereas if
the gores are oblong, they can be reversed so as to expose the

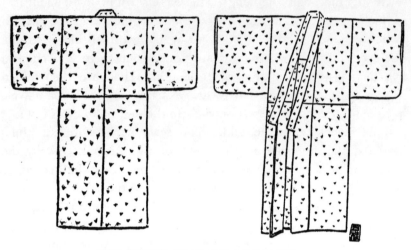

THE *KIMONO*, REAR AND FRONT VIEW.

parts which were formerly folded in and are therefore practically
new.

These dresses can be taken to pieces and remade so long as
the cloth is not worn out; and as they can be made to fit most
persons by judicious tucking in or letting out, they are often
washed and remade for others than the original wearer. As the
maximum length of the body pieces is about ten feet, a cloth of the
usual length would be too short for those who measure more than
four feet ten or eleven inches from the nape of the neck to the
ankles. A spare person, five feet eight inches in height, might just
manage to make himself a dress out of a cloth of the usual length;
but a man of a greater stature or of the same height with more
flesh would have to get a cloth specially woven for him or buy a
double length. Moreover, if a cloth is too short for the height, it
would also be in all probability too narrow for the sleeves, which
would then require a strip to be sewn on to cover the arms.

The unlined dress of coarse bleached cotton, known as *yukata*
or bath-dress, is the simplest and most comfortable for summer wear.
It is worn immediately next to the skin without underwear of any

kind, and is washed whole every few days in midsummer. It is commonly white or blue with stripes, spots, or other simple designs. If the dress is of silk, hemp, or of a better kind of cotton, an underwear of bleached cotton is put on. This resembles the *kimono* in form, only that it is much shorter, coming down only to the thighs, and has open sleeves and no gores. The unlined *kimono* is worn when one goes out in summer; the *yukata* is mostly for home wear or put on for a walk in the evening. The unlined clothes are worn through midsummer from the middle of June until the latter half of September.

The lined *kimono* differs from the unlined in having a lining, which is usually of dark-blue silk or cotton. The lining is first made separately from the covering, and its pieces, which are similar to those of the other with a slight shrinkage in the measurement to allow for its being the inner side, are stitched together, except at the edges of the sleeves, skirt, gores, and the inner border of the body pieces, which are sewn on to the corresponding parts of the outer cloth. The band of the latter covers both cloths; and at the opening of the sleeves a stiff piece of cloth trims the edges as that part is apt to be rapidly worn out from the movement of the wrist. The underwear is the same as in the case of the unlined *kimono*. The lined *kimono* is worn for a shorter time than the unlined, in fact, for about a month at the transition from the unlined *kimono* to the wadded and *vice-versa*. The lined *kimono* was not recognised by the old-time etiquette which did not sanction any intermediate dress between the unlined and the wadded; but of its comfort as a *demi-saison* costume there can be no question.

The wadded *kimono* is the most important of all as it is worn for a longer period than the others. It is simply the lined *kimono* wadded, and is made similarly to it. When the two halves, the outer and the inner, have been stitched separately, they are first joined together at the skirt, turned inside out, and spread on the floor. The wadding is then put on the outer half, the lining is brought over and sewn on, and finally the whole dress is turned back the right side out. The lining is made narrower than the covering as it remains inside, but is slightly longer to allow for the

bulge of the wadding.   The wadding may be of floss-silk as when
it is desired to keep the dress thin and light ; or it may be of ginned
cotton with a thin coating of floss-silk ; the floss-silk is needed
because if the wadding were only of cotton, it would fall in the
course of time and gather at the skirt, whereas the floss-silk adheres
to the cloth with such pertinacity that part of it oozes out through
the texture of the cloth and forms little white lumps on the outside.

The wadded clothes are worn double in midwinter.   The
under dress is of slightly smaller dimensions than the upper.   It is
usual to make its body of a less stiff material than the other, for if
it were as stiff or thick, it would be uncomfortable to wear.   Hence,
the gores, the skirt, the band, and the wrist-ends of the sleeves, that
is, the visible portions, are made of stiff stuff ; but the rest is of softer
silk or cotton.

Under the lower *kimono* is worn a doublet, thickly wadded and
coming down to the knees.   It is made of inferior silk and has a
black silk band.   Under this is the same underwear as in the case
of the lined *kimono*.   The doublet has sleeves like the *kimono*.
The merino undershirt is now frequently worn instead of the Japanese underwear ; it is certainly warmer than the other which lets the
wind and cold enter through its open breast and sleeves, but it
cannot be said to add to the picturesqueness of the national costume.

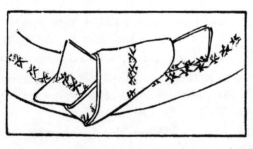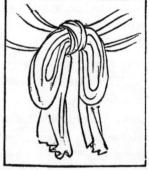

THE *OBI*, SQUARE AND PLAIN.

Merino drawers are also worn ; they are useful as the skirt is often
on a windy day blown aside and exposes the legs to the cold.

The *obi*, or sash, is about four inches wide and varies in length from twelve feet and a half to fourteen. It is usually of the same material on both sides and can be worn either side out. It is stitched along one edge and stiffened with a padding. This is the regular sash, commonly called the square *obi*; but when we are at home, go out for a walk, or visit an intimate friend, we prefer another kind of sash, which is a piece of white crêpe, about ten feet long and varying in width from a foot and a quarter to two feet, and stitched at the ends to prevent their fraying. It is much more comfortable than the other.

The *haori*, or outer coat, is worn over the *kimono*. It comes down only to the knees or a little lower. It has no gores in front like the *kimono*. The neck-band runs down to the skirt. The *haori* is open in front and the band falls straight from the shoulders on both sides, so that there is no need for gores in front which are required only for folding over; but there is a narrow gore on either side coming down from the lower extremity of the sleeve to the skirt. The sleeves of the *haori* are just large enough to enclose those of the *kimono*. At the skirt the body pieces are turned in and form

THE *HAORI.*

the lining of the lower part of the *haori*; and so the full length of a cloth, that is, about thirty-five feet, is taken in the same way as in the making of the *kimono*. The upper part of the *haori* and the sleeves are lined with another material; that for the upper part is often of bright colours or embroidered ; it is, in fact, the only portion of the male dress where the usual rule of sober colours is not strictly adhered to, and people who aspire to be *chic* sometimes use for the lining a more expensive material than the outer cloth.   Unlined *haori* which are made of silk gauze or similar thin stuff for summer wear, are woven shorter than the others to dispense with the skirt-lining.   The *haori* for winter wear is sometimes wadded with a thin layer of floss-silk.   About fifteen inches down the neck, a small loop of the same material as the *haori* is stitched on to the band on either side, and to this a silk cord is fastened and tied in the middle to keep the *haori* from slipping off.   Sometimes the cords are made in a knot or a bow and fastened to the loops by hooks at the ends.

The *haori* worn on a visit or on formal occasions is usually black and adorned with the family crest.   The crest is found on three or five parts of the *haori*, one in the middle of the back over the seam, and one each on the back of the sleeve, and if there are five crests altogether, one each on the breast of the body piece between the band and the sleeve.   The crest is of various forms and is about an inch from end to end.   It is invariably white ; the white cloth is specially dyed for the purpose so that the crest is the only portion left undyed ; but sometimes ready-dyed cloths with white disks for the crests are bought, when the crests have to be drawn on them, or if they have no such disks, the crests are sewn on.

Haori for common wear have no crests and are plain, twilled, or striped and of sombre hues, though not necessarily black. Those for home wear are often much longer than ordinary *haori* and are thickly wadded with cotton.   They are also without crests.

The *hakama* is a sort of loose trousers.   Either leg is made by joining along the nape five pieces of cloth about a yard long, four of which are of the full width of the cloth and the fifth of half that width.   The skirt is sewn by turning in the edge three times to stiffen it.   The two legs are joined in such a manner that the half-width pieces form the inner side and the lowest point of the fork is about twenty-two inches from the skirt.   In front a longitudinal plait is made an inch or so to the left so that its edge is in the middle ; two more plaits are made to the left and two to the right, and a third on the latter leg under the middle fold. A similar but deeper plait is made behind on either leg, that on the right having its edge in the middle. These plaits are not stitched, but merely hot-pressed so that they can be opened at will ; and as they

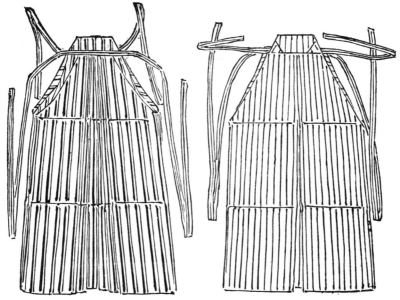

THE *HAKAMA*.

are much deeper at the skirt than at the top, they give free play to the legs when walking and make the *hakama* appear to fit more closely than it would without them. The upper half of the *hakama* is open at either side, the fork at which is of about the same depth as that in the middle. The top of the front half which is about a foot wide, is sewn on to the middle of a band which is folded and turned in to the width of half an inch and is about eleven feet long, thus leaving a free end five feet long on either side of the front half. The back, the top of which is narrower than that in front, is surmounted with a piece of thin board on which the cloth is pasted with starch mucilage. This board has also a narrow band, two feet long, on each side. The *hakama* is lined or unlined, but never wadded.

Socks are made with a thick cotton sole and a cover of common cotton or calico, black or white, which comes up only to the ankle-bone. They are split between the big toe and the next for

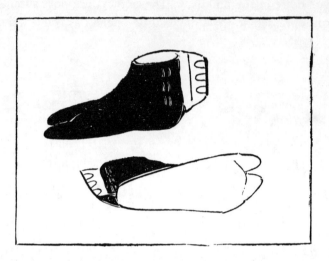

SOCKS.

holding the thong of the clogs. They are kept from coming off by two or three small metal clasps catching a cord behind the heel.

Now the Japanese suit is complete. In summer we wear the *yukata*, or the coarse unlined cotton *kimono*, at home, or an unlined dress of cotton or other material with underwear when we go out. We always put on our clothes by folding the left over the right. The clothes are folded one by one, that is, the underwear is first folded left over right, over it the doublet, and lastly the *kimono* which, if double, are folded in pairs. The principle in putting them on is that their bands shall alternate right and left and the folds form gradations widening with the outer garments, so that from the bands one can tell the quantity of clothing a man has put on. We wind the *obi* over the *kimono*. If it is the unlined crêpe, we merely wind it round and either tuck in the ends under the folds or tie them behind; but if it is the square *obi*, we leave behind one end about ten inches long and winding the *obi* twice round, fold the other end, the tip of which is tucked under the fold, at such a length that a foot or so of the doubled end is left over. The two ends are tied together in a double knot with the two extremities slanting upward one on each side of the knot. The knot is tied behind over the spine, the *obi* being wound just above the hips. Over the *kimono* we wear the *haori*. The *haori* is neither a greatcoat nor a coat properly so called ; for we wear it on all occasions and indoors, and yet we may on informal occasions take it off without breach of good manners. Indeed, a man who walks abroad without a *haori* would be in an entirely different position to one who goes about in shirt sleeves. The crested *haori*, which is invariably worn on formal occasions, is a ready means of identification ; and accordingly, when we are unwilling to attract attention or to risk recognition, the uncrested is commonly put on. The *hakama* is worn when we have to be properly dressed, on occasions, that is to say, when one would wear a frock-coat or an evening dress ; at schools and in government offices the *hakama* is indispensable when Japanese clothes are worn. In putting on a *hakama*, the front band is first brought flush with the upper edge of the *obi* and the ends are each passed once and half round the body and tied behind under the knot of the *obi* ; and then the board at the back is perched over the same knot to prevent its slipping down, and the ends of its bands are tied in front.

The socks are worn with all clothes except the *yukata* ; but many people go about barefooted, save in winter. The white is the colour worn on formal occasions ; but the black is popular as it wears better than the other and does not betray the dirt when it is soiled. Only young children wear socks of other colours, such as red and yellow.

CHAPTER VIII.

FEMALE DRESS.

Attempts at Europeanisation—Difference between Japanese and foreign dresses—Expense and inconvenience of foreign dresses—Japanese dresses not to be discarded—How the female dress differs from the male—Underwear and over-band—*Haori*—*Hakama*—*Obi*—How to tie it—The dress-*obi*—The formal dress—Home-wear—Working clothes—The sameness of form—The girl's dress—Dress and age.

THE late Prince Ito's first administration which lasted from 1886 to 1889, was a period of great pro-European activity when heroic attempts were made to Europeanise the entire social organisation. The most conspicuous of these attempts were the strenuous efforts made to remodel the social life of the nation ; and with that object in view, various social customs of the West were introduced. Balls and soirées were given in official circles and among peers and men of wealth. One of the direct consequences of this innovation was the eager adoption of the foreign costume by ladies of rank and position, whose example was soon followed by their humbler sisters. Women in European dresses were common objects in streets and at public gatherings. And it looked for a time as if the national costume were doomed.

But it was not long before a reaction set in. A cry arose in various quarters for the preservation of national characteristics ; and though there was a section of these reactionaries who would resist the introduction of western innovations in all departments of life, the general sense of the nation was to yield only so far as a change was necessitated by the incompatibility of the old customs with the new conditions imposed by the adoption of western civilisation. And among the first to feel the effect of this reaction was the western style of female dress ; and our women fell back upon their national costume. It was as well that the reversion to the old style took place before the reforming spirit had gone too far, for, to tell the truth, the Japanese woman seldom appears to advantage in a European dress. If she looks graceful in her *kimono*, she cannot be equally prepossessing in a bodice and a skirt ; and those who are charming in a western costume are the reverse in their native dress. The conditions which are needed to give charm to the wearer of the *kimono* are totally different to the conditions which one associates with elegance in European dress. The former require rounded or sloping shoulders, for square ones would put the sides of the dress out of shape and interfere with the graceful disposition of the sleeves. The body should be bent forward, for if it were held straight or bent back, the dress at the breast and the knot of the *obi* would suffer ; and for the same reason full breasts are out of favour. The close-fitting skirt of the *kimono* prevents the feet from being set far apart, and the wearer cannot take long strides. Her feet are turned slightly inward and makes her wobble a little as she walks. Such a gait would be very ungainly when a woman puts on a European dress. It may be possible for her when she dons European garments to assume another gait than that she is used to in Japanese ; but it is naturally very hard to throw off on occasion a habit acquired from childhood.

But what really led to the discarding of the European dress was not so much the uncomely form it presented as the expense and inconvenience it entailed upon its wearer. It necessitates the possession of jewelry which is useless in a Japanese dress ; necklaces and bracelets are not put on with the latter. The foreign dress is, moreover, extremely inconvenient in a Japanese house. A man can squat in European clothes without much difficulty if his trousers are baggy enough to allow the knees to be doubled ; and if they are creased, they may be set right again with a little ironing. He can therefore visit his friends in European clothes. With a woman the case is different. She cannot squat in a European dress. Her corset would inflict on her excruciating tortures as it gets out of shape when the body is bent foward in squatting ; she certainly could not bow her head to the mat in the usual Japanese fashion. What trimmings she might have on her skirt would be irretrievably spoilt; and if she once squatted, she could not get up without assistance or going on all fours. In short, the European dress cannot come into vogue until Japanese houses are remodelled and furnished with chairs instead of mats and cushions. Moreover, the expense of having a fair wardrobe of both European and Japanese dresses deters many women from taking to the former since the latter are absolutely indispensable.

Lovers of the picturesque may then rest assured that there is no immediate prospect of the disappearance of the graceful *kimono*. Largely as are the western clothes worn by Japanese men and boys, there is not much danger of their totally supplanting the national costume while the internal arrangement of the Japanese house remains unchanged ; and that transformation is, as we have already stated, to be looked for in a very dim future. Still less probability is there of a similar change in the costume of our women as it is even more intimately connected than men's clothes with domestic life. It is indeed as well that it should be so, for much as we desire to make use of the fruits of western civilisation, we would emphatically draw the line when it comes to the appearance our wives and daughters shall present at home. We may therefore leave out of consideration the western costume as worn by Japanese women.

The Japanese female dress does not differ essentially from the male ; the distinction lies in its proportions and colours. There is therefore no need to describe it in detail ; it will suffice if we give the points of difference. Thus, the body pieces are a little narrower to fit the slighter forms of women ; but they are longer, the length being from four feet nine inches to five feet. The tuck at the hip is not sewn in as in a man's dress, but the body is left loose so that the dress may be worn with a train or tucked at the hip with a sash. The tuck is usually about eight inches. The neck-band is also much wider than men's, being four inches and a half, and longer by an inch or more. The sleeves too are longer by two inches or more ; but the opening at the wrist is smaller. The sleeves are open for about a foot from the lower extremity so as to allow the wide *obi* to be worn without inconvenience, and sewn on to the body pieces for about ten inches from the top. The front and back edges of the body piece are hemmed for four inches before they are sewn together and leave an aperture of that length under the joints of the sleeve. This opening is made in all female dresses and exposes the sides of the body to the air; but it is hidden from view by the sleeve and the *obi*, and is visible only when the sleeve is held up; the object of this aperture is to give free play to the breast part of the dress. In all female dresses the sleeves are left open and hemmed from their joints with the body pieces to the lower end. The skirt of the wadded *kimono* is more heavily wadded than men's and is rounded to show more of the lining and the bulge of the wadding.

Under the *kimono* a woman wears much the same clothing as a man; but unlike him, she wears two loin-cloths. The lower one, which is the loin-cloth proper, is a piece of bleached cotton wound round the hips and coming down to the knees. It is called in Japanese the "bath-cloth," as it was formerly, and still is in some parts of the country, worn when a woman takes a bath. The upper loin-cloth, called the "hip-wrap," is more ornamental; it is tied round the hips like the bath-cloth, but comes down to the feet. It is usually made of *mousseline de laine* or crêpe, and is red for girls, of a gay colour with fanciful patterns for young women, and white for matrons. This hip-wrap is replaced in winter by what we call a "long chemise," which is practically a *kimono* made without the tuck and of the exact height of the wearer. Over the neck-band is sewn an ornamental band called "half-band," which is usually of crêpe, though some other light silk may be used, red for young girls and of various colours, white, black, violet, blue, or grey for grown-up persons. Flowers, birds, or landscapes are embroidered on it with gold or silver threads or with silk. This ornamental half-band is worn on the chemise or other underwear next to the *kimono*. The *kimono*, the upper one if two are worn, which is for home wear, is usually covered over the neck-band with an over-band of satin.

Women wear, like men, *haori* of various descriptions, the crested *haori* of black crêpe, the uncrested made of silk, striped, spotted, or of other pattern, and the long *haori*, which though often less wadded than men's, reaches like theirs below the knees. A woman's *haori* differs from a man's, like the *kimono*, in having sleeves open on the inner side and a loop-hole under the arm.

The *hakama* is worn by school-girls and their teachers, and by some of the court ladies. The girl's *hakama* differs from man's in not being divided. It is simply round like the European skirt; but it has plaits which are not, however, so deep or so marked as men's. It is open, like theirs, at the sides near the *obi* and tied in the same way.

The Japanese woman's pride, however, is the *obi*. It is often the most costly of all her apparel. It is about thirteen feet long and thirteen and a half inches wide. The *obi* for ordinary wear is made by sewing together back to back two pieces of cloth, of which the face is commonly of stiff stuff like satin and the lining of

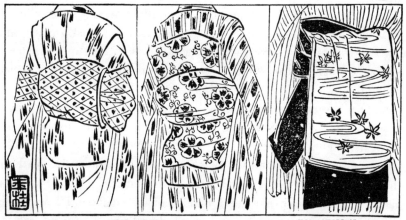

FOR GIRLS.   FOR WOMEN.
THE *OBI* FOR ORDINARY WEAR.

crêpe, or other soft silk or cotton. But the *obi* worn on formal occasions consists of a single piece of double width, which is folded in two lengthwise and seamed; it is made of taffety, satin, damask, or gold or other brocade. The Chinese satin has at one end the name of its loom in red thread; and imitation satins and sateens have similar names at the same end; and this end is always exposed to view when the *obi* is worn. When sewn, the woman's *obi* is padded like men's

The tying of the *obi*, especially of the dress-*obi*, is by no means a simple process. In the first place a woman puts on her dress in the same way as a man, that is, she folds the front edges left over right, and not right over left as in a European dress. When she has thus folded her underwear, which she sometime ties round with a cloth cord to keep it in place, she takes her *kimono*, single or double as the case may be, and catching the two edges near the ends of the band, holds them out behind her and raises them tightly until the skirt is just at her ankles, that is, at the height at which she wishes it to be, and then folding the edges stiffly one over the other, she ties the dress at the hip with a cloth cord to prevent its slipping. Then she arranges the upper half of the dress, putting the band in order and pulling the loose part down so that the breast is pressed almost flat, and ties the tuck just over the hips with a second cord. The tuck is thus tied above and below; for this two different cords are used in formal dresses, but for ordinary wear a single long narrow sash of crepe may be used for both purposes, the sash passing over the tuck at the side. Next, the *obi*, if it is for ordinary wear, is folded in two along its length and wound twice round the waist, thus concealing the cord on the tuck and leaving at the back a foot or so of one end, while the other end is three feet or more in length. The former is folded lengthwise with the lining inside. The two ends are tied in such a way that the doubled end comes out at the side slanting downwards under the knot. The second end is, while being tied, folded once with the lining outside and is pulled vertically so that the folded part is held straight up; and it is drawn out until the length above the knot is about the same as that remaining behind and then dropped over the knot; and so, when it hangs down, its end or the fold is higher than the end of the *obi* just by the width of the knot, that is, by a few inches. The end under the knot displays the face and the fold itself the lining. Some people keep the knot from coming loose by tying a cord over it round the *obi*, while others merely tighten it when it slackens.

The *obi* for ceremonial occasions is tied in the same way, only

that as it is of the same material on both sides, there is no
distinction of face and lining.   When it is tied, a narrow sash with
a piece of board or stiff cardboard in the middle is put under the
vertical fold and raised above the level of the *obi*, and the ends of
the sash are tied in front and the knot is tucked under the *obi*.
This sash is a kind of bustle to keep the fold from falling.   Next,
the fold is refolded inward, while the doubled end, instead of

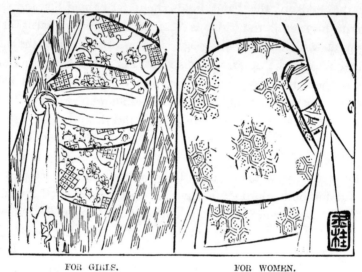

FOR GIRLS.   FOR WOMEN.

THE DRESS-*OBI*.

hanging out as in the ordinary *obi*, is bent back and pushed under
the fold.   A silk cord is then passed between the two faces of the
fold along the middle of the *obi* and tightly fastened in front over
the *obi* by means of a hook or buckle.   This cord is intended to
prevent the doubled end and the fold, after the refold, from falling
off.   The hook or buckle is usually in the form of a flower or
some other simple design in gold.   Thus, it will be seen that in
wearing the ceremonial *obi*, a woman is tied twice each over and
under it.

As the *obi* is the most conspicuous part of a woman's dress,
the *haori*, which would conceal it except in front, is not worn on
formal occasions.   It is only worn at home or on an informal
visit; and in the absence of a *haori* to display her crest on, the

woman has it dyed on her *kimono*, the number being three or five as on the man's *haori*. The formal dress is a suit of three *kimono*, of which the second and lowest have white neck-bands. The skirt is wadded much thicker than usual. Sometimes when it is too warm to wear three *kimono*, the middle one is dispensed with and an extra band is put on the lower *kimono* and a false skirt sewn on to it to make it look as if there were an intermediate *kimono*. The formal colour of the uppermost *kimono* is black, with five white crests ; but except on special occasions less sombre colours may be worn, of which the favourite are blue, grey, and violet, all light-tinted. Underneath the *kimono* is the long chemise which is the only article of clothing that is allowed to be bright-coloured. It is often expensive ; and just as men line their *haori* with costly stuff which may or may not be seen in company, so women expend as much money upon their chemises, the skirt of which may be partly exposed to view as they walk. It is commonly of figured crêpe, *habutaye*, or crêpe de Chine. Under the chemise is the ordinary cotton underwear.

When she goes out on an informal visit, the Japanese woman usually puts on a crested *haori ;* but if it is only for a walk, the *haori* may be plain. The *kimono* may on such occasions be of any pattern, only that when she makes a call, the band must be of the same cloth as the *kimono*. At home a woman usually has on a black satin band as it can be readily renewed, for owing to the liberal use of pomade on her hair, the band is the part of her dress that is soonest soiled, and hence the advantage of a band that can be easily changed. The part of her dress which is, next to the band, most liable to be soiled is the lap ; for as we squat with our knees bent in front of us, we are apt to lay in our laps whatever may be in our hands, and most women therefore, except in families of higher position, wear aprons at home. Those of the middle class take off their aprons when they go out ; but the wives and daughters of tradesmen and artisans wear them even outdoors. Still, as it is not considered good form to have them on when one receives calls, they should take them off before they go into the parlour to welcome their visitors ; as a matter of fact, however, this is done only when the visitor is one of superior position who must be treated with great respect.   The apron covers the front part of the *kimono* below the *obi*, under which it is tied by a cord attached to it.   It is also worn by tradesmen and others whose business it is to handle wares of any kind.

The ordinary *kimono* is inconvenient for active work.   Those whose work requires a free movement of the limbs, commonly

A SERVANT WITH TUCKED SLEEVES.

discard the long sleeves and the skirt.   Coolies and artisans wear tight-sleeved coats and tight-fitting drawers of cotton.   Women,

THE REFORMED DRESS.

too, who labour outdoors have on similar clothes sometimes ; but more frequently they wear tight-sleeved *kimono*, the skirts of which are tucked up to the knees to facilitate their walking. Women, however, who live indoors but have to move about at their household work, do not care to put on tight-sleeved *kimono*, and they tie up their sleeves with a cloth cord when they are actively employed. They are often to be seen dusting and sweeping the rooms with their sleeves tied up and a towel on their heads. The *kimono* appears indeed to be capable of little improvment. The only concession that has been made to the requirements of the latter-day school-girl is the contraction of the sleeves. The " reformed dress," as it is called, has large open sleeves which can be tightened by means of a string. It is found very handy and is worn by many school-girls. Reformed or unreformed, there is this to be said for the Japanese woman's dress that it does not suffer in the matter of pockets or what serve as such from comparison with man's.

There is then very little difference in the dress of a Japanese woman indoors and out, except in the case of the formal dress. Even there the form is the same. This uniformity of cut strikes one everywhere in Japan ; the dresses are all cast in the same mould. There may be variations in the length of the sleeves or in the colour and texture of the apparel ; but even fickle fashion leaves the shape of the dress unchanged ; it only varies the stuff and the pattern.

Children's clothes differ slightly from their elders'. Up to about ten they often wear at home the tight-sleeved *kimono*. Boys, indeed, may continue to put them on far into the teens ; but girls are soon dressed in *kimono* of fancifully-figured crêpe or *mousseline de laine*, the gayest of which are specially made for their wear. Their outdoor *kimono* have sleeves almost touching the ground, and their formal dress is black with light patterns on the lower part of the sleeves and round the skirt. Their *obi* is folded almost perpendicularly behind, the folded end coming close up to the shoulders ; and over it is tied a plain sash, usually of yellow or red crêpe, the knot being tied at the side with the ends hanging down.

A YOUNG LADY DRESSED FOR A VISIT.

The girl, on reaching her sixteenth or seventeenth year, ceases to be a child and becomes a *shinzo*, or maiden ; she no longer puts on gaily-coloured *kimono*, though she still retains the hip-wrap, underwear sleeves, and band of crimson. At twenty-four, at which she becomes a *toshima*, when she is supposed to be married, the colour of her dress becomes more sober ; the hip-wrap is white, the sleeves of her underwear, though sometimes still red for a little while longer, are oftener of a less conspicuous tint, and the band of blue, purple, black, or other dark hues. For the first few years she may, in her desire to conceal her age, affect the *shinzo's* costume ; but when she reaches thirty, she is an unmistakable *toshima*. This stage terminates at forty, when she comes to be spoken of as approaching old age. She is dressed soberly as if to avoid notice. Forty is pretty early for a woman to be classified as old ; but in former days old age began at fifty when a man was considered unfit for business and made over his name and property to his heir. We mature early and decline at the same rate. Indeed, man, says a Japanese proverb, lives but for fifty years and rarely does his span extend to seventy years. Our expectation of life is, then, two decades less than the Psalmist's. Impressed by its brevity, the Japanese woman knows that she ceases to please after two score and unmurmuringly gives up hope. She does not allow herself to be deceived when silver locks begin to appear among the raven ; and by her dress and coiffure she frankly confesses the stage she has reached in the journey of life.

CHAPTER IX.

TOILET.

Queues—Hair-cutting—Moustaches and beards—Shaving—Women's coiffure—Children's hair—"Inverted maidenhair "—*Shimada*—" Rounded chignon "—Other forms—The lightest coiffure—Bars—Combs—Ornaments round the chignon—Hair-pins—The hair-dresser—The kind of hair esteemed—Loss of complexion—Girls painted—Women's paint—Blackening of teeth—Shaving of eyebrows—Washing the face—Looking-glasses.

AMONG the earliest innovations after the Restoration to which the Japanese people took kindly was the clipping of their queues. In the old days men had little queues on the top of their heads. For this purpose they shaved the crown and gathering the hair around, tied it at the top with a piece of paper string; then, they bent the queue and bringing it down forward over the forehead, fastened it with the ends of the same string so that the queue was tied tightly to the first knot. The end of the queue was cut straight. Fashion often changed in the making of the queue, though its general form remained unaltered. The bend, for instance, between the two knots might vary in size and shape, and the queue itself in length and thickness, its girth being regulated by the extent of the tonsure at the crown. Or the hair might be full or tight at the sides and the back. The front was usually shaved. In short, there was a wide scope for taste in the dressing of the queue.

These queues were untied and remade every second or third day, and the head was shaved at the same time. Hair-dressing was therefore a troublesome business, especially as one had generally to get assistance for it. Consequently, when the cropping of the hair came into vogue, people eagerly adopted it as it saved them time and expense. At first they cut the hair long, letting it half hide the ears and come down to the neck behind; but it became shorter by degrees until now the fashion is to crop it to about

a quarter of an inch, presenting a head which is appropriately known
as " chestnut-bur.''

QUEUES.

Although pictures of old Japanese warriors represent them
with moustaches, the custom seems to have been under the Tokugawa rule to be clean shaven about the mouth ; only aged men
indulged in beards, while whiskers grown by themselves were
almost unknown.   After the Restoration government officials began
to grow moustaches, and for a long time the favourite way of
mimicking an official was to twirl an imaginary moustache.   But
professional men of all sorts now let them grow, so that they have
ceased to be characteristic of officials.   Tradesmen, artisans, and
coolies, however, are still clean shaven, or at most have bristles
of a few days' growth.

Japanese barbers shave not only the lips, cheeks, and
chin, and the borders of the hair, but they also pass thir razors

over the whole face, not sparing the forehead, the eyelids between the eyelashes and the eyebrows, the cheek-bones, the nose, and the ear-lobes, and unless their victim objects, they will insert a small narrow razor into his nostrils and ears and twirl it rapidly round with great dexterity. The shaving of the nostrils is easier in a Japanese than it would be in a European on account of their greater width, and another advantage arising from the shortness of the nose is that the Japanese barber does not offer an indignity to his client by tweaking his nose when he shaves his upper lip.

THE " 203-METRE HILL " AND " PENTHOUSE."

Troublesome as was the man's queue in the old days, it was a trifle compared with the woman's coiffure. In the early days of the present régime when men began to cut their hair, many women followed suit and cropped theirs as short. The government, however, interfered and prohibited the cutting of the hair by women other than widows and grandames with whom it was a time-honoured custom. In 1887 when the pro-European craze was at its height, many women tied their hair in European style; but it was subsequently abandoned by those who found that by tying the hair in this manner, they spoilt it for the Japanese coiffure ; for having been accustomed to oil it well for their native style, they discovered that the hair, when bound without any pomade, became very brittle and snapped short.   Still, the European style is now largely adopted because it does not require expert assistance and the services of the professional hair-dresser can be dispensed with.   Various styles are in vogue. Soon after the fall of Port Arthur in 1905, a high knot came into fashion under the formidable title of " 203-metre hill knot," in celebration of the capture of that famous hill which was practically the key to the great fortress.   The favourite at present with our women is a low pompadour known as the " penthouse style." But though the European way of dressing the hair has become very popular, it is not likely so long as the *kimono* remains unchanged that the Japanese coiffure, awkward as it is compared with the European, will be entirely superseded by the other.

Newly-born infants are shaven ; but as they grow up, a little circle at the crown is left untouched.   At first the circle is small, but it grows larger with years ; and at six or seven, boys let all their hair grow and crop them when too long, just like their elders. Girls, before they leave this " poppy-head " stage as it is called,

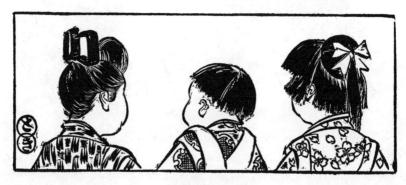

YOUNG GIRLS' HAIR.

have little queues on the crown, tied less closely than men's in the old days.   Next, at ten or more, they have their hair done in a more complicated manner ; sometimes the tresses are tied together at the crown and made into bows, and sometimes the hair is gathered at the top and parted into two tresses, right and left, which are made into vertical loops, joined together at the side, the joint being covered with a piece of ornamental paper. It has of late become an almost universal custom with school-girls to tie their hair with a ribbon and let it down loose or plaited on their backs.

From fifteen to well over forty, the favourite style is that known as "inverted maidenhair." The hair is in this coiffure first combed into one bundle, except a triangular tuft over the forehead. It is tied at the root and divided into two equal tresses, right and left, which are then looped, the end of either tress being combed into the root of the other; and the two loops are turned down and

THE "INVERTED MAIDENHAIR."

brought behind the crown, and kept in place by being tied together to the first knot. The hair at the sides and the back is swollen out by a dexterous jerk of a comb or hair-pin from underneath when it is first gathered. That at the sides is further combed with a rough comb, while the hair at the back is held in place by a spring hair-pin. This is the lightest coiffure as false hair is not generally required; but it is not the formal way of dressing the hair.

For young women the formal coiffure is the *shimada*, so
called from the name of the town on the high road between Tokyo
and Kyoto, where it first came into fashion. In this the hair is
gathered and tied tightly at or near the crown together with a large
tuft of false hair. The tip is folded in forward; the hair is then
folded twice in the same direction as the tip so that the edge of the
fold is half an inch or less behind the knot; and the whole is turned
over the knot in such a way that the edge of the second fold is
forward of the crown. Then, by a string passing over the knot
the fold is tied down. The chignon is formed by spreading out the
hair; sometimes a piece of paper, of the size of the chignon, is well
pomaded and put under the surface of the chignon to help it to
keep in place. The size of the chignon varies with the wearer's
taste; but, generally speaking, a young woman's is larger than her
elder sister's. Its position too varies, as it depends upon that of
the first knot, whether over or behind the crown. In the formal
coiffure of a young lady of social standing it is close to the crown;
but girls in a lower station of life or anxious to be thought *chic*
prefer the chignon to be more to the back of the head.

THE *SHIMADA* AND " ROUNDED CHIGNON."

The *marumage,* or " rounded chignon," of married women is formed by tying the hair at the crown as in the *shimada,* and then making a loop at the end.   This is wrapped round with a piece of ornamental cloth, usually of silk and dyed, and then folded forward ; a small bar is passed through the two sides of the loop and the main tuft ; and the latter is folded forward twice and the bar is brought down near the crown.   The hair behind is spread out into a chignon.   Unlike the *shimada,* this chignon is mostly back of the knot; it is held down by a string tied to the knot and the loop.   False hair is used, but to a less extent than in the *shimada*; and a little paper pillow wadded with cotton is put under the chignon to hold it in place.   A small part of the loop appears on each side of the chignon around the bar and displays the piece of ornamental cloth.   The size of the chignon varies with the age of its wearer, the largest being adopted by young women and the smallest by old matrons.

There are said to be more than a hundred different ways, new and old, of dressing the hair ; and even at the present time there are a score of them in vogue.   But as most of them are combinations or modifications of the three coiffures above mentioned, we need not describe them.   In all three the forelock is taken in a triangular tuft and tied with a piece of string, and held down with a comb just in front of the knot on the crown.

Both the *shimada* and the *marumage* are heavy as they require false hair.   The hair needs also to be well oiled.   The hair is done once in three or four days, but is seldom washed, not more than once a month.   The head is consequently heated and a headache is often the result.   Lighter than either of these is the " inverted maidenhair," which needs no false hair unless the natural hair is too thin.   It is preferred when one is at home, and especially when a long spell of either of the other forms of coiffure has ended in a headache.   It is also in favour sometimes for the reason that it does not, like the others, require hair ornaments.   A Japanese woman has no need of jewelry as it is not the custom to wear brooches, ear-rings, necklaces, or bracelets ; and the only articles of gold or silver are, if we except the watch and chain and the finger-rings, which are all of recent introduction, her pipe, the

clasp of the *obi*-fastener, ornamental hair-pins, and sometimes other articles for the hair.

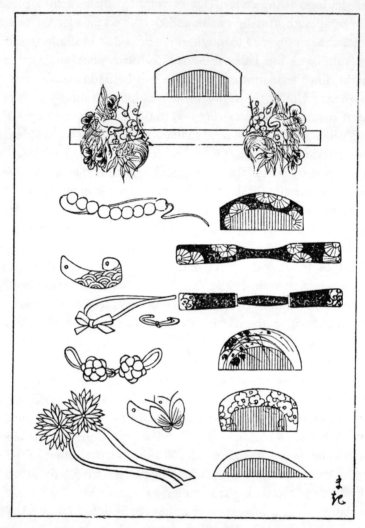

BARS, COMBS, AND BANDS.

The married woman's coiffure requires a bar through the chignon. This bar varies in length with the width of the chignon, beyond which it appears from a quarter to half an inch. The regulation bar is square or oblong in section with flat or slightly rounded ends. It should be made of transparent, light-yellow tortoise-shell; but dark tortoise-shell or lacquered wood with gold figures is also worn. There are artists of high repute who make a speciality of the designing and lacquering of these bars. Inferior kinds are made of black lacquered wood or celluloid. Sometimes floral or other designs in gold or silver are attached to the ends of bars intended for young women.

The comb, on formal occasions, should be of the same material as the bar. Such combs are usually of light-yellow tortoise-shell; they are worn in front of the chignon and hold down the tip of the hair over the forehead. They have curved backs and straight ends, and are thicker than those used in hair-dressing, which are of boxwood. Other ornamental combs are of various shapes; they may be curved toward the tips, or may be longer and narrower or more rounded and wider than the tortoise-shells. They are made, like the bars, of lacquered wood, common tortoise-shell, or celluloid. The commonest kinds are of boxwood. The combs used for combing the side-hair are wider at one end than at the other, while those for gathering in stray locks are only about an inch wide, close-toothed, and with a long, pointed handle, and for removing scurf fine-toothed double combs are used.

In the case of the *marumage* and sometimes of the *shimada*, the knot of the root is hidden from sight by tying around it a thin strip of metal, or a string of paste or coral beads. In the *shimada* a narrow strip of white paper is also sometimes worn. The piece of cloth wound round the loop of the *marumage* is usually of plain common silk crimpled or netted, and often mottled. That worn by young girls in coiffure that requires such pieces is plain red; but their elders prefer quieter tints.

The greatest variety is, however, to be seen in ornamental hair-pins. These hair-pins have mostly two legs, though very simple ones are one-legged. They are made of horn, ivory, wood, metal, or celluloid, and have above the fork, if two-legged, some ornament, a bead, or a design in metal, horn, ivory, bone, or other material. These designs, if of the better quality, consist of figures in gold on lacquer background or on ivory, or chasings of gold or

silver. The hair-pins worn on formal occasions by young girls are
surmounted with a large flower in metal, from which hangs a red

ORNAMENTAL HAIR-PINS.

silk tassel. Grown-up women set most value on silver or gold pins
with a coral bead, about half an inch in diameter. The coral most
esteemed is pink or flesh-coloured, though one of a darker hue is
preferred by some people. In the commoner kinds the legs are of

German silver as wood or horn is liable to snap. There is no rule as to the length of these hair-pins. They are stuck 'in under the chignon, or a little in front or behind, but never in the chignon itself.

Hair-dressing is no light task; and though a woman may be able to do her own hair, she almost invariably gets it done by somebody else as a great deal has to be done at the back of the

THE HAIR-DRESSER.

head. The professional female hair-dresser is therefore an established institution; she visits most houses at regular intervals. She has usually an assistant, or rather an apprentice, who loosens and combs the hair and prepares it for her to dress. A successful hair-dresser probably makes more money than any other professional of her sex. The geisha's receipts may be larger, but her expenses are correspondingly great so that her net profit is comparatively small, whereas the hair-dresser needs neither capital nor stock, beyond a few combs, and even these are often unnecessary as she uses those of her client. Besides her regular charges, which are not heavy, she receives many presents from those who are anxious for her to come at regular intervals or out of turn, as when they are going out to a party, a theatre, or some other place of public resort. She is also a great gossip, a disseminator of scandals, and in this respect she has the advantage over the barber who has himself no mean reputation in that direction in Japan as everywhere else; for whereas the barber has to retail his discourse more or less in public before the other clients who are awaiting their turn, the woman purveys her news in the privacy of the lady's toilet room. And as the discussion of her neighbour's private affairs and the tearing of her character is no less a favourite occupation with the Japanese woman than with her European sister, it is not always for the sole purpose of having her hair done that she eagerly waits for the hair-dresser's visit.

Our hair is always black until it begins to turn gray; and women esteem glossy-black, straight hair. Curly hair is held in such horror that it is said to spoil any face however comely in other respects. And the hair-dresser's apprentice, when she comes to undo her client's hair for re-dressing, first loosens it and combs it to free it of tangles, and then with a cloth dipped in boiling water, straightens it until all traces of former bends and twists have disappeared, and applies to it a pomade to keep it from curling or getting out of shape. Next to the glossy appearance of the hair, its borders receive careful attention. There should be no clusters of short hairs about the borders, which should show a clear demarcation between the hair and the skin. Hairy borders are regarded to be as great blemishes as clumsy hands and feet. The short hair over the forehead is, however, tolerated as hardly any one is free from it ; but at the same time the border over the forehead should rise from either temple in a slight curve until it is right over the forehead when it should meet the other in a faint downward curve. From a fanciful resemblance of such a border to the outline of Mount Fuji, the forehead is then known as the " Fuji forehead," and highly admired as an important feature of personal beauty.

The Japanese woman does not allow any hair or even down to grow on her face, and from time to time shaves the whole face like the other sex. We are not a hairy race, and our women have on the whole very smooth faces. We hardly ever see them with moustaches or stumps of hairs on their faces. It is not improbable that this shaving of the face contributes to the early loss of complexion among the Japanese women ; but the arch-enemy of the clear complexion is certainly the paint, for painting is an almost universal custom in Japan.

Young girls are painted quite white and present a somewhat ghastly appearance, for the paint is a thick paste of white powder, coarser than *poudre de riz*, and is daubed over the face with the hands. The neck and the upper part of the breast are also painted ; but the paint, it must be admitted, is too conspicuous to be mistaken for the natural colour of the skin, and the Japanese girl knows it. If the hair hung over her neck and face in fringes or ringlets, we might suspect her of attempting to pass the paint for her own skin ; but the hair is combed up into a knot at the crown and the borders of the hair are strongly marked on the forehead and the neck. As, however, the hair is usually thick over the forehead, the contrast there between the paint and the natural skin may not be striking ; but at the back it is impossible to conceal the difference, and as if to make a virtue of necessity, the paint is daubed at the borders in a very angular zigzag, which emphasises the difference between it and the brown skin.

The paint is laid on less thickly as the girl grows up ; and though many women, especially those from the country, make a liberal use of it, the custom in Tokyo is to apply a dilute solution lightly so that one can hardly tell at a distance whether the face is painted or not.   The neck, however, is more thickly painted. Vermilion is applied to the lips in degrees varying with the age.

The blackening of the teeth is fast going out of fashion; nowadays in Tokyo, only middle-aged women and their seniors take to it, though young married women among the lower classes are sometimes to be seen with blackened teeth.   In ancient times men of rank and position blackened their teeth ; it was a sign of good birth, and the expression " white teeth " was synonymous with plebeianism.   This custom was subsequently confined to court nobles, and was later still adopted by married women.   The idea seems to be that as black is the only colour that remains unchanged, the teeth were blackened in token of their owner's constancy and fidelity.

The eyebrows are shaven in infants and little children, especially girls, with the object of making them grow thick. Women touch them up with Indian ink or burnt-cork powder. They used to shave them off upon marriage at the same time as the first blackening of the teeth; but this custom is, like the other, dying out.   Many women, however, shave off their eyebrows when they reach the age of forty or thereabouts, as they prefer to have none at all to having them thin and irregular.

Before they commence their toilet, women take a bath or wash their faces, necks, and shoulders over a tub unless it is early morning in cold weather.   Soap is a foreign innovation ; and the same purpose was served by the use of fine bran-powder obtained by sifting rice after its final cleaning in a mortar.   A handful of this powder is put into a little cloth bag, which is then wetted and rubbed against the skin ; and the turbid water which exudes through the texture of the bag is very efficacious in cleaning the skin.   It is now used together with soap.   Young women some-times put other substances with the bran into the bag, such as pulverised egg-shells which are said to remove stains from the skin and the powered bark of a species of magnolia.

Our women, squatting as they do at their toilet, do not need a dressing-table, instead of which they set before them a small wooden box with three or four drawers and surmounted with a square looking-glass hinged on two supports which stand on the box. In the old days when glass was unknown or at least very rare, a metal disk highly polished on one face and with a handle was set on a stand. Now, however, sheet-glass mirrors are very common, though those of plate-glass are less used owing to their higher prices as they have, unlike the sheet-glass, to be imported from abroad.

CHAPTER X.

OUTDOOR GEAR.

Boots and shoes *versus* clogs and sandals—Inconvenience of foreign footgear— Shoes and boots at private houses—Clogs and sandals able to hold their own—How clogs are made—Plain clogs—Matted clogs—Sandals—Straw sandals—Headgear—Woman's hood—Overcoats and overdresses—Common umbrellas—Better descriptions of umbrellas —Lanterns—Better kinds of lanterns.

EUROPEAN clothes are, as we have seen, replacing the Japanese male dress in schools, public offices, and other quarters, and are checked in their advance only by the unaltered state of Japanese homes. In the matter of footgear the case is almost similar, only that boots and shoes have superseded clogs and sandals to a far greater extent than coats and trousers have the *kimono*. For people in foreign clothes almost invariably wear foreign footgear ; it is only in wet weather that one sees sometimes a Japanese in European clothes walking through the mud in clogs instead of boots ; and a great many in native clothes wear boots and shoes. There are plenty of people who go in *hakama* to schools and public and private offices ; but where these buildings are in foreign style as most of them are, people are not allowed to enter with their clogs, and the only alternative is that they must wear sandals or boots. But as the sandals cover the feet with dust in dry weather and with mud in wet, many persons prefer to walk in clogs and change them for sandals at the school or office ; but as this means that they must leave at the entrance their sandals at night and their clogs in the daytime, they run the risk of losing them. Hence, there is a steady increase in the number of those who wear boots or shoes, which if one gets used to them, are easier to walk in than clogs or sandals.

Boots and shoes go very well with the *hakama*, which, being loose and wide, does not rub against them ; but they are not so con venient when we are in *kimono* only. The leather, by rubbing against the *kimono*, wears it, especially if silk-lined, much more quickly than do clogs ; for in a Japanese dress it is not the thongs of the clogs so much as the socks that rub against the lining of the *kimono*. And these socks naturally wear it out more slowly if they are of calico, and not of cotton.

In going into a Japanese house, one has to take off the clogs, sandals, boots, or shoes ; and consequently it is more convenient to go in either of the former two as they can be slipped off without the least trouble. And also, as the socks are visible in wearing clogs, we seldom go out in shabby ones ; but when we put on boots or shoes, we not unfrequently forget there is a hole in the sole of a sock, or it may be that we put up with worn-out socks believing there would be no need to take off our boots until we come home, and then, being suddenly called by business to a private house, we repair thither and on pulling off our boots, see with dismay the toes peeping out of the socks. Another disadvantage of boots when we visit a private house is that felt in winter, which has already been referred to in a former chapter ; that is, though there are braziers for the hands, no provisions are made for the feet which are soon benumbed through the socks, which however thick they may be, are not so warm as the Japanese socks, especially when the latter are under cover of the *haori*. Still, boots and shoes are often unavoidable when we pay a chance visit ; but then the boots should be elastic-webbed, for if we call with laced boots on, the servant who answers the door has to wait patiently in the draught until we take them off. The situation is aggravated when the visitor leaves ; for then the host and his servant, and if he is a friend of the family, the wife and the children, will come to the porch to see him off and remain there until he leaves the house. If the caller has any tact, he will merely tuck in the laces and walk out with his boots flopping and tie them when he is out of the premises. Many visitors, however, think nothing of keeping the whole family shivering in the cold while they leisurely lace their boots, for probably they too are put to the same ordeal when they have visitors in laced boots. For their greater handiness in this respect shoes were at first almost exclusively worn ; but now boots are supplanting them to a large extent on account of their superior ease in walking.

As these disadvantages, then, attach to boots and shoes when we wear a *kimono* or visit a Japanese house, clogs and sandals are able to hold their own against the invasion of foreign footgear, and are likely to continue in favour so long as we are obliged to go indoors barefooted or in socks only, which means, while the interior of Japanese houses is unchanged and people squat on mats instead of sitting in chairs. As it will be a long time before the interior can be Europeanised, the clogs and sandals will for many a year to come remain the national footgear of the Japanese. Our description of the Japanese dress would therefore be incomplete without a reference to the clogs and sandals.

To begin with the clogs, they are either plain or matted. A plain clog consists essentially of a piece of wood, oblong or with rounded ends, just large enough to cover the sole of the foot, and supported by two flat, oblong pieces of wood, running from side to

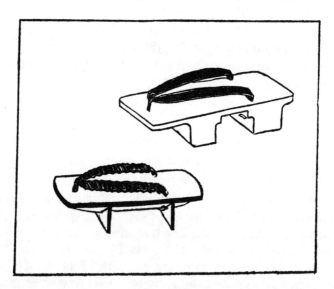

PLAIN CLOGS.

side and one behind the other. The sole-piece has three holes, one on each side just in front of the hind support and one in the middle in front of the forward support. A thick thong of hemp is passed through the side-holes from above and the ends are tied together under the sole-piece ; the part on the upper face of the sole-piece, which is covered with cloth or leather, is just long enough to be stretched out to the third hole ; a similarly-covered thong is passed through a hole pierced in the top of the first thong and its ends are pushed through the hole in the sole-piece and tied in a knot on the nether side. The second thong thus holds down the first, which is separated from the sole-piece by a distance just enough to pass the toes between them. In wearing a clog the toes are slipped in under the side-thong and the top-thong is held tightly between the big and the second toe. The side-thong presses on the joints of the toes and prevents the clog from slipping off. If the top-thong is gripped tightly, the toes will naturally be bent and press down the fore-end of the clog and, the top-thong acting as a fulcrum, the hind-end will press against the heel. Thus, there will be little difficulty in walking in clogs. But if the grip be relaxed, the hind-end will drop and, in walking, be dragged on the ground ; and as it will hurt the toes to be always in tight grip, the clogs are very often merely hanging on to the toes and are consequently dragged along. It is this dropping and dragging of the hind-end which makes the clogs clatter so noisily on the stone pavement and wooden flooring.

Plain clogs vary in height ; they are cut out of a single piece of wood or else have the sole-piece made separately from the supports. Those for rainy weather are five or six inches high ; the supports are made separately and fit into grooves on the nether side of the sole-piece, and the thongs are covered with leather. There is a toe-cap to serve as mud-guard, made of thick waterproof paper or leather and held down by two pieces of twine from its ends, which are tied behind the hind support. There is a similar kind, much shorter and without a toe-cap, which is put on in fine weather. But the favourite form with men at present is cut out of a single piece of wood ; the thongs are covered with cloth or leather, preferably the latter. The rain-clogs for women have their edges and nether sides often varnished black.

Matted clogs are mostly of a single piece ; the two ends are rounded ; the under-side of the toe-end slants downward so that the part touching the ground is a thin, angular edge, while the hind support is comparatively thick. The hole for the top-thong is enlarged on the nether side so that the knot of the thong can be enclosed in it and a metal cover tacked on it to keep the knot clean. This is a wise precaution, because the top-thong is the weakest part of the clog ; if one stumbles, for instance, the thong is strained and often snaps, and it has to be renewed. The matting which is woven fine with rushes, is tacked on the sole-piece. In the clogs for women the hind support is large, being of the same form as the

MATTED CLOGS.

hind-end of the sole-piece and leaving just space enough for tying the thong ends. In those for young girls the supports touch each other with a cavity within for tying the thong ends ; these clogs are painted black, brown, or red ; and those for very little girls have often tiny bells in the cavity, which tinkle as their wearer toddles along. There is another variety for women, in which the hind support is mortised as in the rain clogs. The thongs are covered with leather or dark-coloured silk or hemp cloth for men, while the coverings for women are mostly of silk, cotton, or hemp cloth, the commonest being heavy woven silk, plush, velvet, and velveteen, and those for girls are usually of red or purple velvet or plush. Clogs, especially of the better kind, and thongs are sold separately, and they are fitted while the customer waits. The best clogs are made of paulownia wood and those of inferior quality are of cryptomeria and other common wood, while the supports, if made separately, are of oak for better qualities and beech for inferior ones.

Sandals are made of matting or straw. Matted sandals are the lightest and easiest to wear of all footgear ; but they are apt to cover the feet with dust in dry weather and to become sodden and muddy in wet weather or after rain. They are comfortable

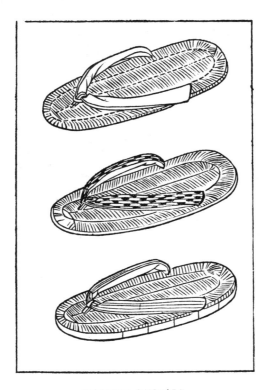

MATTED SANDALS.

only on dry hard ground. Common sandals are lined on the sole with strands of hemp. Another variety has a thick wooden sole in lateral sections so as to allow the matting to bend freely. But the sandals of the best quality, which are at present very popular and

known as " snow-sandals," though they are unfit for walking in the
snow, have soles of untanned hide with a flat piece of iron at the
heels to prevent their slipping; but the feet, especially if socked,
slip on the smooth matting unless the thong is held very tightly,
which defect renders these sandals unsuitable for fast walking.
Still another kind, also very popular, is lined with caoutchouc.

Straw sandals, on the other hand, are fitted for running or
long walks. The thongs, which are of straw, are tied over the toes
and around the foot just over the ankle. Though these thongs are

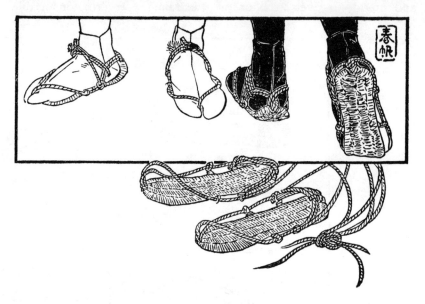

STRAW-SANDALS.

apt at first to cut the feet if unsocked, they are easy and comfortable
when one gets used to them. They are worn by coolies and others
whose business it is to be constantly on their feet. Unfortunately,
they soon become sodden in rain or over a muddy road; but as
they are very cheap, they are frequently changed in a long journey.
Cast-off straw-sandals are among the commonest sights on the road
on a rainy day.

Next to the covering for the feet, the most important article
of outdoor wear is the headgear. In the old times a majority of the

people went bareheaded ; and even now hats are often worn for appearance rather than from necessity. Except in very cold weather, there is little difference in the temperature within doors and without, and one does not feel it necessary to wear a hat in the open air. There are still people who go about bareheaded except in midsummer and mid-winter. With European clothes we natural-ly wear hats, but with Japanese clothes there is no such invariable custom. However, the habit grown with foreign clothes has passed on to the national dress, and now bowlers, wideawakes, chimney pots, Panamas, straw hats, and caps are in their season to be seen

OLD HEADGEAR.

everywhere. The hats used in the old days served as sunshades no less than as mere head-coverings. Of these the black-varnished, wooden hat, shaped like a flattened cone, which was worn by the military class, has entirely disappeared. Street-vendors and pedlars still wear in the summer heat large, flattish, round hats of bamboo-sheaths, which are light but very fragile, while mushroom-like hats of spliced bamboo covered with white or black cloth are extensively worn by coolies. A rush-hat deep enough to cover the whole face but with a peep-hole for the eyes, which was formerly worn by samurai out of employment to avoid recognition, is now worn for the same reason by fortune-tellers at the roadside and by prisoners under trial on their way to the law-court. Convicted prisoners, however, wear the mushroom-hat,

Women wear nothing on their heads except in mid-winter for fear of deranging their elaborate coiffure. The large chignon is as

A HOOD.

great a protection against heat, cold, and wind as any European bonnet. In winter, however, women wear a hood of *mousseline-de-laine* or crêpe lined with common silk. It is oblong in shape, being five feet long by about two wide ; it is folded in two and at one side, about a foot from the fold, the edges are sewn together for an inch. The loop thus formed is the face-opening. The hood is put carefully over the head so that the face is visible at the opening, and a loop of string on either side of the fold is passed over the ear to keep the hood in place ; and the ends of the hood are brought forward, folded loosely over the nose, mouth, and throat, and tied together behind on the neck. The hood which lies lightly on the head can be taken off without deranging the hair to any extent. Women are expected to take off the hood when they meet an acquaintance in the street, though they omit to do so if he is an intimate friend. The hood keeps the head, neck, and shoulders very warm.

At one time shawls were much in vogue and worn together with the hood ; but they have of late fallen out of favour. Their place is taken by " azuma-coats," which are overdresses worn over the *kimono*. They resemble the latter in form, except that they are looser and have much wider bands which come down to the skirt and dispense with gores altogether. In the latest forms the sleeves are very large ; the front is double-breasted with the throat open ; and the overlapping parts button at the breast by means of a loop and knot and are tied at the hip with a string. They are made of silk. They are vulgarly known as " rag-concealers," as many women put them on when they go out to hide the shabby dresses underneath. Men's favourite overcoat for the *kimono* is a kind of Inverness cape, with a long skirt to cover the *kimono* and large arm-holes for the sleeves. These are also made of wool. Among the lower classes there are still men in Tokyo who wear, as do peasants in the country, a straw rain-coat which covers the body and the sleeves, but leaves the legs bare ; they are unpleasant neighbours in an electric car on a rainy day. The majority, however, especially coolies, messengers, and postmen, put on a coat shaped like the *haori* and made of waterproof oil-paper or rubber-cloth.

There is a great variety in umbrellas. The Japanese umbrella, as may be seen from the innumerable samples to be found the world over, has bamboo ribs and stem and is covered with oil-paper and

AN OVERDRESS.

surmounted with a thick paper cap into which the ribs run. It is a heavy clumsy article ; and it cannot be used like the European umbrella, in place of a walking-stick in fine weather, as we should be afraid of knocking the cap off if either end touched the ground. It has to be carried with the handle downward after a rain to let the water drip off. Its only advantages are its cheapness and its size as it is large enough to shelter the whole body from rain. The common kind, such as is used by servants going out on an errand and by the poorer classes, is of plain oiled paper marked with the name, usually the first syllable, of its owner, and his trade sign if he is an artisan or tradesman, and sometimes his address as well. It can be readily identified ; and one cannot therefore put up, as if it were one's own, in broad daylight an umbrella with one's neighbour's name and address plainly written on it. Besides, as these umbrellas are very cheap, it would be hardly worth while making off with them.

Umbrellas of the better sort have black caps with concentric rings in black and red on the covering, though light yellow rings are also to be found among them. They are known as " serpents' eyes" from a fanciful resemblance thereto of these rings. They are, however, being superseded by foreign umbrellas with iron ribs and cloth covers which are more convenient to carry. Gigantic umbrellas are sometimes set up for shading street-stalls. Sunshades resemble the " serpents' eyes" in form, except that the paper is not oiled and the centres and rings are blue or white ; but they too are going out of use. The sunshades which find such a large sale abroad with gay pictures and flowers painted on them, are used in Japan by children only, especially by little girls.

The streets of Tokyo are ill-lighted. Street-lamps set up by the municipality are comparatively few ; and what light there is in most streets comes from the lamps hung over the gates and front-doors of private houses ; and where these houses are far apart, one has to walk in absolute darkness. Hence, at night many people carry lanterns to light them over ruts, mire, and diggings. The general make of the Japanese lantern is too well known everywhere to need special mention. They are all collapsible. The simplest and cheapest form used by wayfarers is the telescopic lantern, which is often given at tea-houses and restaurants to their customers when they wish to walk home. It is cylindrical when open, and the diameter of the body being less than that of the top and bottom which are made of a thin piece of wood, the body is concealed between them when closed and the lantern can be readily carried in

LANTERNS.

the pocket. It is held by a string attached to the top. The lantern used by coolies and errand-boys is similarly shaped, but of stronger material, and has a bow, the ends of which are fixed to the top and bottom to keep the lantern stretched. The top is not open as in the other, but has a hinged lid which when closed, keeps out the wind. The lantern commonly carried in the streets is spherical and has a bamboo handle attached to the top by a piece of wire.

The lanterns which are so extensively exported abroad are similarly shaped; but the red or red and white kinds are in Japan hung only at festivals or suspended in festoons over shop fronts at opening sales and on other special occasions. The lanterns used by tradesmen and artisans, are commonly marked with their trade or firm names in large black characters on the body, while those of private families are adorned with their crests.

There are also round and bulging kinds, sometimes quite spherical and sometimes more elongated, stretched out by a bow and having a hook attached to the top, so that they can be carried about or hung on to bars. They have also lids like the coolies' lanterns. They are especially used at fires; indeed, they form a distinctive feature in the confusion and disorder which invariably prevail on such occasions. There is another kind, known as the horseman's lantern, which is spherical, with a roof over the top which is open; the handle is of lacquered wood, within which is a piece of whalebone with its end attached to the lantern, and by means of this whalebone the handle can be lengthened at will. This lantern is also used by foot-passengers among the better classes. All lanterns have a round nail sticking up from the centre of the bottom, on which the candle is fixed; for the Japanese candle which is made of vegetable wax, has a hollow paper wick. These candles have, when they are set in a candlestick, to be snuffed from time to time; but the swing of the lantern facilitates the combustion of the wick, and the candles rarely need snuffing when they are being carried in the street.

CHAPTER XI.

DAILY LIFE.

Busy life at home—Discomforts of early morning—Ablutions—Off to school and office—Smoking—Giving orders—Morning work—Washing—Needlework—The work-box—Japanese way of sewing—Ironing Remaking clothes—Home duties—Bath—Evening—Early hours.

MANY foreigners think that Japanese women must lead a pretty dull life as they can have little to do in a house bare of furniture. But whether their lives be dull or not compared with the lives of women in other countries, they certainly are not idle. They do not, it is true, go out much; it is a red-letter day with them when they visit a public place in the flower season or betake themselves to the theatre. But at home they are kept all day to their work. The very scarcity of furniture in a Japanese room implies constant sweeping and tidying; and what with the care of children, making and unmaking of clothes, and superintending of the kitchen, the Japanese housewife has by no means an easy time of it.

But to begin with the early morning. In Japanese houses there are, as has been already stated, no rooms exclusively set apart for sleeping. The beds can be laid anywhere on the mats. The bed consists of one or two thickly-wadded mattresses of cotton or silk, usually three feet wide by about six feet long, that is, nearly the size of a mat. These are laid on the mats and over them a large, thickly-wadded cover of the shape of a winter *kimono* with open sleeves and a quilt, also heavily wadded, of about the same length as the bed but wider. They are both of silk or cotton, figured or striped, with linings of a dark-blue colour. They both have a black velvet band where the sleeper's face touches them. The two are used in winter; but in spring and autumn only

THE FAMILY IN BED.

one, usually the *kimono*-like cover, is thrown over the sleeper. In midsummer, even that is too hot, and is replaced by an ordinary lined *kimono* or a thinly-wadded quilt. The pillow for men is a long round bolster filled with bran; but women, whose coiffure would be deranged by such a pillow, lay their heads on a small bran bolster, two inches or so in diameter, which is wrapped in paper and tied on the top of a wooden support. It is very uncomfortable at first, though most women are used to it. As the bolster soon gets hard, the skin about the ear often becomes red and rough if one sleeps all night on the same side. Though the beds may be spread anywhere, their places are always fixed for the members of the family. The master and mistress sleep in the parlour or some other large room with the youngest children, the mother with the baby in her bed and the father sometimes with the next youngest in his. The rest of the children sleep either in the same room or in another and with some other member of the family, unless they are quite grown up. The sitting-room is usually left unoccupied. The servants sleep in a room next to the kitchen and the house-boy in the porch. It is important to group the sleepers as much as possible ; for in summer when mosquitoes are out, nets are hung over the beds by strings attached to the four corners of the room, and to economise these nets the beds are brought together wherever practicable.

The servants get up at five o'clock or later every morning according to season. They first open the shutters of the kitchen ; the cook sets at once to boil rice and then to make the morning soup. The housemaid opens the shutters of all the other rooms, sometimes even of those in which people are still sleeping. Where there is a verandah, the maid reaches it by a vacant room ; but if all the rooms are occupied, she does not hesitate to pass by the beds. In winter the opening of the sliding-doors at the same time as the shutters would be enough to give a cold to any one unused to our way of life. He would sneeze and dive into bed ; and when he goes dozing again, the servant begins to sweep the unoccupied rooms and dust the sliding-doors and shelves in them. The noise would startle him as the partitions between the rooms are thin ; and the servant, usually a country-girl who has hitherto been wading in rice-paddies and carrying loads of grain and faggot, walks about on the mats as heavily as if she were on hard ground, and the shock of her stamping he would keenly feel through the bed. It is therefore but a dog-sleep that he would get after the shutters are opened. This is pretty hard as in all probability he was awakened at dead of night by the rats careering on the ceiling, which, being open between the outwalls of the house, is their happy hunting-ground. In fact, the Japanese house, with its thin walls and sliding-doors, is extremely noisy, sounds from outside being heard as clearly as if they came from another part of the house. Happily for us, however, having been habituated to them from childhood, we are able to close our ears to such customary noises.

The family rise an hour or so after the servants. In that time the breakfast is got ready, and the sitting-room has been swept and put tidy; and that is all we want for the while. We go out upon a verandah, generally one close to the sitting-room, or into the bath-room if there is one, where the servant has already laid on the sink a brass basin for washing our faces and a bowl also of brass for cleaning our teeth. Though the common bristle tooth-brush is now largely used, the old form made of a little bit of willow-wood, pointed at one end and frayed into a tuft at the other, is still found handy. As it is very cheap, it is thrown away after a few mornings, and is especially convenient when we have a visitor who stays only for a day or two. The family wash one after another, the servant bringing a fresh supply of cold or hot water each time. As we are exposed to the cold in winter, we do not bare our necks and shoulders or wash our hair, but dip our faces only; however, as we take baths daily or every other day, this does not matter much.

Now breakfast is ready. Before, however, the family sit down to it, the first offerings of the morning's rice and tea are set before the family shrine, in which are recorded on tablets or in a book the names of the ancestors and other deceased members of the family. If the children go to school early, they sometimes have breakfast before the rest of the family; but as the father, if a government official or a man of business, has also to leave home, the whole family generally take their morning meal together. Breakfast over, the children are packed off to school, and their father, after looking through the papers, also makes for his place of business. When he gets up, he always wears Japanese clothes; and when leaving for his office, he puts on a *hakama* if he goes in the same clothes; but if he prefers European clothes, he has to dress over again. Before he leaves home, he is given a cup of tea, as it is said to protect him from accidents abroad. His wife and servants see him to the front door and speed him.

The wife who has been getting the children ready for school and helping her husband to dress, has now a little respite, during which she may glance through the papers and take a few whiffs of tobacco. Smoking is a general custom among Japanese women; but tobacco is smoked in homœopathic doses in tiny bowls. The Japanese pipe consists of a bowl, about a quarter of an inch in diameter and depth, bent into a tube, and a mouthpiece, both of metal, which are connected by a bamboo stem. The metal is brass for common pipes, while better sorts are of nickel, silver, or gold. The bamboo stem is five or six inches between the metal ends for pipes which are taken abroad, and not unfrequently a foot or more for those used at home. Among the lower classes the wife uses the long-stemmed pipe to emphasise her speech by beating the mat with it when she gives a piece of her mind to her truant husband; and a blow with it is pretty painful, as many an idle apprentice knows to his cost. A small pinch of tobacco is put into the bowl, and two or three whiffs are all that can be got from it. A Japanese does not merely smoke, that is, get the smoke into his mouth only, but actually swallows it and then slowly emits it from his mouth or nostrils. Women generally emit it from their mouths only. The tobacco smoked is dried leaves cut into fine slices. The filling and emptying of the bowl takes about as much time as the smoking of it, so that one cannot smoke while doing something else; but it is an excellent time-killer, as day-labourers will testify.

A WOMAN SMOKING.

The wife, however, has not much time to herself; for before she has taken many whiffs, the tradesmen's boys will be making their daily calls. Those whose bills are settled at the end of the month are usually the dealers in rice, *sake*, and faggot and charcoal, the fishmonger, and the greengrocer. The rice-dealer does not call every day; he brings a bag of rice when required and knows pretty well when it will be exhausted. The *sake*-dealer comes every day; he sells, besides *sake*, soy, *mirin*, and *miso*; and in many cases he deals in faggot and charcoal as well. The fishmonger and the greengrocer call every morning; the former will

cook to order simple dishes of fish. Besides these regular tradesmen, there are street-vendors who bring bean-curd, boiled or
steamed beans, and other food which will not keep long. We
have no grocers properly-speaking in Japan ; the nearest approach
to them is the dealer in " dried vegetables." Tea and sugar have,
like rice, special dealers.

When these tradesmen have been disposed of, it is time to
commence the serious work of the day. The cook washes the
breakfast things and sweeps and scours the kitchen floor. The
housemaid takes up one by one the quilts and mattresses of the
beds, folds them in three, and puts them away in closets ; she then
dusts the paper sliding-doors, shelves, and other woodwork, sweeps
the mats and verandahs, and scrubs the woodwork with a hard-
wrung cloth. Many foreigners think it strange that we should
dust before sweeping ; but we dust the woodwork so as to make
the dust fall on the mats or be blown out, as we always open the
verandah sliding-doors when we dust and then sweep the mats to
get rid of the dust. And finally when some of the dust has fallen
again on the woodwork, we remove it with a damp cloth. When,
therefore, we have finished cleaning a room, all the woodwork looks
bright and speckless. The verandah is scrubbed first with a wet
cloth and afterwards with an almost dry one to make it shine. In
the sitting-room the wiping and polishing of the brazier is a long
job, for the housewives of Tokyo pride themselves upon the appearance of their braziers. The wife superintends the cleaning of
the rooms and also at times lends a hand.

When the rooms have been swept, next comes the washing.
There is always plenty of washing to do, especially in summer.
If, moreover, there are young children in the family, the clothes
they are constantly soiling have to be taken to pieces, washed, and
remade. If the clothes are lined, wadded, or of the better quality
of the unlined, they are taken to pieces and washed, and the pieces
are then spread out on a smooth plank specially made for the
purpose and laid out to dry in the sun. They are next starched,
and when they are dry, they still adhere to the plank and so keep
free from creases and shrinkages. The wadding is never washed.

THE STARCHING-BOARD.

The underwear is also washed; but unless it is of silk, it is not spread out. In summer the unlined clothes, called *yukata* or bathdress, are washed every three or four days; and as every member of the family has two or more changes, there is always something to wash. The clothes and underwear which need not be spread out, are hung up on long poles which pass through the sleeves and are hoisted up on the pegs of two high upright posts. When dry, these clothes are spread out on a matting and starched and folded for use. Silks which require special skill in washing or have stains to be removed are sent to the dyer.

Meanwhile, the mistress of the house may begin her needlework. Needlework is the first qualification of the Japanese housewife. As all clothing for both sexes is made by hand, the wife who is a good needlewoman effects a great saving to her family. Clothes for daily wear are remade every year, sometimes oftener; those belonging to one person may be taken to pieces and remade for another member of the family; and old clothes which show signs of wear are redyed, turned inside out, or resewn to hide the torn seams. The underwear is also subjected to similar transformations. Sometimes a cloth may be remade from the unlined to the lined or wadded, or *vice-versa*. It is no light task to make shifts to enable the whole family to present a decent appearance, so that even in an ordinary-sized household there is no end of needlework to be done, and unless she is very active or well-assisted, the housewife finds it pretty hard to keep abreast of the seasons with a stock of neat, newly-made clothing. Even in a family where she has no need to sew herself, she must have a fair knowledge of needlework so as to be able to cut the cloth before giving it to the needlewoman in her employ or sending it out to a seamstress; for unless she can by her knowledge check the amount of cloth used, she may be robbed with impunity of odd bits and ends.

The Japanese needlewoman's work-box is commonly a square or oblong case with two drawers, one above the other, of nearly the same breadth as the case itself and another pair of half the breadth side by side on the top. Into these drawers are thrown threads wound round square, flat pieces of wood or cardboard, odd bits of rag, scissors shaped like shears, and a bone cloth-marker. On one side of the case is an upright post with a flat hole for inserting a bamboo foot-measure, and on the top of it is a little box for the needle-cushion. To the post is attached a small loop of string, to which the cloth to be sewn is hitched with a needle, as pins are, or rather were until recently, unknown. Sometimes the needle-cushion is on an upright of its own, apart from the work-box, and has a long base which is pressed under the knee while the cloth is fastened to the loop. The thimble is not of metal, but of leather or thick paper and is nothing more than a ring put over the first joint of the middle finger.

In sewing, the needle-cushion upright is put to the right of the worker, and an end of the cloth is hitched to the loop. The threaded needle is held and the tip only is moved up and down while the cloth itself is gathered in small folds on the needle; and when there are enough folds on it, the needle is pushed forward with the thimble and the folds are pulled over the thread and straightened out. The needle is then drawn out until it is stopped by the knot of the thread at the first stitch. The same process is repeated. The cloth is re-hitched to the post from time to time as the stitching goes on. This manner of sewing is often mentioned as a peculiarity of Japanese needlework; but the Japanese woman is so used to it that she can sew very rapidly in this way. It cannot be resorted to when the stitches have to be very close or the cloth is too thick or stiff to be doubled into little creases, in which case the needle has to be passed through at every stitch. The Japanese needle is of a very primitive kind; it is made of iron or badly-tempered steel, for it is very brittle; and it rusts rapidly while the eye is square and apt to cut the thread. The danger of the Japanese way of sewing with beginners is that when they bring back the needle after passing it through, they not unfrequently scratch their right cheeks with it if the thread is long.

After a cloth has been sewn, it is ironed. The iron is a deep metal pan with a flat, smooth bottom and a long handle. Into it red-hot charcoal is put and the pan is heated enough to blacken any paper that it is laid on for a minute or less. It is then moved rapidly over the cloth to be smoothed; sometimes when there is some danger of the cloth being burnt, a piece of paper is put over it before ironing. For ironing edges and corners, a small thick trowel with a long handle is used. The end is put into a brazier

NEEDLEWORK.

under the charcoal, and when it is hot, it is wiped and pressed over the part to be smoothed. The degree of heat is judged by holding it close to the cheek; and the beginner often burns her cheek by bringing it too close.

The housewife, therefore, who is an adept in needlework, has plenty of work before her. The clothes and underwear for herself and her husband and children require making and unmaking. Those for holiday wear do not need remaking every season; but everyday clothes have to be taken to pieces, washed, and remade. For the children she would want two or three suits for each season, as the Japanese children have, notwithstanding their proverbial gentleness and tractability, as great a capacity for soiling and tearing their clothes as the little folks of any other country; besides, Japanese clothes are more readily soiled than European. The wife has also the bed-clothes to make. These, when they are soiled, are taken to pieces, washed, and remade with fresh layers of cotton wadding. Cushions for squatting upon are also remade when they are soiled, which may be once in one or two years. In the matter of sewing, then, woman's work is never done in Japan any more than elsewhere.

Of course a lady who employs servants does not undertake all the sewing herself. She sets the servants between hours to work on clothing and bedding that do not require skill or delicate handling; but she has to assist in putting in the wadding and probably gives the finishing touches to the clothes. In the same way she superintends the kitchen and may at times help in cooking. And with one thing or another she is fairly well occupied all day. A wife, especially a young one, has not unfrequently a middle-aged woman who has come with her as a sort of duenna from her father's family or has otherwise become a permanent member of her husband's household; such a woman would take a great deal of work off her hands and superintend the other servants. But even when they have not a housekeeper of that description at home, many ladies manage to amuse themselves by paying and receiving visits, going to theatres, or occupying themselves in some favourite accomplishments, such as tea-ceremony, flower.arrangement, or playing on the *koto* or *samisen*.   But a mother with little children cannot as a rule gad about or be absorbed in her own amusements like one who is childless or whose children are all grown up.   The Japanese mother does not, if she can help it, delegate her maternal duties to a nurse, and an infant in arms she seldom cares to give in charge entirely to a servant.   She would of course have more time to herself if her mother or mother-in-law is living with her.

Towards the evening, the husband comes home and the children are back from school.   It is the custom to take a bath every day in summer and perhaps once in two or three days in winter.   If there is a bath-room in the house, the inmates take a bath one after another, the master of the house leading.   If there is not a bath-room in it, then they go to the public bath-house ; the wife and the children who are with her would take the bath in the daytime before the others have come home.   In the public bath-house there are baths for the two sexes divided by a wooden parti-tion, at the end of which the bathkeeper or his wife sits on a high platform so that both sections can be watched at the same time. There is in each section a single large bath, eight feet or more long by about four feet wide.   Into this all the bathers dip up to their necks.   In front of the bath is a large slanting floor, on which they sit and wash themselves.   Under the partition between the male and female baths is a square wooden tank each for hot and cold water.   The water is ladled in little wooden pails.   When we un-dress, we first wash ourselves on the inclined floor and then get into the bath; and when we have warmed ourselves, we come out and wash more carefully with soap and, in the case of women, with rice-bran powder as well.   When we have done washing, we get into the bath again, and finally, before we wipe ourselves on coming out of the bath, we pour again upon our bodies the hot water from the tank.   We are then supposed to be always clean when we get into the bath ; and as we do not wash in the bath itself, its water should always remain clear.   But as a matter of fact, the water grows turbid as the day wears ; happily, the lights are dim when the bath-house closes an hour or so before midnight.   In the daytime it is pretty clean; and bathing in the forenoon is very pleasant as only a few bathers have been before us, except in the lower town where it is the custom for workmen to take an early morning bath.

When we have had a bath, we sit down to supper. The master perhaps drinks *sake* with it, in which case it will take some time as we always finish drinking before we attack the rice. Women seldom drink. The children sup at the same time. After playing for a while, the youngest are put to bed. The mother gets into the bed without undressing with the infant and gives it milk until it falls asleep, whereupon she gets out. Other young children are put to sleep by other members of the family. Their elder brothers and sisters prepare the next day's lessons and go to bed about nine o'clock. When the children are thus put to bed, the mother is free for the rest of the evening. But it often happens that she is herself sent dozing while she is trying to make the infant sleep.

As we keep on the whole early hours, the streets are almost deserted at ten or eleven o'clock except on special nights, and most shops are closed by that time. Only in tea-houses are noises to be heard until twelve o'clock when all musical instruments must be put away. In midsummer, however, houses are often kept open till midnight on account of the heat, especially in the lower town where the crowded buildings get very little of a breeze.

CHAPTER XII.

SERVANTS.

The servant question — Holidays — Hours of rest—Incessant work—Servants trusted—Relations with their mistresses—Decrease of mutual confidence—Life in the kitchen—Servants' character—Whence they are recruited—Register-offices—The cook— The housemaid—The lady's maid—Other female servants—The jinrikishaman—The student house-boy.

THE servant question is as great a domestic problem with us as it is in other parts of the world. We too complain of our servants' insubordination, idleness, wilfulness, talkativeness, and general contrariness. Old folk are constantly drumming into our ears that servants are not what they used to be in the good old days and that they have ceased to have their masters' interests at heart and are ready to leave their present situation whenever better terms are elsewhere obtainable. That the character of servants has deteriorated admits of no doubt ; but the fault lies as much with their masters and mistresses as with themselves. However, such as they are, they still retain many good qualities ; and on the whole we are better off in this respect than our fellow-sufferers in the West.

Our servants are usually willing workers ; they do not ask, nor would they indeed dream of asking, for free Sundays. They toil from day to day, week in week out, month after month, without a murmur at being put to incessant work. Like the clerks and apprentices in mercantile houses, they have by immemorial custom two holidays a year, on the sixteenth of January and July ; but as in busy families they cannot all be spared at the same time, they are often given some other days in turn. Those who have homes in town pass the day with their families ; but others from the country, that is, a majority of domestic servants, spend their holiday wandering aimlessly about the streets and parks in gaping wonder at the sights of the city.

The servants are, moreover, expected to work without intermission from morning till night. In some families a fixed time is given them daily for rest; but in most houses no such hour is set apart and they snatch what rest they can in the intervals of their work. They get up early in the morning, about five or half past; but as those from the country are used to early rising, it is no hardship to them. It is the late hours that they succumb to. Where the master has a large social connection, is given to entertaining friends, or is found of cards, chequers, or other games, the house is often kept open till midnight or later. In such cases, however, the cook and others who have to rise early to prepare the breakfast, are allowed to go to bed at ten or thereabouts; but the servant who waits on the guests and brings them tea or wine has to sit up till they leave. It would also be a breach of hospitality for the family to go to bed and leave the host alone to entertain his guests; and so, with the exception of the children, the rest of the family wait patiently till the last guest departs. Indeed, the drowsy servants often resort, as a charm for expediting the lingering guest's departure, to burning a pinch of moxa on his clogs or setting up a broomstick on its handle.

As the servants have no regular hours of work and rest, they have often to take their meals at odd hours. Punctuality is not a Japanese virtue, and the members of the family are not always regular in their meals. The hours are governed by the movements of the master of the house, and they are fairly regular if he is a government official, a professional man, or an employé of a private firm or company, who has to be at his office at fixed hours; but if the master's habits are irregular from necessity or inclination, the family meals suffer accordingly. The servants are also expected to be ready at every beck and call, for a great deal of trivial task is imposed upon them. They are, for instance, often called from the kitchen to the parlour or sitting-room and then sent to fetch an article from an adjoining room. But as most houses in Japan are only of one or two stories and the living-room is always

THE SERVANT AT THE SLIDING-DOOR.

on the ground-floor, it is no difficult matter to clap our hands, which is the usual way of summoning a servant, or to holloa to her, for the sound has merely to penetrate one or two sliding-doors or probably none at all in summer. Thus, from the very ease with which a servant may be summoned, she is made to do a great deal which could be readily done without her help.

The servant is trusted to a great degree. The lack of privacy which is one of the principal characteristics of a Japanese home places every room at the mercy of its inmates ; and when the house is left for the day, as sometimes happens, in the servant's charge, a dishonest domestic could easily purloin articles which would not be missed at the time. That such petty thefts are comparatively rare, must be put to the servant's credit. On the other hand, she becomes a member of the family whose service she enters, to a greater extent than would be the case in other lands. The very lack of privacy makes her a party as it were to the private affairs of the family. She is set to work unmaking dresses or sewing them under her mistress's eye and is often taught needlework, especially on long winter evenings, when mistress and servant talk together with less reserve than at other times, and a close sympathy arises between them, which may last through their lives. And many servants retain their love and respect for their mistress after they leave her service and call on her regularly every year with their husbands or children when they are married.

In the old days it was considered to betoken a lack of fidelity for a servant to change her situation; and many girls remained in the same family until they were grown-up women. In such cases the master would find for them suitable husbands or, if they were married through others' good offices, give them the means to set up for themselves. The servants, too, looked upon it as a great honour to be so assisted by their master as it was a conclusive proof of their faithful service. This close mutual understanding is now less common, because there has been, so their employers complain, a serious falling-off in the quality of the servants; but their masters, or rather their mistresses, are also to blame in the matter, for their attitude towards their subordinates has also changed. They no longer look upon them as permanent members of their household and consequently take them less into confidence than formerly; which, however, is unavoidable since the good behaviour of the servants is not now guaranteed so securely as it used to be. In the old times servants were almost as much under their master's authority as a vassal under his liege's. To disobey a mistress's order or to contradict her was considered an act of disloyalty, and the servant was kept in a state of complete subjection. On the other hand, a conscientious mistress had also on her part a sense of duty towards her servant, and looked after her and cared for her as for her own family.

Nowadays, however, this bond between mistress and maid has been loosened except in rare cases, at least in Tokyo. If the mistress has no definite knowledge of the servant's antecedents, the latter has as vague an idea of the real standing of the family. Formerly, reputable families remained permanently settled in the same locality for generations, so that their social position was well known in the neighbourhood; while as for the samurai who came up to town with their lord, the name of the daimyo whom they followed was a sufficient guarantee of their respectability though they themselves might not be personally known. Hence, the servants could without difficulty obtain any information they desired respecting the family whose service they proposed to enter, and they had only themselves to blame if they were not, upon being installed therein, satisfied with its ways. But there is now in every grade of society such a large proportion of families from the country that the servant is often unable to find out their standing, past or present. She may not suffer from arrearage of her wages, though such a thing is by no means rare; but she does not feel quite so much at home as she would if she entered a family whose history is known to her. There is then mutual reserve, not to say distrust, when neither the employer nor the employée knows anything of the other's antecedents. The servant may be dismissed one fine morning at a moment's notice, or she may obtain leave to visit a sick relative, to whose bedside she would pretend to have been urgently summoned, and a few days later send to her employer's for her belongings. It is not necessary to give warning; a few days' notice may be thought due to the other party, though of course, in the case of old and tried servants, a greater consideration is mutually accorded, the domestic usually consenting to remain until a suitable successor has been found. The servant's tenure of service is, then, generally precarious, and at the same time her mistress is never sure of having permanetly secured a good servant. Indeed, if the servant is honest and diligent, it is seldom the fault of her employer if she leaves her service; for the mistress cannot do without a servant and if she has got hold of a good domestic, she is not likely to let her go willingly. The servant, on the other hand, may be quitting service to live at home, to be married, or to look for a better situation. She has more motives for parting company than her mistress.

The truth is that young women have discovered that there is a great demand for their services elsewhere, as at cotton mills, tobacco and other factories, and for house-industries ; and there is in consequence a dearth of servants, let alone good ones. Still, many prefer domestic service, because they have not to work with mechanical regularity as at factories, and they are on that account content with lower wages. For hard as she is worked and though she is without a young man to console her on Sunday for the week's drudgery, her life is not altogether an unhappy one. There is at least variety in it. The tradesmen's boys come to the kitchen for orders and most people of the artisan and trading classes go in and out by the kitchen. They have therefore plenty of chance company. The tradesmen's boys take it easy and linger in kitchens which find favour with them. When visitors come and are entertained in the parlour, their jinrikisha-men are given a meal in the kitchen. Still another chance of gossip is afforded where a common well is used by two or more families. Here they congregate and discuss the affairs of their respective households, tearing to pieces the character of one mistress and extolling another to the skies. The " well-side council," as it is called, is the great market for scandals of all sorts, though it would not be fair to attribute its notoriety entirely to the servants' love of gossip, for the worst scandal-mongers in such cases are the wives of poorer tradesmen and artisans who bring their washings to the common well.

But the servants are on the whole good-natured, thoughtless, and careless of the morrow. They are satisfied if they are well fed ; they are merry and grow fat. It is comparatively rare to find a black sheep among them. Such a woman usually commits petty thefts ; she dares not steal anything of value, for if she takes it to the pawnbroker, she is sure to be discovered as he is completely under the surveillance of the police who can look over the pawn-accounts and seize any article that they may suspect to have been purloined. The woman may take the stolen article to an accomplice; but sooner or later, it finds its way to the pawnbroker's, or if it is an article of clothing, to the second-hand clothes-dealer's, who is similarly under police control, and so the crime is discovered. She steals most commonly stray coins, or handfuls of rice or other food which can be pilfered without much risk of detection. A woman whose mother or husband is in needy circumstances and comes often to call her out on mysterious business is most likely to be guilty of such dishonest practices.

Servants are recruited from various quarters. They may be daughters of poor artisans or tradesmen in Tokyo, of peasants in the country, or of fishermen on the coasts. They naturally come, many of them, to ease the straitened means of their families and to save up enough to buy clothes to take with them when they marry. Others come from the country to see the town and learn its manners, which they do effectually, though perhaps not exactly according to their original intention. Such girls are of the better class of peasants; for the majority of peasants are kept pretty busy with the cultivation of their rice-paddies, and in spring-time whole families are engaged knee-deep in mud in planting rice, while they are equally busy at harvest-time, so that a girl at home does enough work to pay for her maintenance. It is therefore more often the girl's ambition to see Tokyo and save up something than family necessity that prompts the country lass to seek service. Girls living in Tokyo are in a different position. Here girls in a large family can do little to earn their keep by helping their mother, unless they are engaged in some house-industry which calls for the whole energy of the family. If they have a small shop or an eating-house, one or at most two may be useful at home; while among artisans and labourers an extra girl means only one mouth more to feed, and accordingly she is sent out to service. But even in Tokyo it is not always poverty that supplies the vast army of domestic servants. It may be irksomeness on the girl's part of parental authority which is not unfrequently exercised with severity, or fear on the parents' part that the child would be spoilt under their roof and rendered unfit to bear the trials and hardships which must press on the poor man's wife with a troop of children at her heels. In the latter case she is sent out among strangers to be buffeted and knocked into shape. Sometimes, again, the girl prefers absolute strangers' society to the sway and, too often, ill-treatment of a stepfather or stepmother ; or, being an orphan, she is unwilling to be a burden to a near relative who would as a matter of duty offer to take her in. Again, a young woman who has lost her husband by death or divorce would seek service from a desire in the former case to remain faithful to his memory, which would otherwise be difficult if she has no means of support, and in the latter from disgust of conjugal life or to look for another opportunity of trying her luck in matrimony. Or, she may still be married but has, through inability to make both ends meet, to break up her household and wait in domestic service while her husband knocks about, until fortune smiles upon them when they will keep house again. Finally, even fairly well-to-do tradesmen send their daughters sometimes to a family, noble, wealthy, or noted for its strict management, to learn in service deportment and etiquette. Thus, the domestic servant enters service from diverse motives.

A servant is sometimes engaged on the recommendation of an acquaintance, which is a good plan if she proves satisfactory. But if she does not, her employer is placed in an awkward position ; he hesitates to dismiss her as he would have to account for her discharge to that acquaintance, to whom he is naturally unwilling to speak ill of her, especially if he is related to the girl or intimate with her family. Indeed, friendships have been brought to an abrupt termination by the misconduct of a girl so engaged. Most people, therefore, prefer to engage the servant through a register-office, for there are many such offices in Tokyo as they do not require any capital to start. Word is sent to the register-office, and the woman, for it is generally a woman who runs it, brings a girl who is likely to suit the service required. The girl stays one night ; and if neither she nor the mistress takes to the other, the woman brings another in her place, and yet another, until a suitable person is found. Then the woman draws up the contract of service, usually for six months, fixing the girl's wages. For this she receives a small fee from both parties. If, at the end of six months, the girl elects to stay on, the woman receives her fees again for the renewal of the contract; but apparently, for some of these register-offices a sixmonth is too long a time to wait, for they often make tempting offers to the servant and try to persuade her to throw up her situation. And if she follows the advice by making to her mistress some plausible excuse for the breach of contract, she is introduced into another family, but finds her position in no way improved and herself poorer by the commission she has again

COOKING RICE.

paid the woman. The register-office is naturally responsible for the servant's conduct; but if she is found dishonest and discharged, the office, on being taken to task for bringing such a woman, wriggles out of its responsibility by an eloquent flow of virtuous indignation and profuse apologies to the family, and if called upon to indemnify any loss or damage, asks for time to make necessary inquiries and prolongs the delay until the matter is forgotten or at least given up as hopeless.

Though the number of servants naturally varies with the size, wealth, and social standing of their employer's household, there are usually three in a well-to-do middle-class family. Of these the most important is the cook. In wealthy families there are *cuisiniers* for the preparation of the dishes, in which case the cook proper confines herself to boiling rice and keeping the kitchen tidy; indeed, the boiling of rice is in any case the cook's principal function, as is implied by her Japanese designation, which means " rice-boiler "; but in middle-class families she undertakes general cookery as well. If, mroeover, she is the only servant in the house, she sweeps the rooms, scrubs the verandahs, lays and puts away the beds, sets the meal-trays, washes the clothes, and does many other things which are of daily necessity in a Japanese household. Her mistress, however, naturally helps the maid-of-all-work. But if there is an upper servant, the cook boils rice and prepares meals, scrubs the wooden flooring of the kitchen, washes the meal-trays, bowls, and crockery, and helps in washing clothes. The tea-pots and tea-cups, being in constant requisition, have to be often washed in the course of the day. The cook gets up early as the rice has to be boiled for breakfast, and if late hours are kept in the family, she is sent to bed before the others; but as soon as the day's work is over, she is generally found nodding over the brazier or snoring aloud stretched out on the mats. As the cook's duties are of the simplest kind, girls fresh from the country become " rice-boilers " and are noted for their dull wits and rough manners.

The housemaid's chief duty is to keep the rooms tidy. She is called in Japanese the " middle-worker," as she stands midway between the cook and the lady's maid. She dusts the paper sliding-doors, shelves, and other woodwork, sweeps the mats, and scrubs the woodwork, especially the grooves of the sliding-doors, the shelves, the wooden edges of the alcoves, the pillars, and the verandahs. She lays the beds every night, takes them up in the

THE HOUSEMAID AT WORK.

morning, and puts them into the closets.   She has plenty of work in keeping the rooms tidy, above all the sitting-room where almost everything, except the brazier and tea-shelf, has to be cleared immediately it is done with.   Besides, the shelves have such a knack of getting untidy as all sorts of things are for the moment put on them.   If there are children in the family, she looks after them, which is no light task as they roam all over the house and after their nature scatter things about wherever they go.   She also does a great deal of needlework ; she mends the clothes and does most of the work where skill or delicacy is not required. Washing, too, is no child's play in a large family.

The lady's maid is in most cases a young girl from thirteen to sixteen years old. She looks after the clothes ; as soon as they are taken off, she folds them and puts them into a chest of drawers or hangs them up if of daily wear. She waits at meals and does work about the sitting-room. She attends to the visitor, sets the cushion for him, and brings in tea, cake, and the brazier and " tobacco-tray." She helps, too, to look after the children. Where there is a nurse for the little children, she naturally attends to them and carries them about ; but generally the housemaid and the lady's maid divide the duty between them ; and as the latter is a young girl, she has to be very much helped by the housemaid.

The infant is commonly fed with its mother's milk and is not as a rule weaned until its position as the pet of the family is threatened by a new arrival. Where the mother has no milk or is too sickly to give healthy milk, a wet nurse is engaged who has to be well fed and royally treated to make sure that her charge does not fare ill at her hands. Where there is a great deal of needle-work to do, a needlewoman is employed. She is usually a woman of mature years, a widow, probably, and ' a lone 'lorn creetur,' who acts as a damper upon the exuberant spirits of the younger servants. In a large and well-to-do family there is sometimes a head-servant, a sort of housekeeper, who came in all probability into the family as the bride's waiting-woman at the marriage of the present mistress or her mother-in-law. As the oldest servant with the authority she exercises over her younger fellow-domestics, she is held in hardly less reverence than her mistress, and every opportunity is seized to please her ; for to cross her would be worse than to offend their mistress, and she is certainly more touchy than the other. She knows her power, too, and enjoys it to the full. She lets them serve her even more assuiduously than her lady ; and they help her to dress, and when she is tired, offer to shampoo her. She plays, in short, the retired lady more completely than her mistress's honoured mother-in-law.

Of male domestics there are only a few. The jinrikisha-man is the only servant of that sex worth speaking of, that is, in a well-to-do middle-class family. He is in most cases engaged from a jinrikisha-master, who has a number of young coolies under him. He is well fed, as his is a severe physical work, and going as he does with his master to all sorts of places, he has to be treated well for fear he should give exaggerated accounts of petty family affairs at the houses where he waits for his master. He has his faults ; but on the whole, he is a faithful, diligent, and willing servant.

THE HOUSE-BOY.

In many houses, especially of government officials and professional men, there is a young fellow or two, who would probably object to being classed with the servants, but who certainly do menial work. They are as a rule gentlemen by birth, distant relatives from the country or sons of friends in narrow circumstances. They are willing to do the house-boy's work in return for their keep; and they are allowed to attend school or college. When they graduate, they are able to set up for themselves. Of this class of young men come a majority of those who have risen by tact or ability to high and responsible positions in the government and in the professions.

CHAPTER XIII.

MANNERS.

Decline of etiquette—Politeness and self-restraint—" Swear-words"—Honorifics—Squatting—Kissing—Calls made and received—Rules for behaviour in company—Inconsiderate visitors—Woman's reserve before strangers—Hospitality—Reticence on family matters.

IN Japan as in most other oriental countries, etiquette is an extremely intricate art which can be mastered only by diligent study under a professor. It is an important item in a girl's school curriculum and is among her most valued accomplishments. It is not, however, commonly studied in detail by men, unless they have been brought up under the old régime ; they feel in consequence like fish out of water when they have to assist at elaborate ceremonies and fall into many blunders through their nervous efforts to steer clear of *gaucheries*. Men could well spare the time in the leisurely days of the feudal government when they could live in competence by taking up their hereditary offices, professions, or trades and working in the same grooves as their ancestors had done ; but in these days of fierce competition when every man must strike out for himself to earn a living, we have little or no time to go into the intricacies of etiquette. Hence, the more complex forms are gradually falling into disuse ; and the knowledge thereof, and that too not very deep, has become the monopoly of women. Indeed, though there are plenty of books on etiquette for women, hardly one, certainly none of any note, has been published of late years for the use of the other sex.

It is generally conceded that the Japanese are among the politest people in the world ; and some writers go so far as to contrast our politeness with French by observing that the latter is only skin-deep while ours is natural and spontaneous. Such a contrast may be flattering to our national vanity ; but we are inclined to doubt whether it is just. The truth is, we fear, that courtesy is with us as with the French a matter of education and is to a great extent a mechanical habit which its enforcement from early childhood at home and at school has almost made a second nature with us. That self-control which we possess in common with other Asiatic nations from its having been instilled into us from generation to generation by the precepts of our sages, enables us to repress all expression of emotion whenever necessity arises and even to wear a mask under the most trying circumstances. Politeness is then with us a great restraining force in our social life ; but once that force is removed or overpowered by an emotional outburst, we are hurled along as helplessly as any other people by the master passion of the moment and betray like them the hooligan in us, as the police reports too often prove. Our women, from the fact that the outcome of their education is self-effacement, possess this power of control in a far greater degree than men. They will go on smiling in the face of insulting remarks and completely conceal their wounded feelings. This has led many foreign visitors to imagine that they can address without offence any remarks however gross to a Japanese woman. She may put up with them without any sign of anger ; but could politeness permit her to retort, these foreigners would learn with astonishment what cutting sarcasms are capable of being expressed in " the politest language in the world that has no swear-word in it."

Apropos of " swear-words," their absence in a language is, it may be observed, no criterion of the gentleness of the people speaking that tongue. The suave diction of diplomacy can convey a threat far more effectively than the bluster of Billingsgate ; innuendo is a much more telling weapon in polemics than a direct attack ; and courteous or veiled language gives no key to the moral character of the speaker. And so it does not necessarily follow that a nation whose language is rich in honorifics and other terms of respect and reverence is of a gentler disposition or less robust than one which does not recognise such niceties of speech ; the only difference between the two lies in the manner in which they give vent to their passion or emotion. For the former can convey any degree of discourtesy or insult by a wilful omission of these honorifics in a way which would be well nigh incomprehensible to people to whom such discrimination is foreign.   There is no need to resort to blasphemy or profanity to express strong feeling since these honorifics, by their absence or ironical use, serve all purposes of emotional language.   In fact, the words of insult which are used in common speech sound very mild when translated into English. An Englishman would probably smile at a Japanese hurling at his opponent's head words like fool, beast, and dunderhead as opprobrious terms, while the Japanese would be equally amused at the Englishman's readiness to invoke God's curse upon everybody and everything that may fail to please him.   Since, then, honorifics play an important part in Japanese speech, their proper use requires considerable art and tact.   The blunders of the labouring classes in their use are stock jokes with professional story-tellers ; but with the educated classes solecisms of the kind are of comparatively rare occurrence.   From long practice their right use has become a settled habit.   It would be difficult to explain precisely the force of these honorifics in common speech ; but suffice it to state that words, or rather syllables, signifying respect are prefixed or affixed to the words directly referring to the person addressed or spoken of, if he is a superior or an equal whom it is customary to treat with consideration.   There are also special words and phrases to be used on such occasions.

These prefixes are commonly translated "honourable" or "august" by English writers on Japan ; thus, phrases which merely mean "your face" or "his hand," for instance, are renderd by "the honourable face" or "the august hand."   But the use of honorifics being, as already stated, almost a matter of habit, they do not usually convey to the Japanese the same import and significance as the word "honourable" would to an Englishman.   No doubt, they practically mean that ; but the common honorific prefixes, which are monosyllabic, such as *o, go,* and *mi,* are glibly uttered. If the Japanese, however, had to use each time in their place the tetrasyllabic "honourable," he would soon grow out of the habit, just as in all probability an Englishman would cease to swear if the word "damn"

were not such an easily pronounceable one, short, abrupt, and capable
of great emphasis. This word has no equivalent in Japanese and has
to be rendered by a periphrasis which would sound as strange to
an English ear as the word " honourable" does to a Japanese as a
rendering of his common honorific prefixes.   Indeed, the use of the
English comminatory word is far more eccentric when the word
comes to be translated ; the Japanese honorific has at least sense,
which is more than can always be said for the English swear-word,
when it is uttered as indiscriminately as it commonly is.   Mr.
Mantalini, for instance, would be hard put to it if he were asked to
explain what he meant by the little "dems" with which he peppers
his speech, while such an expression as " a damn sight " is meaning-
less, and " a damned good fellow " is an even more hopeless
contradiction in terms than " an awfully sweet girl."

Politeness is early taught in Japanese homes. It is no show-
quality to be exhibited only in company, but is daily practised at
home and in school as an indispensable aid to *savoir-vivre.* Thus,
at home every one bows to his superior in bidding good-morning or
good-night. The servants bow to the children, the servants and
children to the master and mistress, and all to the father or mother
of the master or mistress, who may be living with them. When the
last, or the master or mistress goes out, they are seen to the porch
and sped with a bow, and when they come home, they are met
again at the porch with a bow. We bow squatting with our heads
on the mat. This has appeared to many Europeans to be a more
obsequious way of greeting than a hand-shake, probably because
they associate such a bow with grovelling in the dust, which would
certainly be a humiliating posture to a European. But the two are
quite distinct. With us, from our way of squatting on the floor, no
other form of greeting is possible. In fact, until we cease to squat,
that is, until we reform altogether our mode of life, hand-shaking is
out of the question. In Europe courtesy impels a man to rise to
greet a new-comer, but in Japan he greets him squatting ; in Europe
a man who comes into the presence of his superior remains
standing until he is bidden to take a seat, but in Japan he squats at
the door of the room until he is invited to come in, whereupon he

shuffles in and makes his salutation. He remains squatting and does not approach close enough to his host to take his hand ; for to shake it he must squat with his knees almost touching the other's, and then, before they could talk at ease, he would have to shuffle backward, which would look very ungainly. Thus, as we squat too far apart to shake hands, we can only bow ; and politeness prompts us to bow with our heads on the mats.

Squatting is an art which needs practice from early childhood. The easiest way is to sit Turk-wise with our legs crossed in front ; but this can be done only when we are alone or before inferiors,

BOWING.

and would be the height of impoliteness before a superior or an equal unless he is a very intimate friend. It is permissible now, however, when we are in European clothes, to sit in this manner at a friend's house or at convivial gatherings. But this posture can hardly be called squatting. Of squatting properly so called, there are two ways. One is to sit on our feet. This is done by doubling the knees and crossing the feet behind and laying on them the whole weight of the body. Unless we have been used to it from childhood, this mode of squatting would give us pins and needles in a very short time ; the feet would go to sleep and if we tried suddenly to rise, our legs would refuse to support us. Men squat in this way ; but women resort to the other method, which is to double the knees as in the first case, but to keep the legs and feet straight out behind without crossing, so that less weight falls upon them. As the legs are pressed down obliquely and the tendons are brought into a state of extreme tension, this method is more trying than the other; but Japanese women can sit in this style for hours on end without feeling any fatigue. There

SITTING WITH CROSSED LEGS.

can be little doubt, however, that this habit of squatting is injurious to the development of the body. Most Japanese, if they are not exactly bow-legged, have at least slightly bent legs owing to the weight of the body constantly resting on them. The pressure on the heels also stunts the growth of the lower limbs; for though our trunks are of ordinary length, it is the shortness of the legs that makes us a nation of small stature. We have been told by a Japanese medical authority that we lose at least two inches and a half by this habit of squatting. Now the average height of a Japanese male adult is five feet three inches and a half and that of a female is four feet nine inches and a half, so that if we could abolish squatting and take to chairs, the average heights of our male and female adults would, according to this authority, be five feet six inches and five feet respectively.

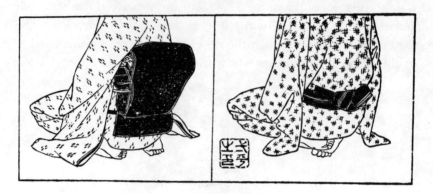

SQUATTING.

We may here add that the reasons which we have given for the impracticability of hand-shaking in a Japanese house, apply with equal force to the practice of kissing. A French writer has charged Japanese lovers with a lack of tenderness as they neither kiss nor shake hands. But what can the poor lovers do to kiss each other? They cannot fall into each other's arms while they remain squatting, for squatting is not like sitting together on a sofa. When we sit up straight with our feet under us, the equilibrium of such a posture is as unstable as if we were perched on a high stool. It is very rude to remain standing and even to speak before squatting, so that kissing while we are on our legs is not to be thought of. To squat side by side may be pleasant, and it may be possible to snatch a kiss; but when they are locked in each other's arms, the lovers would run a great risk of sprawling on the floor. To squat face to face with the knees touching, would require the body to be bent forward as if we were going to wrestle; and if the lovers were then to take each other's arms, there would be a regular tussle and their balance would be more uneven than before. As they could not get at each other without finally rolling on the mats, sweethearts with any sense of decorum would have to forgo the pleasure of kissing; for when we squat, it is much easier to lie down on the floor than to get up again. Lovers, however, are not altogether without the means of approaching each other and feeling the electric thrill which the mere touch appears to give them ; for, on the stage at least, their favourite position is to squat back to back and lean against each other. They are satisfied if their cheeks touch, for kissing is difficult without twisting the neck enough to sprain the muscles. Kissing, then, as a mode of salutation among lovers and near relatives, has never been recognised in this country, because the internal arrangement of our houses and other conditions of life have militated against its practice ; and perhaps, could some means be found to bring about its appreciation by the bulk of the nation, that would be more efficacious than any other measure for the westernisation of our domestic life.

Though good manners are insisted upon at home, they are, needless to say, exhibited to the full in company when one makes a call or receives visitors. The usual manner in which a call is made and received is as follows :—The visitor, on going up to the front-door, does not knock or ring as there is neither a knocker nor a bell-handle. He bawls out ; and as the doors are all sliding-doors, he is easily heard, though he has sometimes to call out again and again before his voice reaches the kitchen. When the door is answered and the master of the house apprised of the call, the visitor is shown in ; he leaves his hat, greatcoat, and umbrella in the porch and is ushered into the parlour. A cushion is immediately set for him and another for the host ; but the visitor does not, unless he is an intimate friend, sit on it until his host comes in and urges him to do so. We often stand very much on ceremony in this respect ; we take the cushion only upon repeated invitation ; one who wishes to show great respect will decline to squat on it however much he may be pressed. The host and the visitor then bow to each other with their hands and foreheads on the mat. They apologise, if they are acquaintances, for past neglect to visit each other, ask after each other's family, and probably, make a few observations on the weather, bowing with each remark, inquiry, and answer. A brazier is brought in if it is cold ; but in warm weather a " tobacco-tray " is set before the host and the visitor.

Tea and confectionery are also invariably offered. When the visitor leaves, there is another succession of bows, and the host and a servant see him to the porch and there bid him good-bye.

As to behaviour in company, the following quaint directions are given in an old book on etiquette for women, which though primarily intended for the instruction of the gentler sex, are also applicable to men, among whom the tendency is, as has already been remarked, to be somewhat lax in the observance of the minutiæ of etiquette :

"A woman should always get up early, wash her face, and carefully comb her hair, for it is rude to appear with dishevelled hair.

"Do not stare at other people, male or female, and be very careful in your speech. Do not tell anything without being asked, make confessions, or speak boastfully of yourself, and above all, on no account speak ill of others.

"When you are in the presence of your superior, do not scratch yourself; but if any part of your body itches so badly that you cannot help scratching it, put a finger on the spot and give it a hard scratch so that the itchiness may be absorbed in the pain so caused. Do not wipe sweat off your face or blow your nose ; but if you must do so, run into the next room or turn your face away from your superior. In blowing your nose, first blow gently, then a little louder, and finally gently again. But you should, if possible, do these things before you come into your superior's presence.

"Do not use a toothpick in company, for it is extremely rude to talk with one in your mouth.

"Do not pare your nails, comb your hair, or tighten your *obi* in company, or glance at a letter that another is reading or writing.

"Do not step upon other people's cushions, beds, or feet ; but always bear in mind that the only things you may tread on are your clogs and the only things you may step over are the grooves of the sliding-doors.

"If any one invites you to go out with her, do not put on a finer dress than hers ; you should ascertain by previous inquiry what she is going to wear. Do not scent yourself too much or have strong scent-bags about you.

"It is not good form when you make a call to sit in the middle of a room, and it savours too much of a novice to sit in a corner. Do not make a noise by opening and folding a fan, or fidget with a tea-cup ; and do not show a tired face and yawn or pretend not to hear what is being said to you. Moreover, when you have a visitor, do not be constantly looking at the clock and let her suspect that you are impatient for her departure.

" When you meet a superior in the street, bow low so that the tips of your fingers, with your hands extended downwards, may touch your feet. Do not get flurried and give incoherent answers ; but steady yourself by fixing your eyes upon the lady's knees if she is one whom you wish to treat with the greatest respect, upon her *obi* if the respect is to be of a slightly lesser degree, and upon the crest of her *haori* if that respect is still less. Look your equal in the face.

" In handing a knife to a superior, if it is hers, take the handle in your left hand with the blade pointing towards yourself; but if it is yours, take the handle sideways so that the blade points to her left. In either case the right hand should rest on the mat as you bend forward. Always use the left hand before your superiors.

" Never enter another's house unannounced, however intimate you may be with her ; for if you were to come upon an untidy room, your intrusion would be no less unpleasant for yourself than for your hostess.

" In leading a blind man into a room, let him rest a hand on your shoulder, or catch hold of a fan in your hand or of your sleeve. It is rude to lead him by the hand.

" It is extremely rudé to send a caller away when you are at home ; but some people go so far as to decide whether they shall be at home or not, only after they have heard the caller's name.

" Nothing is more displeasing to a hostess than to have a a visitor who stays on without having anything particular to say. We should not therefore pay a needlessly long visit or make too frequent calls. Intimate friends should, however, call occasionally ;

but neither the hostess nor the caller is without business of some kind ; and if a person is offended with another for not calling on her often enough, there is no need to become intimate with her. If you have business to do with any one, consider the hour of your visit ; do not call too early in the morning or too late at night or at meal-time. If there is a caller before you, wait till she leaves before broaching your business, or else call again."

.The women of Japan probably talk as much as those of any other country. They chat freely with their friends, but they are reserved before strangers and open their mouths only when they are addressed. They are taught not to boast of their knowledge or try to show it off. Hence, if a stranger asks them a question out of the common, they generally profess ignorance. A Japanese knows this ; and when he makes a woman's acquaintance, he takes care not to lead the conversation outside the merest commonplaces ; but the foreigner who has no idea of this custom is apt to get a false impression and has indeed not unfrequently pronounced her to be little better than a doll with no thought beyond dresses and trivialities of life.

Another misapprehension prevails among European writers who praise Japanese hospitality, but complain that a Japanese, while he receives a foreigner at his house, maintains at the same time strict reserve on the subject of his family. Some have attributed it to an anti-foreign feeling ; but whatever other indications of a bias against foreigners these writers may have detected in individual cases, the fact which they adduce cannot in itself be regarded in that light, for a Japanese guest is placed in much the same position. The host, in his desire to show an interest in his guest, often asks him minutely about his people at home, which some Englishmen have resented as impertinence ; but touching his own family affairs he is usually very reticent. He is anxious to keep his private concerns in the background and will assume a cheerful countenance even in the midst of the most pressing difficulties. His idea of hospitality is that nothing should be allowed to interfere with his guest's enjoyment. Even personal grief is concealed under a smile, and a member of the family may be seriously ill without the guest getting an inkling of the fact. A visitor to any member of the household is considered to have a claim upon the hospitality of the whole family ; and he is royally entertained though the rest may suffer inconvenience, as when the parlour in which the guest squats is the family bed-room and they have all to sit up till he leaves.

Our hospitality is admitted ; but what a European visitor misses is the appearance of the wife and other members of the family at the dinner or supper to which he is invited. The husband, as the head of the family, is its sole representative, and his presence is sufficient for doing the honours. The wife seldom appears unless the visitor is a family friend or she is acquainted with his wife. Such an invitation as taking pot-luck is seldom given ; politeness requires us to depreciate our offering, but we treat to our best. We therefore entertain and are entertained without our wives' participation. It is nothing extraordinary to have friends of many years' standing, whose wives we have never seen. It is then absurd to attribute this reticence respecting our family affairs to any sentiment hostile to our foreign visitors. Our social point of view is indeed so different to the occidental that a European generally falls into an error when he tries to judge our customs from his own standpoint.

CHAPTER XIV.

MARRIAGE.

ARRIAGE is the turning-point of a woman's life in Japan in a far greater degree than it is in western countries, for the simple reason that she has as yet few openings for earning an independence. Girls are brought up with a view to marriage and are early taught the duties of wife and mother. They look upon the wedded state as their lot in life and are prepared to enter sooner or later into matrimony. There are not many women who remain single all their lives. Girls of the poorer classes find employment at factories, if they are strong enough; others become waitresses at inns, restaurants, tea-houses, and other places of entertainment, or enter domestic service ; but even these find mates in time. Of women in other callings, such as hair-dress-ers, midwives, and seamstresses, the majority are married or widowed. For girls of the better classes the scope outside of matrimony is narrow indeed. They may teach in elementary schools, or take private pupils, if they have the requisite knowledge, for instruction in needlework, etiquette, flower-arrangement, tea-ceremony, or music, or else they can only be dependent on parents or relatives. But as the latter alternative which would be the fate of most girls is irksome, they naturally choose wedlock as the best means of escape from dependency or precarious livelihood. And that they, however homely they may be, succeed in finding husbands is due to the go-between system.

But it is not the girls alone who feel the inevitableness of marriage. Men are also in a like predicament. Bachelorhood has none of the ease and comfort which often attach to it in the West. Life in hotels and lodging-houses is both uncomfortable and insecure ; for the doors, being all sliding-doors, cannot be locked, and consequently one is always liable to intrusion at any hour of day or night by other inmates of the house. Flats are, from the very structure of Japanese houses, impracticable. In some houses there are rooms to let ; but meals are seldom provided. The only way is to rent a house, but then housekeepers as such are unknown. To leave the house in the care of ordinary servants is both uneconomical and inconvenient, for they are not likely to stint themselves or be thrifty ; they would, on the contrary, rather be wasteful so as to be popular with the tradesmen ; and far from keeping the house tidy as all Japanese houses need to be, they would not sweep or clean more than they could help. Indeed, from the appearance of the house one can always tell if it has a mistress or other responsible overseer. A bachelor can have a comfortable establishment, it is true, by placing it under the management of a near relative ; but a sister would herself wish to marry and would not therefore be its permanent head, while a mother or aunt would prefer to put it under a wife and lead a life of greater ease and leisure. A mother, moreover, would naturally wish to see her grandchildren. Besides, a bachelor in fair circumstances is as a rule so pestered by go-betweens that unless he is resolutely set against marriage, he is often mated before he knows his own mind.

Thus, marriage is looked upon as an inevitable fate by both sexes.

In a country like Japan where ceremony envelops every phase of life, such an important event as a wedding is, as may be expected, governed at every step by strict etiquette, and to celebrate it in proper style one needs to call in a regular professor of etiquette. But though weddings in high society are still perplexing tangles of formalities, the tendency to-day among the middle classes is to strip them as much as possible of unnecessary ceremony. It is, in fact, difficult at the present moment to give

BETROTHAL PRESENTS.

(FROM A PICTURE BY SUKENOBU, 1678–1751)

the exact procedure which is followed in an ordinary wedding as it is frequently modified by mutual agreement between the parties concerned ; but the following may be taken as a fairly accurate description of the usual procedure in these days.

A young man in search of a wife, or oftener his parents, would ask friends to look for a likely girl ; or it may be the father of a marriageable girl who asks his friends to find an eligible young man ; or a man who thinks a match might be made between two young people of his acquaintance may propose a marriage to their parents. If, in these cases, the parents think a suitable match may be made, they ask a mutual friend to act as the go-between ; or in the absence of such a friend, it is almost always possible to find some one who knows the acquaintances of both parties. The go-between must be a married man, as the duties of the office at the wedding devolve more heavily upon the wife than upon the husband. The go-between then brings about a meeting between the proposed lovers. This takes place at a theatre or other place of entertainment, or in temple-grounds, a restaurant, or some public resort, especially where the flowers of the season are in bloom. Both parties, consisting of the young people and their parents or relatives, meet there as if by accident, and the go-between introduces them casually to each other as his friends. Here the would-be lovers have a good look at each other ; and if they are mutually pleased, they signify that fact afterwards when the go-between calls at their houses to hear the result of the meeting. But before the final decision is made, the two families make private inquiries through their friends in each other's neighbourhood, usually of the tradesmen the other deals with, as to its social standing and repute and the life and character of the young man or girl in question. They must be quite sure that the information thus obtained bears out the go-between's statements ; for the go-between so frequently draws too favourable a picture of the standing of the families and the ability and accomplishments of the proposed couple that the expression " the go-between's fair words " has become synonymous with gross exaggeration. If the families are not satisfied, the match is broken off; but if they are pleased with each other, the go-

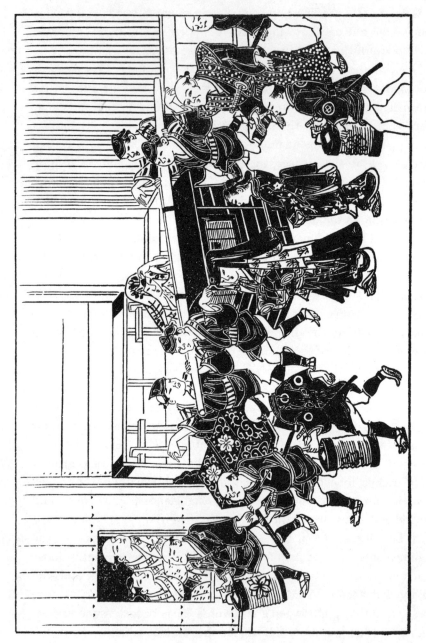

THE BRIDAL PROCESSION.

(FROM A PICTURE BY SUKENORU)

between is asked to look up a lucky day for the formal proposal. Nowadays the photographs are first exchanged and if they are found satisfactory, inquiries are made before the meeting is arranged.

On the appointed day a messenger, a trusted friend or servant of the young man's family, calls on the girl's father and makes a formal proposal, bringing at the same time a present of silk dresses, an *obi*, fish, and *sake* ; the father accepts the present and gives a receipt for it. This acceptance constitutes the consent to the marriage. He also makes a present to the other family. Soon after, he invites his relatives and intimate friends to a dinner, at which he announces the betrothal of his daughter. Preparations are then made forthwith for the wedding ; and when they are completed, another gathering of relatives and friends with their wives takes place and the dresses and other requisite articles for the marriage are exhibited ; and the meeting, especially the female section of it, criticise and offer advice if necessary on these preparations.

Now all is complete ; and an auspicious day has been fixed for the wedding. The bride's property is sent on to the bridegroom's a day or two previously. It consists of chests of drawers and several boxes containing her dresses, bedding, toilet articles, various utensils needed for tea-making and flower-arrangement, a *koto,* and work-boxes, and sometimes even kitchen utensils. In the evening she leaves her father's home. Formerly she went in a palanquin ; but now she is conveyed in a jinrikisha or carriage. She is accompanied by friends and relatives. She is dressed in white or some other light colour. In the country a bonfire is lighted at the door, and she is escorted by torchlight ; but in the city only lanterns are carried.

On reaching the bridegroom's house, the bride is led into the toilet-room to rest herself a while and touch up her toilet. Then she is shown into the room where the wedding ceremony is to take place. The arrangement of the room varies with the school of etiquette ; but usually there are offerings to the Gods on the dais of the alcove. They comprise two round cakes of pounded rice in the middle, with a stand of consecrated *sake* a little in front on either side, and at the back a stand each of fish (a carp or *tai*) and fowl (a

TAE WEDDING PARTY.

(FROM A PICTURE BY SUKENOBU)

pheasant or snipe). There are, besides, a couple of black-lacquered cabinets with writing materials, a small wash-basin, and tea-utensils. There also stands a large flat porcelain dish with legs, on which are planted a miniature pine, bamboo, and plum-tree, with a tortoise at the base and a crane flying above. The pine, being an evergreen, signifies longevity, the bamboo, from its pliancy, gentleness, and the plum-tree, which blooms while there is yet snow on the ground, denotes fidelity in adversity. The crane which is supposed to live a thousand years and the tortoise whose life is said to last ten times as long, both symbolise longevity. In the foreground are an old couple, Takasago by name, who are the Darby and Joan of the Japanese legend, the husband with a rake and the wife with a broomstick. The whole stand is then emblematic of long life, happiness, and conjugal fidelity.

As soon as the bride takes her seat, the bridegroom enters and sits too, in front of her according to one school of etiquette, or beside her according to another. They are attended by waiting-women, by children, or by the go-between and his wife only. Two trays each are set before the new couple. The plats which have each a special significance it would take too much space to describe here. But the most important part of the ceremony takes place after the trays have been carried in. A set of three flattish wooden cups are brought, and the top or smallest cup is filled with the consecrated *sake* which has in the meantime been taken down from the dais and poured into a couple of iron or bronze pots with long handles. It is handed to the bride who drinks it; the same process is repeated twice, so that she drinks from the cup three times. Then the bridegroom, too, drinks three times from it. The second cup is next given to the bridegroom who again drinks three times and is then handed to the bride who does the same. Finally, the third and largest cup is set first before the bride and then before the bridegroom, who each again drinks three times. Thus, both the bride and the bridegroom have drunk three times from each of the three cups. This process, which is called "three times three," constitutes the essential part of the ceremony and joins the two in wedlock.

THE EXCHANGE OF CUPS.

(FROM A PICTURE BY SUKENOBU)

When they have exchanged cups, the bride and the bridegroom retire and change their dresses. They then enter the room where the wedding guests are being entertained. They receive their congratulations and sit with them for a while. They are expected to eat and drink with them; but they retire before long to the bridal chamber. The go-between and his wife assist them and come down afterwards to report to the assembled guests that the happy couple have been put to bed. The guests then take their departure shortly after this announcement.

Next morning the bride is up betimes to send a messenger to her father to announce that the wedding has taken place without a hitch; and the father too, before the arrival of the messenger, sends to ask after the welfare of his daughter and son-in-law. He sends presents to the members of his daughter's new home. She receives the congratulations of her friends.

On the following day the friends and relatives and their wives are invited to the bridegroom's house, when the dresses and other articles brought by the bride are exhibited. The guests are entertained often till very late at night. The bridegroom sends rice-cakes to his father-in-law who distributes them among his friends and relatives. On the fourth day after the marriage, the bride goes to her father's house and stays there a day or two. After her return to her husband, her father invites the young couple and the friends and relatives of both families to dinner. This gathering is called "the unbending of the knees," because the guests are expected to unbend themselves and stretch their knees and legs which they kept rigidly bent during the marriage ceremony and subsequent parties. They sing and dance and enjoy themselves without constraint. This is the last of the gatherings connected with the marriage. During all these ceremonies the exchange of presents is interminable so that a marriage in the regular style is very expensive, and people of moderate means curtail the proceedings as much as possible. Some even have weddings in a tea-house, especially if their own houses are not large enough to seat all the invited guests. It has become the fashion of late to hold the wedding ceremony in a shrine in imitation of the Christian mar-

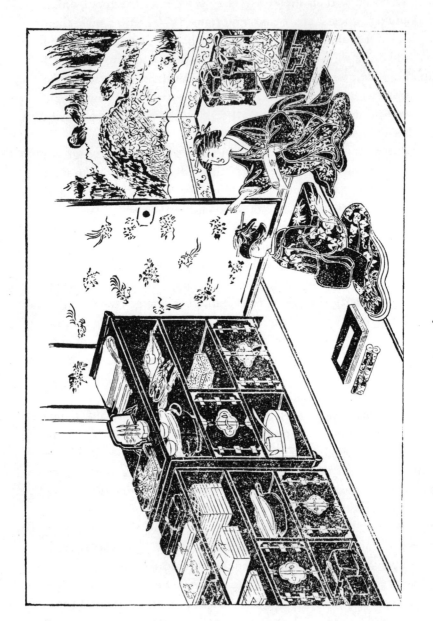

THE BRIDE'S CABINETS.

(FROM A PICTURE BY SUKENOBU)

riage service at church.

It will be seen from the above brief account how much a Japanese marriage differs from a European. The reader who considers that free choice is essential to a happy marriage, will naturally wonder at the employment of a go-between and the comparatively passive part played by the parties most concerned. It is true that the young couple have little opportunity of knowing each other before they are joined in wedlock ; for the short time, often half an hour or less, for which they see each other before making a definite decision can hardly be said to afford them an opportunity of mutual acquaintance full enough to inspire them with confidence in the momentous step they are about to take. The knowledge of each other that meeting is supposed to give them is of the most superficial kind ; for besides the shortness of time, the consciousness of what is to result from the meeting naturally puts the two on their best behaviour and prevents their being caught at unguarded moments, which alone can give any insight into their character. In their prim and stiff attitude, it is only their personal appearance that can be considered ; but even that is disguised on the girl's part by the paint and fine dress she has put on for the occasion. The intended lovers have in fact to trust blindly to luck in their bid for conjugal happiness.

But there is, on the other hand, something to be said for the go-between system. Free choice is certainly most desirable when the lovers are old enough to have a definite knowledge of their own minds and may be expected to make a judicious choice ; and upon the marriage of a man over thirty with a woman of more than five and twenty, the parties would not deserve much sympathy if they subsequently found that they had mistaken each other's character. But in Japan we marry young as a rule, men being under thirty and not unfrequently a little more than twenty and women at the latter age or less. If they were left to themselves, they would be as imprudent in their choice as those of the same age would be in other countries. They would, if pleased with each other's looks, be quite content to take their chance of the other elements that go to make a happy marriage ; and only by bitter experience would

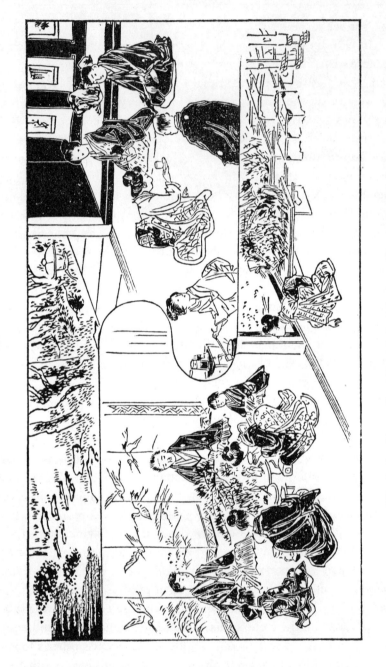

THE FIRST MEETING AND WEDDING AT THE PRESENT TIME.

they discover that they cannot live on love alone, but that divers worldly considerations must be taken into account. Many a life would, as in countries where marriage is freely contracted, be blasted by an early imprudent marriage, which is with us obviated in a great degree by the employment of the go-between. The father of the young man or girl, in looking for a suitable partner for his child, would naturally have prudential considerations foremost in view; the one would wish for a girl, well born if possible, but certainly educated enough to be a worthy ruler of the household, while the other would be equally anxious to have for his son-in-law a steady young man who would always be able to maintain his family in comfort. And the go-between, by looking himself or through his friends for an eligible partner, would be able to search on a far larger scale than would be possible to the unaided efforts of the father and his child.

This ability to make an extensive search brings out another advantage of the go-between over the free-choice system. The custom in the West which requires the woman to wait till she receives a proposal entails upon her great hardships. Sometimes, as her circle of acquaintances is generally small, she throws herself after long waiting upon the least uncongenial of the lot and prepares for herself years of disappointment, disillusionment, and heart-burnings. Or, where personal appearance counts for much as it almost always does, a woman with no pretension to beauty must often suffer many a year to elapse before the gallant comes to woo her; perhaps he never comes at all, and the qualities which might have made her a model wife are allowed to run to waste for being concealed under a homely face; and she who might have helped a husband to fame and fortune becomes a soured old maid with bitter hatred of men, or that other and more pathetic figure, the kindly maiden aunt who lavishes on her little nephews and nieces that wealth of love which a wise man would have taken to his heart as an inestimable treasure despite the plain casket in which it is enclosed. From such compulsory spinsterhood a woman is saved in Japan by the go-between; she need not set her cap at any one, for being the deputy for the woman as well as for the man, the go-

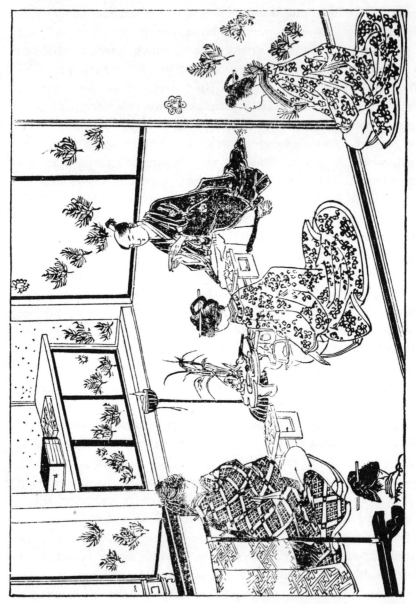

A DAIMYO'S WEDDING.

between can carry proposals from her as if he were making them on his own initiative and so can meet with a rebuff without bringing upon her the shame of a repulse. He can also find for her a suitable husband even if she is far from pretty or gentle, or has defects which may make an ordinary man think twice before rushing into her arms. "For the cracked pot a rotten lid," as we say in Japan, and for a pot however cracked or imperfect, we can always find a lid to match. So with men and women. A woman with imperfections can thus get without much difficulty a husband with similar defects ; but it would be no easy task to catch such a man without the go-between's assistance.

There is still another benefit accruing from the go-between system. Upon a squabble taking place between the husband and the wife, they may in the heat of the moment wish to separate ; and if left to themselves, they would at once get a divorce as it would not be difficult to bring their own families to take up their cause. But before they can resort to such an extreme step, they must consult the go-between, whose duty it is to make arrangements for their separation in the same way as for their union ; and the go-between, bearing in mind the interests of both parties, will do his best to patch up any differences that may have arisen, and if he is a man of tact, usually succeed in restoring peace. In minor matters he is also always appealed to ; he hears the complaints of both the husband and the wife, and advises them to yield or compromise. He is really even more useful after the marriage than before ; and he is always treated with great respect by the couple he has joined. But if, in spite of all his efforts to the contrary, the divorce does take place, his position is an unenviable one, for not unfrequently he would be thought by either family to have purposely deceived it by introducing a person whom he had known from the first to be unsuitable.

With us marriage is a civil contract. All that the authorities require is that the heads of the two families should report the marriage and request the girl's domicile to be transferred from her father's house to her husband's. The registrar of the local office complies accordingly, and the couple are legally married. There

A LOWER-CLASS WEDDING.

is no ceremony connected with it. Perhaps this absence of religious sanction may tend to make a marriage less imposing ; but as to its being less binding on that account as some have alleged, such a contention is open to question as the divorce court proceedings in the West seldom appear to be stayed by any considerations of the sanctity imposed upon marriage by religion. The exchange of cups in our weddings is a tacit vow of love and fidelity ; and when we have in view the possibility of a divorce thereafter, it is as well that we do not lay ourselves open to the charge of perjury by coming up for a second marriage after having at the first sworn before God that we would " love and cherish each other until death us do part."

Finally, the new couple do not go on a honeymoon, but proceed at once to enter upon their household duties. The honeymoon is undoubtedly an excellent institution for giving the couple an opportunity of enjoying themselves unreservedly in each other's company before taking up the serious business of life ; but at the same time it not unfrequently happens that they return from it sadly disillusioned and with an outlook far from rosy upon wedded life. The Japanese bride has an advantage over her western sister in that respect, for she has no illusions to be dispelled.

Here, then, is the essential difference in the point of view taken of wedded life. In the West it is through romance that people enter into matrimony, and that is apt to melt before the hard facts of life ; whereas in Japan we regard it in a more prosaic light, and the Japanese bride takes up the burden of married life at the threshold to lay it down only at the grave. Again, in the West a man may in a vague way think it time for him to marry and then look for a suitable partner ; but more often it is the sight of the woman with whom he would willingly share the pleasures and pains of this world that awakens in him the desire to marry and prompts him to propose to her. The possession of the woman he has set his heart upon is the immediate motive of his marriage. In Japan, however, the young man finds life lonely by himself, or is pressed into marriage by his parents or friends, or fails to win the confidence of his circle while he remains single ; and accordingly he or his parents ask friends to look for a suitable wife. The impelling cause is here the desire to have a well-ordered establishment, and love is something to be aroused and developed after marriage. As fewer elements of happiness enter into our method of wife-seeking than into the European, it may be conjectured that marriage is naturally a more risky venture with us in respect of domestic felicity. But then, we do not, when we marry, look so much for the fire and heat of love ; we are content if the common cares and joys of conjugal life induce in the course of time the warm, equable glow of affection.

CHAPTER XV.

FAMILY RELATIONS.

The family the unit of society—Adoption—The wife's family relations—The father—Retirement—The retired father—The mother-in-law—A strong-willed daughter-in-law—Tender relations—Domestic discord—Sisters-in-law—Brothers-in-law—The wife usually forewarned—The husband also handicapped—His burdens—Old Japan's ideas of wifely duties—The Japanese wife's qualities—Petticoat government—The ·wife's influence.

WHEN a woman marries, her union with her husband is not more considered than her entry into his family. Marriage, it is true, has in all countries this twofold character ; but it is especially the case in Japan where but a few decades separate us from the feudal times when, as in medieval Europe, the family was the unit of society ; and it is only in recent years that the individual has begun to receive equal consideration with the family as an element of society. The Chinese sages laid down with great emphasis that the primary object of marriage is the perpetuation of the family line and that nothing is more unfilial than the failure of issue. Thus, feudalism and Confucianism combined to impress upon the nation the importance of the family succession. More-over, every man has a natural desire to preserve his blood from extinction ; and there is a still greater incentive towards the same end in the ancestor-worship which lies at the root of Shintoism. It is every man's duty, according to that cult, to keep alive the memory of his ancestors, a duty which naturally devolves upon the head of the family ; whence arises the necessity for every house of having a recognised head. And consequently, under the old régime primogeniture flourished in its strictest form ; and younger sons and brothers were held of no account. In the feudal times the offices in the central government and in the daimiates were conferred only on the head of the family, the rest of which were merely his dependants. Cadets, therefore, could only acquire independence by being adopted into other families and becoming their heads, or in rare cases by founding branch families.

This system of adoption prevailed largely in the feudal times, and still exists, though not to so great an extent. For whereas adoption was formerly almost the only means of procuring independence open to the subordinate members of a family, now no one

HUSBAND AND WIFE.

who is able to shift for himself would care to be adopted and to assume another's surname unless some great advantage were to be gained thereby. Yet families without male issue must resort to adoption to prevent self-extinction. They adopt therefore from a family on a lower social level or one afflicted with too large a progeny. It is often a little child they undertake to bring up and so have a claim on its gratitude. A man who has daughters but no son, adopts a young man as his eldest daughter's husband and makes him in due course the head of the family. Sometimes, the adoption and the marriage take place at the same time, when the bridegroom comes to the bride's house and the usual relations between the two are reversed. The husband naturally assumes the wife's surname. His position is not an enviable one ; for though as the head of the family, he has a legal right to its property, still he is constantly reminded that he is an outsider and has to ingratiate himself with the members and relatives of the family. It is always possible to convene a meeting of these persons ; and this council is all-powerful in the disposal of family affairs. In the old times, if a member of the family misbehaved himself disgracefully, the family council met and took measures for his punishment. It would act even against the will of the head ; indeed, the head himself was not always exempt from its censure, and there are many instances of his being forced to retire in favour of a son or another member, and in military families, of his being required to wash away with his own life-blood the stain he had brought upon the family name. If one who had become the head by birth was so powerless in the presence of the family council, it will be readily surmised that the head by adoption would often be in a far worse plight than the other ; he could be divorced from his wife if she was the daughter of the house, and driven out of the family. He would naturally be more liable than any other member to the censure of the family council.

If the adopted head of the family sometimes finds his position an irksome one, the wife who marries into another family has often, if it is a large one, as hard a time of it with her husband ; she must not only put up with his whims and caprices, but she may have to bear with equal patience the humours of the rest of the family, who have her at their mercy as any one of them might by false represen-tations easily prejudice her husband or his parents against her. She is constantly put on her mettle and has to guard against giving umbrage to any of her husband's numerous relatives. Of course he may not happen to have a member of his family with him ; but if he is living in his native place, a parent or some other near relative would probably be with him. Those who have come up from the country and made their way in the metropolis would more likely be by themselves as their parents would prefer to live at home and content themselves, if need be, with monthly remittances from their sons. If a man from the country has any one with him, it is commonly some young fellow, a relative, who lives with him to complete his education. Hence, as chances of discord increase with the size of the family, a girl or her parents not seldom stipulate, in looking for a husband, for a countryman rather than for a native of the capital. But as that condition cannot always be satisfied, the girl finds herself saddled with a father, mother, and other connections by marriage with whom she has to reckon if she would get on with her husband. Of these the most important are, needless to say, the parents.

Apart from the question of the continuation of the family line, the father and, more especially, the mother are naturally anxious to see their son married and fondle their grandchildren before they die. They have, moreover, as a rule, another motive in his marriage ; which is, to make over the care of the household and live free from all anxiety. The father, if a samurai in the old days, would retire from his office in favour of his son, for many of the offices in the central and provincial governments were hereditary, unless he forfeited it by his own fault or through the caprice or displeasure of his lord. A merchant or tradesman would also, by making his son the head of his family, transfer to him his business and his name, himself assuming another name ; for it was the rule in the old times, and still is to some extent, for a merchant to have a business-name, so to speak, which was handed down from father to son, each being distinguished from the rest by the degree of descent. This retirement is a long-established custom in this country and makes our habit of taking life easy such a contrast to the strenuous, hard-working ways of the western peoples who pride themselves upon dying in harness.

In the middle ages it was a common custom with the Emperors to abdicate. Many of them resigned their high office in the prime of manhood. Some retired to a monastery and lived in complete seclusion, while others resigned in name only and, putting upon the Throne a son or a near relative who was amenable to their will, exercised the authority without the responsibilities of sovereignty. This political retirement was imitated by many of their subjects. Among the most powerful leaders, both warriors and statesmen, not a few left their marks upon their times in nominal

A DOMESTIC QUARREL

AND RECONCILIATION.

retirement from active life. There were men, also, who were, really or nominally for some fault or indiscretion committed, compelled to retire and make room for others more pleasing to the authorities. Many retired of their own will completely from the world. In short, retirement might be due in those days to four causes, namely, weariness of the world which led men to seek repose in the solitude of a hermitage or monastery, political reasons which left men better able to work their ambition under cover of retired life, official orders which imposed retirement as a disciplinary measure, and physical infirmities which disabled men from taking an active part in life. Among the military class all these causes were at work ; but nowadays only the first and the last may be said to be effective.

In ancient times the officially-recognised minimum age-limit for retirement was seventy years ; but later, in the feudal days, the limit was lowered to fifty years. Subsequently, however, such limits were ignored and men retired at what age they pleased. The usual pretext among the people was that they were compelled to retire by reason of physical infirmities ; but not unfrequently the real reason was indolence and love of ease, to which they could yield the more readily since they knew that their sons would provide for them, serve them, and treat them with respect and reverence as all dutiful sons should, so that they could pass the rest of their lives free from care and anxiety. The retired father, who nowadays hardly ever withdraws into solitude, is a harmless old gentleman who takes to innocent amusements, such as playing chess or *go* with his friends or entering into prize contests for Chinese poems or Japanese odes ; he is contented so long as he is provided with his *menus plaisirs*. At worst he sits up late at home or at tea-houses with his cronies. He appears to be calmly awaiting his end with such little pleasures as his means permit ; and if he is a sensible old fellow and can afford it, he will, while his wife is with him, live apart from his son and daughter-in-law so as not to give any occasion for family differences.

The mother, too, is harmless generally if she is over sixty ; and even when under that age, she can do little mischief if she lives apart with her husband, beyond complaining perhaps to her neighbours that her daughter-in-law or son-in-law, as the case may be, does not treat her with the consideration that is her due. Of course she thinks like all mothers that no partner however unexceptionable in disposition, ability, or personal appearance, can be good enough for her child ; and her complaint is taken for what it is worth by her neighbours unless they really detect any flagrant breach of filial duty. But it is the widow ranging in age from forty to fifty who is the greatest disturber of domestic peace. She is too old to attract, and yet not old enough to realise that fact and abandon hope ; and jealous of a younger woman in the house, she rebukes her in a dog-in-the-manger spirit for any demonstration of love when she is with her husband. She is the worst of mothers-in-law ; but others run her hard. A widow under forty cannot readily acquiesce in the relegation of household authority to another woman and often wreaks vengeance for thus supplanting her by an ill-natured tongue and the imposition of degrading work ; for mistress as she is of the house, the young wife has in all things, as a matter of filial duty, to submit to her mother-in-law's will.

In the present stage of Japanese society, the lack of sympathy between a man's wife and mother is aggravated by the difference in their education. The older woman, being separated from the younger by the yawning gulf which divides Old from New Japan, cannot perceive why the ideas in which she was herself brought up should not be good enough for the other and finds fault with what are in her eyes outlandish ways introduced by the new era. She is loud in praise of the old, harping upon the ideal state of things that would have prevailed if the world had remained unchanged, and thinks that it has retrograded socially, morally, and even physically in the interval, grumbling that the weather itself has been affected by the innovations of these latter days and refuses to bring storm and sunshine in the good old downright fashion. Such women cannot be reasonably expected to get on with those of the younger generation who have passed the primary school and probably the girls' high school and acquired a smattering of western knowledge. The instinctive antipathy between the mother-in-law and the son-in-law, which is a stock joke with the European comic press, dwindles into insignificance when compared with the feeling which sometimes arises between the former and her daughter-in-law.

But armed as she is with the unlimited authority with which custom has invested parents, the mother-in-law has not always the best of it in the tussle with her daughter-in-law. She may be

good-natured and submit to the other as readily as she has submitted
all her life to her husband ; or she may be accessible to flattery and
be made the other's tool by judicious coaxing. She is under the
thumb of her superior in wit, will, or tact. She may be made to
consent to live apart from the young couple if her husband is still
living, or to content herself with the use of a single room in their
house if she is a widow ; and sometimes she becomes little better
than an upper servant. A daughter-in-law who can make her a
willing slave, exercises as great an influence over her husband
and can persuade him to acquiesce in any proposal that she may
make with respect to his mother.

It must, however, be admitted in justice to the mothers-in-law
and daughters-in-law that there are many pleasant exceptions.
Mothers-in-law there are in abundance who are willing to give the
young wife any help in their power and afford her every chance
of establishing herself in the household. They recognise the
change in the times, and with the vague optimism of old age, hope
for the best and cheerfully resign themselves to the lead of their
sons' wives. The wife too, on her part, is not insensible to these
kindly advances and serves her mother-in-law with all her heart,
ministers to her wants, and guides her gently as she totters to the
grave. In many a household such peaceful relations subsist.
Then, again, the child-birth pain is the purgatory out of which the
young wife rises to be received with deeper love by the whole
family, and by right of motherhood, strengthens her position in the
household.

The child being, as a Japanese proverb says, the chain that
binds the husband and the wife to each other, the latter's hold on
her husband's affection becomes stronger when she is a mother ;
but a Japanese work on etiquette warns the wife that as her
husband's parents, brothers, and sisters, however well-intentioned
they may be towards her, are not after all of her blood, she must be
careful never to give cause for offence and be on her guard against
any thoughtless deed or word likely to set their tongues wagging,
and that she should consider herself to be in the enemy's country
and be prepared for surprises and ambuscades. The advice is no

doubt sound ; but it implies the possibility of family disturbances when too many of the husband's near relatives live with him, and the inference is that however well-disposed such relatives may be, the wife cannot count for a certainty upon a life of unruffled calm, and their dwelling under the same roof with her must always be a factor, actual or potential, of domestic discord ; in other words, so long as this custom holds, conjugal happiness must be more or less problematical.

Besides her husband's parents, the wife has to reckon with his brothers and sisters. If he is the head of the family, he is probably the eldest child of his parents, and his sisters would have to treat his wife as an elder sister though she may actually be younger than themselves. Girls, however, being naturally impressionable, are, if they are well treated, easy to manage unless they are particularly ill-tempered or maliciously disposed ; but if they think they are slighted, they become the most malignant of spies and exaggerate to their parents any fault she may be guilty of. The wife has therefore to win them over. Happily for her, the girls will be sooner or later disposed of in marriage ; but her trials will be more than doubled if any of them leave their husbands and come home. They are then no longer innocent, chattering hobbledehoys ; but having had an experience, unpleasant in all likelihood, of married life and lived in discord with their husbands or mothers-in-law, for otherwise they would not have been divorced, they look with envy upon any demonstration of conjugal affection and attempt to sow dissension in the family.

With her brothers-in-law the wife is on easier terms. They are not as a rule inquisitive ; they treat her with indulgence ; and in a quarrel they will cheerfully take her side against their brother. But she is put to her hardest task when there is a scapegrace among them. The trouble is of another sort than that which confronts her in dealing with a sister-in-law. The ne'er-do-well is usually, as in other countries, the youngest of the family and his mother's spoilt child. His brother, knowing his evil ways, forbids his wife to have anything to do with him. But the scamp is smooth-tongued and, making up to her with offers of service, worms himself into her favour. The wife, too, knows that his enmity will certainly endanger her standing with his mother and, willing to give her pleasure, yields to his importunities and from time to time supplies him with money by cutting down the household expenses. Thus, with the best intentions she is placed in an awkward position ; she must defraud her husband to please his mother, and if she is found out, she will be sharply brought round ; and meanwhile, she lives in fear and trepidation.

With all these encumbrances in her home, the wife's life may appear to be well-nigh intolerable. Fortunately for her, however, her husband's family is not always so complete ; it is not often that she finds there both parents, brothers and sisters in full force, and children by a former marriage. It would under such circumstances have been better, had she remained at home, though it may of course happen that the whole family are taken with her, or are easy-going and kindly-disposed, or are won by her tact, gentleness, and sweet temper. But even if they are not all that may be desired, the wife goes into the family with her eyes open ; for when the proposal of marriage was informally made by the go-between, she could easily have ascertained through friends by inquiry in the neighbourhood the size and general character of the family with which her union was sought : and it was only by gross carelessness or wilful misrepresentation on the part of her agents that she could have been kept ignorant of the fate that awaited her.

If the wife is handicapped in her bid for conjugal happiness by the size of her husband's family, he is under no less disadvantage for the same reason. If she finds it difficult to get on smoothly with all the members of his family, he encounters quite as much difficulty in feeding so many mouths ; for the whole family are often dependent upon him, as in all probability his parents pinched themselves to find means for his education so that when he completed it and made his way in the world, he might make up for their sacrifices. But even if they had done nothing for him, he would still be expected to support them. The new Civil Code recognises this right on the part of the parents ; and the head of the family has also to support his brothers and sisters and other members of his house, in addition to his wife and children. Besides these possible dependants whose claims are admitted by law, there are others whose appeals on the score of kinship however remote he cannot altogether ignore, as custom allows those related by blood or marriage to look for help to the least unfortunate among them. Thus, the father of a family has to spend the money he could otherwise save up for his children in maintaining his uncles, aunts, and cousins and some of his wife's near relations, who, as long as he supports them, stick to him like leeches and follow him about with all the pertinacity of Sir Joseph Porter's female relatives.

From the social point of view this is undoubtedly an excellent system, for the nation at large is not burdened with the support of its poor ; only the comparatively few without relatives to whom they can turn have to be maintained at the public expense. We have not, therefore, so far been confronted by the pauper question, as the poor are provided for by their own people. But it cannot at the same time be denied that the system bears hardly upon the individuals on whom falls the duty of maintaining their poor relations ; and especially is this the case with a young man at the threshold of his career. He marries, as we have already observed, not because he can support a family without embarrassment, but because he is in need of some one to manage his house. In the matter of marriage the Japanese is ordinarily improvident ; he does not allow financial considerations to enter into his matrimonial plans. It is generally with great difficulty that he can afford to help his relatives. So that under the circumstances a young man married is often with us, if not actually a man that's marred, at least one that is heavily handicapped and forced to struggle against great odds. A man who has to earn his own living must sweat and starve, slaving from morning till night, to support these drones ; and whatever ambition he may have harboured in the flush of youth is ruthlessly dashed to the ground, and his life is frittered away in sordid cares and petty troubles.

The great authority for two centuries on the conduct of women who enter into matrimony was a work written by a Japanese scholar and based on the teachings of the Chinese sages. This book enjoins upon the wife unconditional obedience to her husband. She is told that she is in every respect his inferior, and she is expected to be so overwhelmed with the sense of her own unworthiness that she must in all things submit to her husband who is the absolute lord and master of her body and soul ; whatever he may do, she is not to murmur against it, but she is to be humble when she is in the right ; and all the while, over her hangs the Damocles' sword of divorce. The position to which she is relegated by the Japanese guide to wifely conduct is merely that of an upper servant ; for no matter how many domestics there may be in the house, she must do menial work. She must share with her husband all the hardships of grinding poverty ; and when fortune smiles, he may live in luxury and entertain many friends, but she must not frequent public resorts or go sight-seeing. Wealth may bring her more conveniences, but not more pleasure ; and until she is forty years old, she is not to be seen in company, but to remain at home minding her house and children.

Such are the injunctions of the Japanese authority on female conduct ; but happily the practice is better than the precept. There may be, thanks to these teachings, furniture wives, as Lamb calls them, who are of little use beyond filling their places in their households ; but human nature breaks even through the cast-iron rules which hold it down, and, the sages and moral guides notwithstanding, there are countless happy homes which are unfortunately less heard of than those in which dissensions are rife for the same reason as that our attention is always more drawn to careers of crime and adventure than to quiet, eventless lives. Had our women become what the old teachers wished them to be, it is certain that we should not have retained our vitality through the centuries of feudalism and burst out after ages of inert isolation into all the vigour and energy of a freshly-sprung nation. It is an indirect tribute to our women that the race has preserved un-impaired those high qualities which have since raised it to its present position among the nations of the world.

Japanese wives are gentle, docile, and obedient ; but let not the western husbands who groan under petticoat government, imagine that Japanese benedicts always have it their own way, for even in Japan the grey mare is sometimes the better horse, as many a henpecked one knows to his cost. There are termagants and viragoes with us as in other countries ; the only difference is that our scolds are not so obtrusive as those of the West, and yet do enough to convince the luckless wight that he has caught a Tartar. Just as the omission of honorifics in Japanese speech is as rude as the use of profane language in English, so the absence of those gentle manners with which we invariably associate our women is an even surer index of coarseness and vulgarity than the violence of a western shrew. The Japanese vixen can therefore, without any roughness of manners, nag and harass her husband quite as effectually, though her methods may be quieter than those of the occidental species.

Labouring as she is under many disadvantages, the Japanese wife does not get credit for her good qualities, because she always keeps in the background. Neither she nor her husband ever sings the other's praises in public ; on the contrary, mutual depreciation is the custom. And yet all her efforts are directed to her husband's cutting a creditable figure among his acquaintances. A good, sensible, tactful wife is a jewel with us no less than with the wise man of yore ; and her adroitness covers a multitude of defects in her husband. And for all his brave show, often, as our proverb says, " 'tis the hen that tells the cock to crow."

CHAPTER XVI.

DIVORCE.

Frequency of divorces—The new Civil Code on marriage and divorce—Conditions of a valid marriage—Invalid marriages—Cohabitation—The wife's legal position—Her separate property—The rights of the head of the family—Care of the wife's property—Forms of divorce—Grounds for divorce—Custody of children—No damages against the co-respondent—Breaches of promise of marriage—Few mercenary marriages—Widow-hunting also rare.

IN the old days divorces took place on the slightest pretext. Among the higher classes, it is true, the family connections which a marriage brought into existence could not be dissolved without more or less serious consequences, and the parties were, as in other countries, expected to sacrifice their personal happiness to family considerations ; but among the other classes which were not influenced, as a rule, by such worldly motives in their marriages, divorces were of pretty frequent occurrence. And moreover, as they often took place from no fault of the persons divorced, they came to lose to some extent the stigma which usually attaches to them. Still, those women who had been brought up with a strict, old-world sense of honour, looked upon divorce as a stain upon their reputation ; for if it did not necessarily imply misconduct, it was attributable to want of tact on the part of the *divorcée*, and although it arose not unfrequently from the husband's caprice, she was not, until that could be proved, held altogether free from blame. As she was from the first supposed to be prepared for a wilful, cross-tempered mother-in-law, it signified a certain defect in her character that she should have failed to get into her good graces ; and the girl, therefore, ashamed to be exposed to the ignominy of divorce, did her best to please her husband's family and would put up with almost anything rather than be sent away. But the family relations sometimes became so strained that she ran away or was packed home. Divorce was, moreover, easy to effect; it needed nothing more than the re-transfer of the divorced wife's domicile from her husband's home to her father's. There was no official inquiry, and a remarriage could take place at any time.

This unsatisfactory state of affairs was to a certain extent remedied by the new Civil Code which came into operation in 1898, though it is too early yet to say what permanent reform it has brought about in our system of marriage and divorce ; and it may be well, before entering into the grounds on which a divorce may be sought under the new law, to consider the conditions requisite for a valid marriage as they will give some idea of the position taken by the legislature in regard to matrimonial relations and so help us to understand its attitude towards divorce.

A marriage, in the first place, is valid only if the parties are married of their own will. This condition may at first sight appear superfluous ; but it is formulated to enable the parties concerned to nullify a marriage contracted through mistaken identity and to prevent unions with persons who have lost control of their will or are otherwise in a disordered state of mind. Only such marriages are valid as are contracted between those who are not deceived in making their choice and are in full possession of their faculties. The object of this condition is then to protect those persons who are joined in wedlock against their will ; but, as a matter of fact, many marriages are arranged by the parents before their children are old enough to know their own minds, and the betrothed, upon coming of age, acquiesce in the engagement which they would consider unfilial to refuse to carry out. So that in many cases free will in marriage is merely formal. The second condition of a valid marriage is that it must be reported and registered at the local district office. The bride's father reports to the local office of his district that she has ceased to be a member of his family and requests her name to be struck off and transferred to the local office of the district in which her husband lives. This is accordingly done, and at the same time the husband's report confirms the father's request and the girl's name is registered as that of his wife. This transfer of the domicile constitutes the official act of marriage.

A defect in either of these two conditions naturally renders a
marriage void, for it cannot then be recognised as a lawful union.
But a marriage may subsequently to its registration be annulled in
various ways. Such annulment is not, however, a divorce, because
the marriage was not complete and cannot be said to have been
consummated. In the first place, the parties must be of the legal
age for marriage, which is for the male seventeen years and fifteen
for the female. This is a great advance on the old limit which was
fourteen years for the male and twelve for the female. The right
of annulling a marriage in which either party is under the legal age
expires in three months after the marriage or when the age-limit is
reached. Marriages contracted by force or fraud may be annulled
upon application by the victim. The application must be made to
a court of justice within three months after the discovery of the
fraud or removal of the force ; the right of application is forfeited by
condonation. A marriage is naturally invalidated by a previous
marriage ; the right of application for its annulment is vested in the
aggrieved party, the head of that party's family, the relatives, and
the public procurator, and also in the first wife or husband ; and as
bigamy is a criminal offence, there is no time-limit for the application.
One who has been judicially divorced for adultery cannot marry the
other party to the offence ; that is, marriage is forbidden between
the respondent and the co-respondent. It may appear somewhat
unjust that a man whose conduct has led to the divorce of a married
woman should be disqualified from making to her the only repara-
tion in his power for her loss of home and honour ; but the idea is,
as in the Scots law, that the ability to marry each other would
rather encourage such illicit connections and make the offenders
brave the ignominy of judicial divorce for the prospective pleasure
of a lawful union. The prohibition is therefore intended to be a
deterrent against infidelity. Marriage is also forbidden between
ascendants and descendants in the direct line and between those
down to the third degree of consanguinity in the collateral line,
that is, it is prohibited with one's parents, grand-parents, children, and grandchildren, and between brother and sister, uncle
and niece, and aunt and nephew, but permitted between cousins

german and more distant blood-relations. It is also prohibited between similar relations of affinity in the direct line, but not between those in the collateral line, so that while one cannot marry a parent or a child of one's deceased spouse, there is no impediment to a marriage with the deceased wife's sister or the deceased husband's brother, or their uncle, aunt, nephew, or niece.

A son up to thirty years of age and a daughter up to twenty-five years cannot marry without the consent of their parents. If either parent is dead, irresponsible, or has left the house, the consent of the other is deemed sufficient ; but if both parents are dead or of unsound mind, or if their whereabouts are unknown, only those parties who have not yet reached the majority-age of twenty need ask for the consent of their guardians or appeal to the family council for approval. If the parties are afflicted with a stepfather or step-mother who refuses to consent to their marriage, the approval of the family council will suffice as these persons cannot always be presumed to have at heart the interests of their step-children. A woman cannot for obvious reasons remarry until after the lapse of six months from the annulment or dissolution of her first marriage ; but if in the interval she gives birth to a child, there is no hindrance to the second marriage taking place immediately after. Lastly, in the case of a man who has been adopted as husband to the daughter, the severance of his connection as adopted son may be brought forward as a ground for the avoidance of the marriage. As he has twofold relations as son and husband, the dissolution of either relation would lead to that of the other, for the only alternative would be for the daughter to leave her family at the same time as her husband ; but as it was to keep her in the family that the husband was adopted, her father would not consent to such a step. The usual procedure is to adopt for her another husband.

Upon the consummation of marriage, the wife is obliged to live with her husband, who is required by the Civil Code to make her cohabit with him. Thus, cohabitation is in the eyes of the law an indispensable condition of matrimony ; and therefore, such a thing as judicial separation is unknown in Japan, and there is no middle course between cohabitation and divorce. The wife usually takes her husband's surname ; but if she is the head of the family or the heiress to it, the husband by adoption assumes her surname.

If the wife is under age or judicially pronounced incapable of managing her own affairs, the husband becomes her guardian for the time being; but if the husband is pronounced incapable in a similar manner, the wife becomes his guardian and takes charge of his affairs. The wife, however, in ordinary circumstances is under the husband's control. Her disabilities arise not from her sex as such, but from her status of *feme-covert* ; for though political rights are still denied to women, no discrimination is made in the private rights of the two sexes. It is only when she marries that she cedes to her husband many of her rights as *feme-sole*. There are certain acts, for instance, for which she is required by the Civil Code to obtain her husband's permission, such as the receipt and use of a capital sum, contracting of debts, bringing of actions at court, carrying on of a trade or business on her own account, and making of contracts binding herself to service for a specific term ; but the permission may be dispensed with if her husband's whereabouts are unknown, or he has wilfully deserted her, is pronounced incapable, is under restraint for lunacy, or is serving a term of imprisonment exceeding one year, or if his interests clash with hers.

The wife may have separate property. She is at liberty to make any arrangement with her husband for its management and disposal ; but such arrangement must be registered not later than the registration of the marriage itself, or it cannot be upheld before her heirs or set up against third parties. In fact, all contracts between husband and wife may by mutual consent be altered or cancelled at any time ; but such alteration or cancellation cannot be upheld to the prejudice of a third party. This right to hold property in her own name is a great concession to the wife, for such rights were formerly utterly ignored. In the old days, everything belonged to the husband as head of the family, not only any property that the wife might bring or inherit, but also any estate, real or personal, that might be acquired by any other member of the family. All its members were supposed to work for the benefit of the family, and the head as its sole representative had absolute control of the property so acquired. But now in recognition of the rights of the individual as against those of the family as a whole, the Civil Code permits the separate registration of property by its subordinate members.

Where no special arrangements have been made between husband and wife with respect to either party's property the law directs a certain course to be followed in its use and disposal. In the first place, while the owner of any property is naturally deemed to possess absolute right to the interest or profit arising therefrom, any property which has been acquired but cannot be definitely credited to either party, is to be taken, pending production of proof to the contrary, as belonging to the head of the family. The head has also the right to put to use the other party's property and derive profit therefrom, provided the character of such property remains unaltered. Thus, the head may cultivate the other's fields or rent them to a tenant and occupy or rent the other's houses, but may not, for instance, convert a field into building land or a dwelling-house into a godown. This power is given to the head to offset the obligation he or she is under to bear all expenses resulting from the marriage, that is, to defray all household expenses, support the family, and pay for the bringing up of the children. If, however, the head is in needy circumstances, the other party, if possessed of separate property, must support the family.

The husband, whether head of the family or not, has the management of his wife's property. He may make improvements in it; but he cannot without her consent rent her land for more than five years running or her house for more than three. And if the wife is afraid of her husband's abusing this discretionary power, she may request the judicial authorities to order him to deposit security against any loss that the estate might suffer through his mismanagement. The wife is to be considered as her husband's agent in household matters, such as the provision of food and raiment. The husband may, however, reserve the right to repudiate partially or wholly her acts as his proxy; but he cannot thereby cancel his obligations to those persons who have been dealing with her in good faith, believing her to possess the powers usually delegated to the wife.

Having thus given an outline of woman's legal position in matrimony, we may now pass on to the conditions of divorce. The laxity of the custom in regard to divorce was, as we have already observed, partially remedied by the new Civil Code, which is based on European laws and modified by existing Japanese usages. In the matter of divorce, it makes many concessions to the customs hitherto prevailing in Japan, as a strict adhesion to the European laws on the subject would call for a too drastic change in the habits of the people who have for the most part been accustomed to think lightly of divorce. In the old times it was sufficient to give the wife a declaration of divorce, which, from its shortness, came to be known as "the three lines and a half."

In these days, however, when the supremacy of law is universally recognised, such an informal process cannot be tolerated ; and formalities as full as at marriage must be gone through. For divorce in its simplest form judicial intervention is not needed. It is enough that the parties agree to separate. All that is necessary is to make a declaration attested by two reputable witnesses at the local office that the divorce takes place by mutual consent. If there is sufficient cause which would be recognised by a court of justice, the offending party would readily consent to this form of divorce, for few people would care to wash their soiled linen in public when the same end could be gained more quietly in private. Hence, judicial divorces are comparatively rare. The attestation of two witnesses is of considerable use in preventing rash divorces made in a moment of passion and repented immediately after, as the witnesses who may be expected to be cooler-headed than the principals, would do their best to patch up the quarrel or difference before finally setting their seal and signature to the deed of divorce. Moreover, if the parties are under twenty-five years of age, they must obtain the consent of those persons, that is, parents, guardians, or family councils, whose consent would be necessary for a marriage in which the bride is under twenty-five years of age and the bridegroom under thirty. In a divorce the domicile of the wife or the adopted husband is re-transferred from the domicile of the family into which they were married to that of their original family ; the process is reverse of that required upon marriage.   In a divorce by mutual consent the request for re-transfer is voluntarily made by the parties concerned, while in a judicial divorce, since the appeal to law is made in consequence of the refusal of one of the parties to sign the request to the local office, the re-transfer is made by order of the court.

Judicial divorces are granted on several grounds.   First, for bigamy.   Bigamy is punishable with penal servitude for a term not exceeding two years, and the second marriage is annulled ; but the offence may also be made the ground for the dissolution of the first. Thus, the bigamist may, when he has served his term, find himself single and be ready for a third marriage.   Secondly, the wife may be divorced for adultery, but not the husband.   He may be divorced if he is convicted of adultery with a married woman.   The unfaithful wife and her paramour are liable to penal servitude for a term not exceeding two years if the charge is brought by the outraged husband.   The lover cannot be punished alone ; the woman must share his fate ; and only such a lover's wife can bring a divorce suit for adultery against her husband.   But it is very seldom that the husband applies for divorce from his wife on the score of infidelity ; such divorces are generally effected by mutual consent unless the husband is ready to expose his family affairs for the mere gratification of wreaking vengeance.   The delinquent wife, if brought before court, is, as has already been stated, both punished and debarred from marrying her paramour.   Besides infidelity with a married woman, the husband may be divorced for immoral crimes.   Divorce may also be sought if the other party is guilty of forgery, theft, burglary, fraud, embezzlement, and other heinous crimes.   As the guilty party is usually the husband, the wife may refuse to live any longer with one who has brought dishonour upon the family.   She may also bring an action for divorce if her husband is imprisoned for three years or more for offences other than those mentioned above or if she has been so ill treated or grossly insulted by him as to make cohabitation intolerable.

The common custom in Japan of the couple living under one

roof with the parents of either party is doubtless responsible for two other grounds for divorce, which are that an action for divorce lies if either party ill-treats or grossly insults the ascendants of the other or is ill-treated or grossly insulted by them. Thus, without there being any strained relations between the couple themselves, either of them may seek divorce if ill-treated or grossly insulted by the parents or grand-parents of the other, or be sued for it if similar treatment is offered to them. Mothers-in-law are proverbially hard to please, and once a quarrel takes place, it is always easy to detect insult in the high words that may pass between them and their children's spouses or ill treatment in their subsequent behaviour to each other. If they lived apart, such occurrences would be rare. Though the wife may keep her temper and submit as far as possible, adopted husbands are not so amenable to parental authority, and their divorce is not unfrequent.

Wilful desertion is a valid ground for divorce. The term of absence justifying such action is three years. An adopted son who severs his connection with the family is divorced from his wife if she is the daughter of the house ; but if she is not, she may leave it with her husband. If she is the head of the family, the divorce of her adopted husband dissolves both family and marital relations at the same time ; and if she wishes to follow him, she must give up her position as head of the family and be married to him afresh.

Any arrangements may be made for the custody of the children after divorce ; but in the absence of special agreement, the principle followed is that the children belong to the family in which they were born. Thus, they belong as a rule to the father ; but if he has been adopted as husband, they fall to the care of their mother.

Judicial divorces are, as already stated, seldom applied for. There have been a few cases of divorce for adultery, which, where proved, always ended in the imprisonment of the unfaithful wife and her paramour. These criminal suits have not so far been accompanied by civil actions ; the Japanese husband is satisfied with the incarceration of the destroyer of his domestic happiness. Seeing that his wife is party to the ruin of his home, he would not dream of being indemnified for it, as a woman who is capable of infidelity is in his opinion bound sooner or later to dishonour her husband. To the Japanese there is something repugnantly mercenary in claiming damages for his wife's forfeiture of chastity in the same way as he might for the loss of any piece of property.

Pecuniary considerations enter as little into actions for breach of promise of marriage. Since the new Civil Code came into operation, there has been only one such case brought into court. It was decided in favour of the plaintiff; but the court merely ordered the promise of marriage to be carried out and did not enter into consideration of any pecuniary compensation for the breach. But then there is really nothing to assess when an engagement is broken off in Japan. All that is necessary when the other party consents to its being broken off, is to return in kind or value the betrothal presents. As the engaged couple, if they ever do write to each other, only send formal letters with the compliments of the season or inquiries after each other's health, these epistles afford no means of measuring the suffering entailed by the breach of faith. Neither do the lovers go out together ; and on the very rare occasions when they walk with each other, they are accompanied, not by a conniving gooseberry, but by an Argus-eyed chaperon who frowns upon the least departure from strict propriety. So that their behaviour in each other's company gives as little guidance as the letters in the assessment of the damage done to the jilted lover's heart.

In a similar manner mercenary marriages are not so numerous with us as in other countries. Many men marry, it is true, with ulterior motives daughters of wealthy or influential families ; and these latter naturally do their best to promote the interests of their sons-in-law. By judicious marriages young men have risen to high and influential positions in official and commercial circles. But marriages that are crudely, unblushingly mercenary are rare for the simple reason that it is not the common custom to give away daughters with large dowries. The wives bring with them plenty of dresses and personal articles, but seldom money, though their fathers may give them something to start with when they marry. There is still a strong prejudice against dowries ; and a man who marries a woman with a *dot* is often considered very mercenary and, still worse, even suspected of having taken the money as an offset against some personal defect in his wife. There is of course the possibility that the wealthy parent would help his daughter in difficulties and when the worst came to the worst, keep her and her family from starvation. But the most effectual way in which a man may make money by marriage is to get adopted as a husband by a wealthy family ; it is indeed the only means a poor man has of acquiring wealth without any exertion on his part ; the difficulty is to find a well-to-do family willing to adopt him. If he has nothing to expect from his father, he need not hope for a legacy from an uncle, aunt, or any other relative, as an estate is seldom allowed to go out of the family. A bachelor or a childless person adopts some one to succeed to his name and property.

In the same way a settlement is seldom made on the wife. A widow is, as long as she remains in the family, maintained by her son or daughter's husband. Until recently she had, if she wished to remarry, first to return to her own family and become a spinster again, so to speak, by re-assuming her maiden name ; but the new Civil Code allows her to marry direct from the family in which she has become a widow ; this is merely to save her the trouble of needlessly removing to her old home. She must, however, secure the consent of the heads of her own family and her late husband's to her second marriage. As the widow brings from her husband's home only her clothes and other personal property, she is not courted by fortune-hunters. A girl does not in Japan give her hand to a dotard with the object of enjoying his property after his death with a husband more suited to her age.

CHAPTER XVII.

CHILDREN.

Child life—Love of children—Desire for them—Child-birth—After-birth—Early days—The baby's food—The " first-eating "—Superstitions connected with infancy—Carrying of babies—Teething—Visits to the local shrine—Toddling—Weaning—The kindergarten and primary school—The girls' high school—The middle school—The popularity of middle schools—Hitting—Exercises and diversions—Collections.

JAPAN has been called the Paradise of Babies ; and certain it is that childhood passes very happily in this country. In every family its children have a free run of the whole house ; there is neither a nursery to which they can be confined nor any room which is exempt from their invasion. They are the real masters of the house ; and father, mother, elder brother and sister are their willing slaves. They will romp unchidden into the parlour and interrupt the visitor whom the father or mother is there receiving ; and the visitor too, be he friend, relative, or comparative stranger, never takes such intrusion amiss, but on the contrary, pays court to them as he knows well that through them the softest spot in the father's heart is reached and the mother's goodwill won. The parent, following the common custom of the country, deprecates any words uttered in their praise, for it is considered as great a breach of good manners to extol one's children, or for that matter, husband, wife, or any other member of the family, as to belaud oneself. The mother, burning as she may be to expatiate upon her children's marvellous sharpness or sagacity, will to the last speak disparagingly of them, but in a tone which clearly expects from the hearer an emphatic protest against her depreciation of her own offspring. Indeed, to take her at her word would be to incur her undying displeasure.

Children too, on their part, brighten every household ; and were it not for their enlivening presence, the Japanese home with its staid manners and cold civilities would be intolerably dull. The wife, debarred as she usually is by household duties from social distractions, would if childless lead a monotonous life ; and the absence of little ones she would take to heart as if she were personally to blame for it and feel that she has missed the primary object for which she entered into wedlock. She would also have to put up sometimes with the reproaches of her husband or his parents for this failure of issue and consent to the adoption of a child to whom she must concede the love which she had hoped to reserve for her own flesh and blood. But happily for the wife, we are on the whole a prolific nation untroubled by the phantom of race suicide, and every woman is prepared to bring up a family, which is in her eyes as much the wife's destiny as in girlhood she looked upon marriage as her inevitable fate. Her absolute con- centration upon her own home, though it is a serious obstacle to her social development, brings its compensation when her wedded life is crowned with maternity, and in the smiles of infancy she finds ample consolation for the monotony of her home. This intense love of children is one of the brightest traits of Japanese home life, and with the reverence for old age, gives it a tone of quiet, undemonstrative happiness.

It will therefore be readily imagined with what eagerness the arrival of the little stranger, is awaited and how the childless wife will move heaven and earth for the blessings of motherhood. She will try nostrums of every kind, submit to any regimen however irksome, that may be prescribed for her, and visit watering-places and other resorts for the improvement of her physical condition ; she will offer prayers at one temple after another, or sometimes make long pilgrimages for the purpose, in defiance of the popular belief that a child born in answer to prayer is either itself doomed to early death or destined to cut short its parents' lives.

When the unpleasant symptoms of morning-sickness warn the wife that she is about to become a mother, a midwife is called in from time to time to examine her and relieve her pain. In the fifth month an auspicious day is selected on which her relatives are invited to dinner to hear the formal announcement of her interesting state. On this day the midwife girds her under her clothes with a wide strip of bleached cotton, with the object of keeping the child as small as possible so as to ensure a light delivery. This girdle is worn up to the moment of birth. With the same object the wife does considerable amount of active housework, such as cleaning and sweeping the rooms, until the beginning of the last month when she ceases from all work and calmly awaits the delivery. Meanwhile, the midwife pays periodical visits, and in a well-to-do family she is often made to live in the house during the last month. She usually assists alone at the birth, for a doctor is seldom called in unless complications have set in or surgical operations are necessary. The accouchement, if indeed it can be so called which in Japan takes place in a sitting posture, is effected, if in the daytime, in a room darkened with half-closed doors and a screen round the bed. The delivery is left as far as possible to nature. The midwife, who is deeply versed in the intricacies of the lunar calendar, can always tell the exact hour at which the tide begins to flow, when the delivery oftenest occurs; and until that time she merely soothes and alleviates. On the whole, the curse of Eve sits lightly on her daughters in Japan, for which we have probably to thank the simplicity of our diet and mode of life. The woman who dies in child-birth is an object of infinite pity; her fate is supposed to be the consequence of her sins in a former state of existence. In lonely country-sides, in memory of such a woman, a piece of white cloth supported on four sticks is set over a stream, together with a ladle, with which passers-by are entreated to pour water into the cloth, because only when the cloth rots away completely will she be purged of her sins and enabled to enter Paradise.

Immediately the child is born, the midwife cuts off the umbilical cord, washes the child in warm water, and dresses it in swaddling clothes, after which it is shown to the mother and the rest of the family. The after-birth is put in an earthen dish and covered with another of the same material; the whole case is buried at the front entrance, inside the door if a boy and outside if a girl, the reason for the discrimination being that the latter is destined

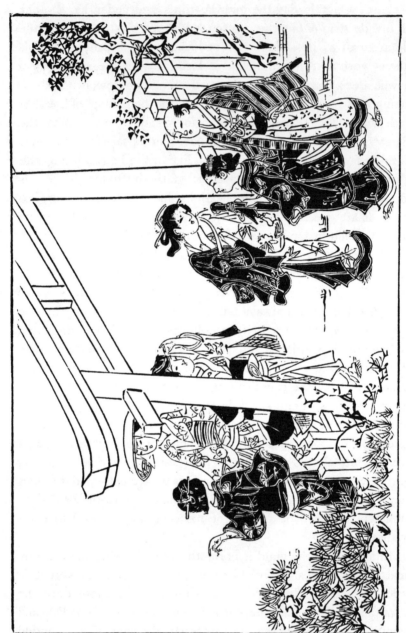

THE FIRST VISIT TO THE LOCAL SHRINE.

(FROM A PICTURE BY SUKENOBU).

to leave her home and, therefore, is not a permanent member of the family. It is the custom now to have the case buried in a special ground by a company formed for the purpose.

For the first day or two the child is given an infusion of a sea-weed which acts as a purgative ; and if the mother is yet too weak, she gets another woman to give it her milk until she is strong enough. She lies with her head propped up high, and the child sleeps with her. On the second day after the birth, the baby is washed again ; and on the sixth, friends and relatives are invited to a dinner to celebrate the birth when the child's name is given to it. The birth is also reported on that day to the local office. The mother does not leave her bed until the twenty-first day ; and she is kept at low diet until the seventy-fifth day when she can take the usual food and is considered to be herself again. Until then she is supposed not to be purified and cannot enter a temple or a shrine. On the same day she resumes her household duties. In the meantime, the child is taken on the thirty-first day if a boy and on the thirty-third if a girl, to the shrine of the tutelary deity of the district, where prayers are offered for its welfare. Then calls are made on those friends and relatives who gave presents upon the child's birth ; and it receives from them various toys, the principal of which is a papier-maché dog. Such a dog is always placed at the head of the child's bed at night as a charm against evil influences.

The child is at first fed entirely with its mother's milk ; if she is weak or sickly, a wet nurse is engaged in a family which can afford one, but in poor homes the child is nourished with a very thin rice-gruel. Cow's milk is now largely used in Tokyo, and in many families given together with human milk. Very often the former is drunk in the daytime, and at night the mother who sleeps with the baby, suckles it with her own milk. In Japan the mother, unless her place is taken by the wet nurse, invariably sleeps with the youngest child, and never leaves it by itself in a cot or bed. This has the advantage that any ailment that the child may happen to suffer in the course of the night is not left to be discovered in the morning when it may be too late, but is detected

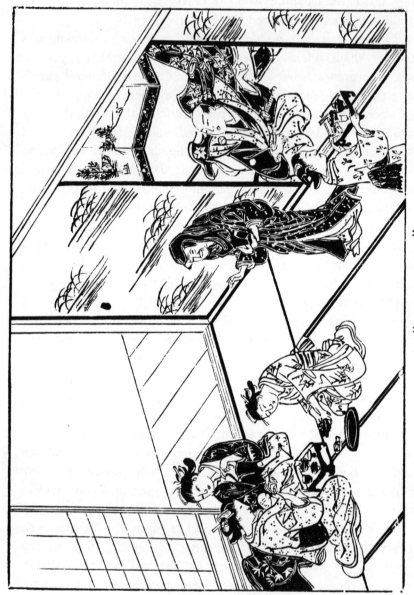

THE " FIRST—EATING."

(FROM A PICTURE BY SUKENOBU).

at once and attended to before it becomes serious. Thus, for instance, any rise in temperature is immediately felt when the child gets its milk, and measures are taken accordingly.

On the hundred and ninth day after the birth, occurs the " first-eating," at which a tray of food is set before the baby. Friends are invited to take part in the ceremony. A lady friend who has a large family of her own is asked to feed the child. She puts into its mouth a little paste of boiled rice and wets its lips with a drop of soup. Though the child generally spits out the paste, the fiction of its eating is maintained, and the ceremony closes with feasting among the invited guests. This " first-eating " is usually deferred for five or ten days as a postponement is supposed to bring luck to the child.

The infant is expected not to be able to walk in less than a twelvemonth ; but if it toddles within a year, a bag holding about three pints of uncooked rice is laid on its back, and the child is made to stumble and fall, because to walk before the first birthday augurs, according to one authority, early death and according to another, residence in a distant land. There are many other superstitions connected with infancy. Thus, a child that begins to suck its fingers before the thumb which represents the parents in Japanese palmistry, will not be an encumbrance upon its father when it grows up ; if it pushes itself out in sleep beyond the head of its bed, it will rise in the world, while a downward course is in store for the one that slips in under its bed-clothes. The baby which eats fish before it can say *toto*, the child's name for fish, will stammer when it talks. In a family in which children have one after another died in infancy, the birth of a healthy infant is ensured by such charms as making a dress for it with thirty-three pieces of cloth collected from as many families, shaving the child's head till its seventh year, and giving a boy a girl's name and *vice-versa*. A sovereign remedy for prickly heat is to hang over the front door by a piece of red thread a small egg-plant before any member of the family eats one that season. Crying at night is stopped by suspending over the child's bed a picture of a devil beating a prayer-gong. Immunity from measles is secured by putting over the child's head for a moment the rice-pot still hot after the removal of the rice, while a similar treatment with the bucket for feeding the sacred horse at a shrine is said to be equally efficacious against small-pox. The child's face is wiped with a wet scrubbing-cloth to cure it of shyness before strangers. For whooping-cough there are several remedies: for instance, a wooden spatula with the child's name and an invocation against the disease is nailed over the front door; the inked string used by carpenters for marking lines is tied loosely round the neck; a slender piece of nandina wood, just long enough for the child to grasp, is hung by a red thread to its neck; or a pair of small square wooden blocks are obtained from a temple dedicated to Jizo, the protector of children, when the child is suffering from whooping-cough and clapped whenever it coughs, and when it has recovered, the blocks are returned to the temple with another pair bearing the child's name. If the infant stands up and bending down its head, peeps from between its legs, another child will soon be born in the family; and if it has a single streak on its thigh as a birth-mark, the next to be born will be a boy, but if the streaks are double, the next will be a girl. Mothers are especially warned against leaving their children's clothes out to dry at night, for the souls of women dying at child-birth fly in the form of birds at dead of night and if they see children's apparel, they will, from envy, drop their blood upon it and the wearer of the clothing so soiled will surely sicken and die. Infants in arms must, when out at night, be covered with their own loin-cloth to avert the malign influences of the night-demon.

Japanese babies are at first carried in arms. When they fall asleep in the daytime, they are laid on a bed in a room where they can be watched. They get early used to noise, and slumber on though the watchers may talk aloud to each other. When they are a month or more old, they are carried not only in arms, but on the back as well. In the latter case, the child is tied by a long piece of bleached cotton which is first passed under its arms and over the nurse's shoulders and after crossing in front, one end is passed under the girl's arm and over the child's thighs and tied at

CARRYING CHILDREN.

the side to the other end. Thus, the piece is carried over the child's back in parallel lines and crosses on the nurse's breast. In cold weather, the nurse and her charge are covered with a kind of *haori*, thickly-wadded, before being tied with the cotton. It keeps them both warm, while the child's breast and stomach are even better protected by the contact of the nurse's back. Very young babies are tied down straight with their legs close together; but when they are older, they ride astride and their feet dangle on either side. The nurse who is specially engaged for the purpose is twelve or thirteen years old; but in poor families the elder brother or sister takes her place. Little girls are often to be seen in the streets, carrying on their backs sisters and brothers only a year or two younger than themselves, whose feet, as they dangle, almost trail on the ground. At first the girls can hardly walk with such burdens; but they soon get used to them, and they run, romp, and dance with their companions without much concern for their charges, who are often put in very uncomfortable positions. These, however, fare worse when they are on their brothers' backs; for these urchins, being rougher and more careless than their sisters, fly kites, climb up trees, flourish bamboo poles to catch cicadas, run after dragon-flies, and even snowball one another, utterly regardless of the discomfort they occasion their charges, who, if they cry, are knocked with the back of the head, and seem soon to become habituated to the dangers they run through the recklessness of their carriers. This manner of carrying on the back is only possible with Japanese clothes, for the knot of the *obi* behind prevents the child from slipping down; and it would be difficult to try this method with European clothes, with men's because the tying down of the coat would hamper the movement of the arms, and with women's because of the multiplicity of pins at the neck and the waist. Nurses tie a towel round their heads so as not to let their back-hair fall on the babies' faces. When the children are older and able to walk, they are carried without being tied down, for they can catch hold by the shoulders or by putting their arms loosely round the nurse's neck, while they are kept from slipping by the nurse's passing her hands under them.

Among little toys given to infants is a wooden whistle with either end rounded into a ball. It is given to the child to suck and bite and like the coral, hardens the gums, thereby facilitating the teething. The time for teething varies of course with the individual child and is the source of as much anxiety to the Japanese mother as to that of any other country.

On the fifteenth of November in the second year after the birth, the child is again taken to the shrine of the tutelary deity of the locality. A small offering of money is made ; and in return the consecrated *sake* in a flat unglazed earthenware is given to the child to sip, while the priest purifies its body by waving over it a sacred wand adorned with strips of paper. The ostensible object of the visit is to invoke the God's blessing upon the child ; but it is really made the occasion for dressing up the child in finery, when parents vie with one another in the richness of their children's apparel. Calls are then made on the friends who made congratulatory presents to the child. The shrine is visited again on the same day of the same month two years later in the case of a boy and four years later if the child is a girl.

As soon as the child is able to toddle along, sandals or plain clogs are tied to its feet when it walks on the ground. It learns first to walk indoors. As there are no go-carts in Japan, it tries to stand up by clinging to pillars and sliding-doors, for it may stumble and flop down on the soft mats without hurting itself ; it is when it runs, as children will do, without being able to stop, that the greatest care has to be taken that it does not tumble over the edge of the verandah. In Tokyo perambulators are now pretty common ; but in the old days there was no special means of conveyance for children, and they had to be carried in arms or on the back.

There is no fixed time for weaning. After its first birthday, ordinary food is given to the child little by little until in a year's time it is able to do without its milk. Generally-speaking, however, the time for weaning is governed by the arrival of a younger brother or sister ; but the youngest is often allowed to take its mother's milk up to its fifth or sixth year, though of course, as it can t ke common food, it goes to its mother only for diversion.

At three or four years children are sent to kindergarten, that is, if they can gain admission, for these useful institutions are still few even in Tokyo. There they are kept in good humour, everything being done for their amusement. They sing together simple songs, have object lessons, are set to make little things out of paper, and are also allowed to romp about as they please. At six years, the minimum school-age, they enter the primary school, the course at which extends over six years. Here they are taught Japanese, arithmetic, elements of history, geography, and natural history, elementary drawing, singing, and gymnastics, and hand work for boys and needlework for girls. This six years' course is compulsory for all children; and there is a higher primary school with two years' course for those boys who cannot afford to receive any higher education. The pupils who have completed the course at the ordinary primary school are qualified to present themselves for the entrance examinations of the higher schools, the middle school for boys and the high school for girls.

Although a women's university was established not long ago in Tokyo, a girl's education generally stops with the high school, if it goes so far. As she has been six years in the primary and four in the high school, she has had ten years of schooling if she has passed every class satisfactorily from the first to the last, and she is sixteen years old when she leaves the high school. And as a Japanese girl usually marries at eighteen or nineteen, she has not much time to spare before she has to think seriously of matrimony. Two or three years of home life are all that is left her before she will have to take charge of a household of her own. And further, as she is supposed to pass the flower of her youth at four and twenty, a college course would bring her dangerously close to the lower limit of spinsterhood, and so, as things stand in Japan, female universities would, even were they plentiful, not be so popular as they should deserve. In the high school the same subjects, more advanced, are taught as in the lower school, the only new subject of importance being domestic economy.

The middle school has a course of five years, in which the pupils are taught, besides the advanced course of the subjects studied in the lower school, Chinese classics, algebra, geometry, physiology and hygiene, physics and chemistry, law and political economy. English becomes a subject of importance, being taught seven hours a week. When the course is completed satisfactorily by regular promotion every year, the pupil is seventeen years old. He is now ready to commence his secondary education, for which he will enter the special higher schools for the professions or the preparatory high school for the university.

A very large percentage of children of the school-age pass through the primary school; but of these a comparatively small proportion enter the middle school, partly because many of them are too poor or cannot be spared at home where they must help their fathers, and partly because there are not middle schools enough to take in all the applicants, though of late years these schools have greatly multiplied. Formerly, parents were content to let their children stop their education when they had passed the primary school unless they intended to fit them for the professions ; but now a general recognition of the importance of education on modern lines has done much to increase the demand for middle schools. There is still another motive for entering the middle school. To the Japanese mother the greatest source of anxiety on her boy's account is his liability, when he comes of age, to compulsory military service. Of course, he may upon medical examination be pronounced unfit for service, or he may, though strong enough, be exempted when lots are drawn among those who have been passed by the medical examiners. But the former contingency is naturally distasteful while the latter is too uncertain to be hoped for with any degree of confidence. However, a comparatively easy way of escaping some at least of the rigours of military service was opened when the authorities permitted those who had completed the middle-school course to offer themselves for a year's voluntary service. As such volunteers leave service with the rank of sergeant at least, and even of commissioned officer if they pass certain examinations, they are, needless to state, better treated than the common soldiers. Moreover, though the prescribed age for conscription is twenty, the students who enter colleges and other institutions for secondary education are permitted to postpone their enlistment until they graduate or reach the age of twenty-eight.

Children, as we have said, are very much petted. They are never whipped or kicked, but occasionally slapped. Even at school they are hardly ever subjected to corporal punishment; caning and birching are unknown. Formerly they used to be made to stand on a school desk or in a corner with a cup of water for half an hour or more; but now the severest punishment is detention after school or suspension from attendance for a certain period. Of course, at home or at school, among their mates they may be knocked about; the hitting is done with a swinging blow on the head or on the back, and very rarely with a forward blow, for the art of boxing being unknown, the hits peculiar to it are seldom resorted to. Kicking is not practised because, with the clogs on, the kicker is as likely to hurt himself as the kicked, while with the sandals or bare socks it is naturally out of the question. People stamp with their clogs, but that can only be done on a fallen foe.

Girls, when they congregate in the open air, play at blindman's buff, Puss-in-the-corner, and hide and seek, sing in a ring, and romp about much in the same way as do their western cousins. Their amusements are social, but quieter than those of boys, who though they play with their sisters at first, develop, as in all other countries, sovereign contempt for girlish sports when they approach their teens and engage in rougher games of their own. Japanese boys do not box or use single sticks, but they wrestle and fence. In wrestling, their object is to made their adversary touch the ground with any part of his body or to push him out of the ring, just as is done by professional wrestlers, while the great point in fencing is to hit one's opponent in a way that would be fatal if a real sword were used. The fencing-sword is made of four pieces of spliced bamboo bound together with a stout string and capped at the tip with leather; it has a sword-guard between the handle and the hilt. The combatants put on barred visors with sides of thickly-wadded cloth, which is tightly tied at the neck. They have also on thick gauntlets and body-pieces of stout leather around the waist. The

FENCING.

legs are unprotected. Blows are given on the crown, arms, waist, and legs, and a thrust is made at the throat. Sometimes the fencers throw down their weapons and wrestle, when the victor must bring down his opponent on the ground and getting astride of him, untie the band and pull off his visor. It is an exercise more exciting and fatiguing than fencing with foils.

Birds' nesting is unknown ; but if birds are exempted from the Japanese boy's cruelty, their place is taken by the cicada and the dragon-fly, and in late summer and early autumn, boys are to be seen running after these insects with long lime-tipped bamboo poles and catching the cicada as it emits its stridulous cry on the trunk of a tree and the dragon-fly as it flits and flutters in the air.   As these boys flourish their poles in the open street, they not unfrequently catch the unwary passers-by in the face, or their hats and clothes. But butterflies and moths, in which Japan is especially rich, are free from their pursuit.   Indeed, Japanese boys do not as a rule go in for collection of natural objects.

CHAPTER XVIII.

FUNERAL.

Unlucky ages—The Japanese cycle—Celebration of ages—Respect for old age—
Death—Preparations for the funeral—The wake—The coffin and bier—The funeral
procession—The funeral service—Cremation—Gathering the bones—The grave—Prayers
for the dead—Return presents—Memorial services—The Shinto funeral.

WHEN the Japanese child has passed through its teens without
any serious mishap, its mother is not yet altogether free
from anxiety ; for there are certain stages of its life at
which it is threatened by misfortune. Superstition has fixed certain
ages, different according to sex, which must be passed with utmost
circumspection if one would escape calamities ; these ages are the
twenty-fifth, forty-second, and sixty-first years for men and the
nineteenth, thirty-third, and thirty-seventh years for women. Here
we may note a curious way of counting years commonly practised
in Japan ; in official reports and legal documents one's age must be
given according to the number of full years and months one has
lived, but on other occasions we have a very loose way of comput-
ing our ages. Thus, when we say that a man is thirty years old,
we do not mean that he is full thirty years of age or that he is in
his thirtieth year, but we mean that he has seen thirty solar years
of the almanac ; that is, if we say in 1910 that he is thirty years old,
we mean that he was born some time in 1881, and if his birthday
is the New Year's Day, he would be twenty-nine years old on the
same day of 1910, but if it is the thirty-first of December, he would
be only twenty-eight years and a day on the first day of 1910, still
we speak of him in either case as being thirty years old. A baby
born on the last day of the year would be two years old the next
morning ; its second year according to our mode of computation is,
in short, the solar year in which it completes its first twelvemonth.
When, therefore, we say, for instance, that a man's first inauspicious

age is his twenty-fifth year, we mean the solar year in which he completes his twenty-fourth year. Thus, the twenty-fourth, forty-first, and sixtieth years of a man and the eighteenth, thirty-second, and thirty-sixth years of a woman are really their climacteric years ; and of these the most critical are the forty-first for a man and the thirty-second for a woman, for not only these years themselves, but the years immediately preceding and following each of them also, are considered inauspicious, so that the crisis lasts in either case for three years, during which period men and women refrain as much as possible from acts that may appear like tempting Providence.

The sixtieth year is our grand climacteric, after which a man must be prepared for death at any moment ; but this age is treated as one for congratulation and never for sorrow or anxiety, because it completes our cycle of years. To each year is assigned an element of nature, namely, wood, fire, earth, metal, or water, each of which is divided into two kinds, elder and younger, so that there are practically ten elemental signs by which the years are successively designated. Again, there are twelve signs of animals which are also applied to years ; these animals are the rat, ox, tiger, hare, dragon, snake, horse, sheep, ape, fowl, dog, and boar. The years are designated in order after these animals. Since, then, the years are named in succession after the ten elemental and twelve animal signs, the same combination of an elemental and an animal sign recurs every sixty years ; the year of the first sign of metal and the sign of the rat, which last coincided with the year 1852, will come again in 1912, that is, sixty years after the other. Our cycle, therefore, comprises sixty years ; and a man who has completed this sexagenary cycle is supposed to return to childhood, and often wears red under-garments or red-lined clothes and a red cap after the manner of children. He invites friends and relatives to a dinner to celebrate the occasion.

The next celebration takes place when a man has reached his seventieth year, which is named " a rarity since antiquity," after the saying that man has seldom since antiquity reached seventy years. The septuagenarian distributes among his friends and relatives large, round, red and white rice-cakes with the character signifying longevity written on them. The seventy-seventh year is celebrated as the fête of joy, because the characters for seventy-seven resemble the character for joy when written in a certain style. On this occasion fans, cloth wrappers, and rice-cakes with the character for joy written on them are distributed among friends and relatives. The eightieth year is celebrated in the same manner as the seventieth ; and the celebration of the eighty-eighth year, which is called the fête of rice because of the resemblance of the characters for eighty-eight to the character for that useful cereal. The ninetieth and hundredth years are also celebrated when such opportunities occur.

When a man whose days have exceeded threescore years and ten passes away, the words that his friends come and sometimes utter to his surviving family sound more like congratulation than condolence ; it is not, however, as a cynic might suppose, that they congratulate the family upon having ridden itself of a peevish old man who was a damper upon all its innocent enjoyments ; it is because they consider it a matter for congratulation that he should have lived to such an age, and since death must come to all, he was to be envied for having succeeded so long in keeping off that unwelcome guest. They often add the wish that similar good fortune may be theirs. The aged as a rule live happily, except such as have no relatives nor any one else to depend upon ; and though they may complain of the infirmities that come with years, they never lack sympathy and, so long as they do not make themselves disagreeable, are treated with tenderness by their friends and neighbours. The respect for old age, which is one of the fundamental precepts of Confucian philosophy, is a national characteristic in Japan no less than in China.

When an illness takes a serious turn or an injury is likely to prove fatal, the members of the family are, if they live apart, summoned home and gather around the death-bed. It is considered unfilial, and unfortunate if unintentional, not to be present at a parent's death, as, for instance, children are warned not to go to bed with their socks on even in the coldest weather since, in that case,

they would be unable to attend at their parents' death-bed.   When
the patient is in the last article of death, his wife and children put
their mouths close to his ear and call him by name ; recalled by the
dear voices, life flickers for a moment and then goes out.   And
when the glazed eyes and rigid face show that all is over, his lips

OFFERINGS BEFORE A COFFIN.

are wetted with drops of water ; so universal is this custom that the
expression " to wet the dying lips with water " has come to signify
the tending of a patient in his last illness, as when we say that the
wife should be younger than the husband since it is her duty to wet
his dying lips with water.   The folding screen which is usually set

around the head of the bed to soften the daylight in the sick-room, is put upside down. The bed is replaced by a matting, and the quilt is put over the body with its ends reversed so that its foot is over the dead man's breast; and a white cloth is laid over the face to hide it as its exposure is believed to be an obstacle to the soul's journey on the road to Hades. A table of plain white wood is set at the head of the bed. At the furthest end is placed a tablet of white wood, on which the Buddhistic name of the deceased is written in Indian ink. The Buddhistic name is the name by which the deceased will be called in prayers and at his temple; he may have received it in his lifetime as many people ask priests of high virtue and reputation to give them such a name, or more often, the superior of the temple where the funeral service is to be held, is communicated with immediately and desired to give the name, which he fixes upon according to the deceased man's social position, calling, and services to the temple. In front of the tablet are ranged in a line a vase with a branch of the Chinese anise or oldenlandia, a cup of water, and a lamp lighted with rape-oil; all these utensils are made of unglazed earthenware. On the nearest edge is set an earthen censer in which incense-sticks are kept constantly burning, with a box of the sticks beside it. A sword or a knife is placed on or near the corpse to avert the malign influences of evil spirits.

Meanwhile, the family shrine is not unfrequently covered to prevent the ingress of the air polluted by the presence of the dead body. The front gate is closed and, in shops and tradesmen's houses, a reed-screen is hung inside out over the front entrance with a notice of the family bereavement and, often, of the date of the funeral. A similar notice is sent to friends and relatives, and also advertised in the papers. The family temple is notified and a priest comes from it and recites prayers before the tablet. In the evening the body is washed in a tub; first, cold water is poured into the tub and then hot water is added to the required temperature. Superstitious people insist at other times upon pouring hot water into any vessel and then adding cold water even when the reverse process would be more convenient, simply because the latter is the rule at the body-washing. The washing is done by near relatives; sometimes the body is merely wiped with water; and, in the case of a woman, the water is simply poured on the body by inverting the dipper outward with the left hand instead of inward with the right as on other occasions. The head is shaved after washing by touching it with the razor in small patches instead of running the razor continuously which may presage a succession of misfortunes in the family. Next, the grave-clothes are put on; the garment is made by two female relatives sewing with the same piece of thread in opposite directions without knotting the ends. Around the neck is suspended a bag containing Buddhist charms and a small coin or picture of a coin to pay the ferriage on the road to Hades. A rosary and a bamboo staff are also put into the coffin. Mittens, leggings, and sandals are worn, the last being tied with the heel-ends to the toes to signify that the dead shall not return drawn back by love of this world. The wife, if the deceased is her husband, sometimes cuts off her hair and puts it in the coffin in token of her resolve never to marry again. Into the child's coffin a doll is put to keep it company on its lonely journey to the other world. The coffin is then filled with incense powder or dried leaves of the Chinese anise.

On the eve of the funeral a wake is kept. The body must be kept for at least twenty-four hours after death. In great families where elaborate preparations must be made for the funeral, it is often kept for several days; but in most other houses the funeral takes place as soon as possible. In the summer heat it is naturally important that the body should be buried with the least delay. When more than one night intervene between the death and the funeral, the wake is sometimes held every night. Friends and relatives are invited, and they burn incense before the coffin and offer prayers; and in the interval the conversation turns upon the deceased and every effort is made to console the bereaved family. A priest is called in from the family temple, and he recites three or four prayers in the course of the night. In a separate room a slight repast is offered to the persons gathered in the house, and though *sake* is drunk, it is taken very quietly.

The coffin is among the better classes a double box of wood, oblong in shape to allow the body to lie in it. Sometimes the box is single and almost square, the body being made to sit in it, and sometimes an earthen jar is used; and among the poorest it is no more than a barrel with bamboo hoops. The coffin is wrapped in white cloth. The bier may be only a rest with poles extending at both ends; but in most cases, especially if the coffin is oblong, it has a curved roof with a pair of gilt lotus flowers in front and behind. The square coffin has usually a baldachin over it;

COFFINS AND AN URN.

formerly it used to be carried in a palanquin. The pall differs in colour according to the sex and age of the deceased. It is made of two square wadded covers like quilts; and the upper or outer cover is light blue for a man and the lower one is white if he has not yet reached his forty-first year and red if he is past that age, while the outer cover is white for a woman, and the inner red or pink according as she has or has not passed her thirty-second year. The lower cover differs in colour according as the deceased is under or over the age which is considered most critical for one of the deceased's sex.

The funeral usually takes place in the afternoon; but in summer the *cortège* leaves the house at an early hour of the morning. In the country the mourners gather before the funeral and take a meal; but in Tokyo it is usually the chief mourner who has a meal before starting. At such a meal a second helping is never taken as it may presage another death in the family. One bowl of rice on which clear bean-curd soup is poured, is eaten with a single chopstick. At other times, therefore, it is considered unlucky to take only one helping of rice.

A BUDDHIST

The funeral procession is not always in the same order; but in a middle-class funeral the order is commonly as follows:—The procession is led by a person who acts as its guide; he is followed by men carrying white lanterns on long poles, huge bundles of flowers stuck in green-bamboo pedestals, birds in enormous cages, and stands of artificial flowers which are almost always large gilt lotus plants; these men always march two abreast with the exception of the caged birds, for the flowers, natural or artificial, are invariably presented in pairs, while the cages are single. They are the presents of friends and relatives and their names are given on the wooden tickets attached to these presents. The birds in the cages are taken to the temple and there set free as an act of mercy, while the natural flowers are thrown away or pulled to pieces by the children of the poor in the neighbourhood who invariably come

FUNERAL PROCESSION.

and beg when there is a funeral. After the flowers comes the priest who has been sent from the temple to return with the funeral procession; he is in a jinrikisha. Then follow persons carrying incense and the tablet, and if the deceased was a government official, a military or naval officer, or otherwise a man of rank and position, the decorations which he may have received are also carried. The tablet is carried by the chief mourner or some other member of the family ; in the latter case the chief mourner follows the hearse. In the wake of some flags, on one of which is inscribed the deceased's Buddhistic name, comes the hearse beside which walk the pall-bearers, generally persons in the deceased's employ. It is immediately followed by the family and relatives, and then by other mourners. The mourners should properly follow on foot ; but frequently they go in jinrikisha and carriages ; moreover, it has become the custom for mourners who are not intimate friends of the deceased to proceed straight to the temple and wait there for the arrival of the procession.

When the funeral procession reaches the temple, the bier is placed in front of the shrine, which stands at the furthest end of the temple hall. The chief mourner, family, and relatives take their seats usually on one side of the hall and the other mourners on the opposite side, leaving a space between the shrine and the front entrance of the hall for the officiating priest to hold the funeral service. When all have taken their seats, the officiating priest, who is as a rule the superior of the temple, enters with his assistants. With gong, bell, drum, and cymbals the prayers are recited and sutras chanted. The officiating priest then recites alone a prayer which is to guide the spirit of the dead on the road to Hades. After this prayer, the chief mourner, family, and friends and relatives advance in front of the bier and, taking a pinch of incense, drop it into the censer to burn. Where there are many mourners, two or more censers are placed close to the bier and the incense-burning is begun simultaneously so as not to keep the mourners waiting a long time for their turn. The chief mourner and his nearest relatives come forward and thank the mourners in the hall, or stand at the entrance and thank them as they leave. Sometimes, an address expressive of sorrow or in eulogy of the deceased is read by a relative or friend.

The bier is then taken to the crematory by the chief mourner and his relatives. There are a few public cemeteries on the outskirts of Tokyo, where the body may be taken immediately from

SERVICE AT THE TEMPLE.

the temple and buried as it is.   But for burial in a temple yard in
the city the body must be first burnt ; and accordingly it is taken to
a crematory.   There are seven crematories just outside Tokyo,
none being permitted in the city.   The body is taken to one of

AT THE CREMATORY.

these and put in an oven ; the fire is lighted ; and the door of the
oven is locked and the key taken home by the chief mourner.

Early next morning, the relatives return to the crematory, and
in their presence the oven is opened.   The bones and ashes are
gathered into a tray, which is brought out and the mourners pick
the bones from among the ashes.   Every piece must be picked up
by two persons holding it with two pairs of chopsticks and put into
the urn.   When all the bones have been picked out, the urn is
closed with a lid and taken to the temple.

The grave may be dug in a small plot bought by the family in
a public cemetery when the body is to be buried with its coffin.
In that case a separate grave is dug for each body ; but if it is to be
interred in a temple yard, one grave will serve for the whole family,
for there is a hollow under the tombstone which is closed with a
stone, and at each burial the stone is removed to put in the urn.

The tombstone is an upright stone, square in section and with a tapering top, which stands on a stone pedestal. The front inscription merely gives the name of the family with, perhaps, the family crest over it, and the Buddhistic name of the deceased is engraved on a side. In a public cemetery where the grave-enclosures are larger and a tombstone is set up for every member of the family, the tombstone naturally cannot be got ready in time for the funeral,

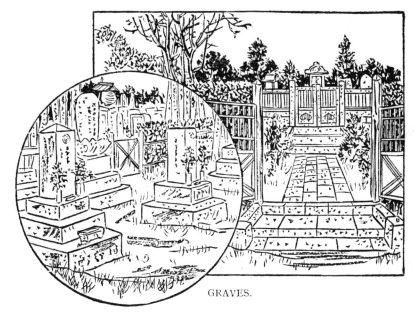

GRAVES.

and a wooden grave-post is stuck in the grave with the Buddhistic name in front and the lay name and date of decease on the sides.

After the funeral, the tablet of the deceased is set on a table at home, and a light and incense are kept burning before it until the seventh day from the day of decease ; and prayers are offered at the grave every day for the same length of time, after which a priest comes from the temple every seven days until seven weeks are passed. For forty-nine days the spirit of the dead wanders in the dark space intervening between this world and the next, and every seven days it makes an advance forward, in which it is materially helped by the prayers of those it has left behind ; according to some, the spirit hovers for the same period over the roof of its old home, for which reason many people dislike to remove until the period has terminated from a house in which a member of the family has died, as his spirit would have to hover over a house deserted by those he loved.

At the end of the fifth week, packages of tea and boxes of cakes of wheaten flour stuffed with red-bean jam are sent as return presents to those persons who brought offerings to the dead. On the forty-ninth day, forty-nine cakes are taken to the temple; in old times the human body was believed to contain forty-eight bones, and if to these the skull is added, the total becomes forty-nine, and as emblematic of these bones, one of the cakes is made much larger than the rest. They are offered before the dead, and after prayers have been recited and incense burnt, the large cake is taken home and divided among the family. A wake is sometimes kept on the night of the forty-eighth day; and on the following day, after the service at the temple, those who attend are taken to a restaurant and entertained, when the near relatives, who have hitherto abstained from animal food in token of their mourning, take it as this day ends the period of deep mourning.

A memorial service is next held on the hundredth day. On this day the provisional tablet which has hitherto been set up in the family shrine is exchanged for the permanent one; and at the temple also, the tablet which is there kept is taken down from the shelf on which are placed the tablets of the recently deceased. On the day of decease every month prayers are recited and a meal-tray set before the tablet in the family shrine. The next memorial service at the temple takes place on the first anniversary, after which comes the second anniversary which, after the method of reckoning mentioned at the beginning of this chapter, is called the third anniversary, so that a second anniversary is unknown in the commemoration of a death or any other event. The later anniversaries on which services are held are the seventh, thirteenth, seventeenth, twenty-third, twenty-seventh, thirty-third, thirty-seventh, fiftieth, and every fifty years thereafter.

We have given above an outline of the ordinary Buddhist funeral, though the procedure varies slightly with each sect of

Buddhism. There is, however, another form of funeral, which is performed with Shinto rites. As, however, the two forms resemble each other in the main, we may here give a few points of difference between them.

When a death takes place, it is reported at once to the shrine of the local tutelary deity, and a Shinto priest called in. The date of the funeral is then fixed. The body is laid in the upper part of a room, and the face is covered with a white cloth; before it is set a table, on which are put some washed rice, water, and salt, and a

A SHINTO FUNERAL PROCESSION.

lamp is lighted; and perfect silence reigns in the room. A tablet is placed before the body and the ceremony of transferring the spirit of the dead to the tablet is performed. Then a new bed and pillow are put in the coffin and the body is laid on them with the face covered and a new quilt put over it; and at the same time many favourite articles of the deceased are laid beside him. The coffin is then filled up, and the lid nailed on it. The body is never washed, but it is sometimes wiped with a wet cloth if it has lain long; in the sick-bed. The coffin is laid on wooden rests, and rice,

A SHINTO FUNERAL SERVICE.

water, and salt offered before it; it is next placed in a bier which has a roof like that of a Shinto shrine. The funeral procession is led by the guide, who is followed by bearers of lanterns and branches of *cleyera japonica ;* after them come priests and carriers of red and white flags with a box of offerings between them. Next comes the officiating priest and after him is carried a flag bearing the name of the deceased with his court rank and title, if he had any ; and then, more lanterns, followed by the hearse and the rests behind it. The grave-post is carried next, and after it marches the chief mourner, behind whom walk the near relatives and after them, the general mourners. When the procession reaches the hall for burial service, the bier is laid on the rests and the *cleyera japonica* and the flag with the deceased's name are set up. Offerings of food are made before the coffin and the officiating priest reads out a funeral address giving a short sketch of the deceased's life ; and then all the priests, the chief mourner, the relatives, and the rest of the mourners take each in turn a *tamagushi*, which is a branch of *cleyera japonica* with strips of paper hanging from it, and laying it before the coffin, makes a bow to the dead. The food is removed and the coffin brought down and buried, the relatives throwing the earth into the grave. The grave-post is next set up and fenced round with bamboo poles, which are connected with sacred rope. The priest announces the burial and bows to the grave, in which act he is followed by the mourners present. Before leaving the burial-ground, all the mourners are purified by the priests with a sacred wand. On the night of the funeral, when the house has been purified by sprinkling salt water over it, the *cleyera japonica* and flowers of the season are put in vases before the tablet, a lamp is lighted, and food is offered to it ; and the priest reads a prayer and, together with the others present, offers the *tamagushi* and bows to the tablet, after which the food is removed, and the service ends.

CHAPTER XIX.

ACCOMPLISHMENTS.

THE greatest accomplishment, and the most useful, that the Japanese woman can possess is unquestionably the art of sewing ; but the knowledge of needlework is so generally recognised as an indispensable equipment of the housewife, forming as it does an important subject of study in girls' schools, that it is not often included in the accomplishments recommended in Japanese books for women. The first place among them is given to composition, that is, the art of writing, more particularly, of letter-writing, for in Japan where considerable difference exists between the spoken and written languages, composition has to be specially learnt. In letter-writing, moreover, there are many conventional phrases and turns of expression which must be used though they may not add to the meaning ; they give an artificial character to Japanese letters and call for great diligence if one would become a good letter-writer. A skilful and expressive transcription of characters is also looked upon as an art of no mean order. Middle-aged men, especially of the old school, often spend hours on end in writing for practice ; and a well-written piece on a *kakemono* is frequently hung in an alcove in place of a picture and as highly appreciated. Many skilled caligraphists make a respectable living by writing.

A WRITING-TABLE AND BOOK-CASES.

The writing-table is a low piece of board, three feet long and about one wide, supported at either end or a few inches from it by a wooden prop; and the writer, in sitting at the table, puts his knees under it between the props. The paper used for letter-writing is rice-paper in a long roll, which is unrolled as one writes. Most people can write with the roll in their hands, letting the written portion drop as the paper is unrolled. The ink is made by wetting and rubbing the Indian-ink stick on a stone slab with a hollow at the upper end as reservoir for the ink. The pen is a hair-pencil with a bamboo holder. A paper-weight of metal is used to hold the paper down when we write at the table ; and the writer sits straight at the table and, dipping the brush in ink, writes with it held almost perpendicularly and lightly touching the paper.

Another literary accomplishment is the composition of odes. These are short verses of thirty-one syllables, made up of two sets of five and seven syllables each, closed by a line of seven syllables. To be expressed within so small a compass, the idea must be at once single and simple. It is commonly an epigrammatic presentation of a mood, it may be, of love, longing, appreciation of nature, or consciousness of the uncertainty of life. Sometimes it is didactic or expresses a moral truth in simple or metaphorical language. Our national anthem is an instance of this form of verse and runs as follows :—

> *Kimi ga yo wa*   *Chiyo ni yachiyo ni*
> *Sazare-ishi no*   *Iwao to narite*
>   *Koke no musumade;*

which may be literally translated : " May Our Lord's reign last for a thousand, eight thousand ages, until little stones become rocks and are covered with moss."

A celebrated minister of state who lived a thousand years ago, composed the following :—

> *Kokoro dani*   *Makoto no michi ni*
> *Kanainaba*   *Inorazu totemo*
>   *Kami ya mamoran.*

"If only our hearts follow the path of rectitude, the Gods will protect us without our prayers.

An Emperor saw one day in a private garden a plum-tree with a bush-warbler's nest in it. He took fancy to it and ordered it to be transplanted to his palace-ground. The owner, who was a poetess and court lady, obeyed as a matter of course, but to show her reluctance, she hung to a branch of the tree a piece of paper with the following ode :—

Choku nareba	*Itomo kashikoshi*
Uguisu no	*Yado wa to towaba*
	Ika ni kotaen.

"Since His Majesty commands, I obey with joy; but when the bush-warbler comes and asks for his home, what answer shall I give?" The Emperor, upon reading this ode, felt sorry that he had deprived her of her favourite tree.

There are also other combinations ; but all Japanese verses are composed of pentasyllabic and heptasyllabic lines. What is known as the long ode is a series of the two in alternation, closing with an extra heptasyllable. Another verse is formed of a pair of sets, each containing a pentasyllable and two heptasyllables ; and still another comprises four couplets of a heptasyllable and a pentasyllable each. From these combinations has been evolved what is called poetry of the new school, which is an indefinite series of five and seven syllables in alternation. It is now very common ; and almost all songs written to the accompaniment of European music are in this form. In the following children's song which has for the last half-dozen years been popular in Tokyo, the English reader will recognise a very old friend :—

Moshi moshi kame yo	*kamesan yo*
Sekai no uchi ni	*omae hodo*
Ayumi no noroi	*mono wa nai*
Dōshite sonna ni	*noroi no ka*
Nanto ossharu	*usagisan*
Sonnara omae to	*kakekurabè*
Mukō no oyama no	*fumoto made*
Dochira ga saki ni	*kaketsuku ka*
Donna ni kame ga	*isoi demo*
Dōse ban made	*kakaru daro*

Kokora de chotto   *hito nemuri*
Gū gū gū gū   *gū gū gū*
Kore wa nesugita   *shikujitta*
Pyon pyon pyon pyon   *pyon pyon pyon*
Anmari osoi   *usagisan*
Sakki no jiman wa   *dōshitano ;*

which may be rendered :

    " Please, please, Tortoise, Mr. Tortoise,
    There is in all the world no one
    So slow-footed as you ;
    Why are you so slow ?"
    " What do you say, Mr. Hare ?
    Then, I will race with you and see
    Which will be the first to reach
    The foot of yonder hill."
    " However the Tortoise may hurry,
    He will take at any rate till night;
    And here I will take a nap."
    Snore, snore, snore, snore, snore, snore, snore.
    " I have slept too long ;   I have blundered."
    Leap, leap, leap, leap, leap, leap, leap.
    " You are too late, Mr. Hare ;
    Where is your boast of a while ago ?"

Finally, there is a verse of two pentasyllables with a heptasyllable between, which is more popular among men than any other form. The *haiku*, as it is called, can hardly be given the name of poetry. It is simply a suggestion of ideas which it is left to the hearer to clothe with poetical sentiment ; but the suggestion itself is far from explicit and needs a person used to this form of verse to interpret it in the sense intended. It is, in short, little more than a *tour de force* in the art of compression. For instance,

    Furuike ya   An old pond
      Kawazu tobikomu   A frog jumping in
    Mizu no oto.   The sound of water.

It pictures the loneliness of an old pond, around which all is so still that the jumping of a frog into the water may be heard.

The composition of Chinese poems by Japanese is one of the most artificial processes of poetising. Chinese characters are divided according to their intonation into those of even and oblique sounds, that is, characters which are pronounced straight and evenly and those in the pronunciation of which the voice changes in tone. A Chinese poem is composed in various combinations of these two kinds of characters, and certain lines in a verse have to to rhyme. Now, the Japanese pronunciation of Chinese characters makes no distinction in their intonation; they are all pronounced in the same tone, Hence, whereas a Chinese can tell at once by its pronunciation whether a character has an even or an oblique sound, a Japanese must learn by heart the tone-quality of every character if he wishes to compose Chinese poems; the knowledge of this tone-quality is of no use to a Japanese for 'other purposes. Moreover, the Japanese pronunciation of Chinese characters differs entirely from the Chinese; it is believed to be a corruption of the Chinese pronunciation in ancient times. The normal grammatical order in a Chinese sentence is that the verb precedes the object, whereas in Japanese the object usually precedes the verb; the result is that in reading a Chinese poem in Japanese the rhyming words do not always end the lines. As the Japanese simply composes according to rule, his lines are sometimes unrecitable in Chinese. Now, to show the difference between the Chinese and Japanese manner of reading a Chinese poem, we will first give a poem in the original Chinese.

(8)	(7)	(6)	(5)	(4)	(3)	(2)	(1)
檻	閣	物	間	朱	畫	佩	滕
外	中	換	雲	簾	棟	玉	王
長	帝	星	潭	暮	朝	鳴	高
江	子	移	影	捲	飛	鑾	閣
空	今	幾	日	西	南	罷	臨
自	何	度	悠	山	浦	歌	江
流	在	秋	々	雨	雲	舞	渚

The Chinese would read the poem in this style :—

(1) *T'eng wang kao kê lin kiang chu*
(2) *P'ei yü ming luan pa kê wu*
(3) *Hua tung ch'ao fei nan p'u yün*
(4) *Chu lien mu kuan hsi shan yü*
(5) *Hsien yün t'an ying jih yu yu*
(6) *Wu huan hsing i chi tu ch'iu*
(7) *Kê chung ti tzu kin hê tsai*
(8) *Kien wai ch'ang kiang k'ung tzu liu.*

The Japanese would read it in an entirely different manner :—

(1) *Tō-ō no kōkaku kōsho ni nozomeri*
(2) *Haigyoku meiran kabu wo yamu*
(3) *Gwatō ashita ni tobu nanpo no kumo*
(4) *Shuren kure ni maku seizan no ame*
(5) *Kan-un tan-ei hi ni yū-yū*
(6) *Mono kawari hoshi utsuru ikutabi no aki*
(7) *Kakuchū no teishi ima izuku ni zo aru*
(8) *Kangwai no chōkō munashiku onozukara nagaru.*

We will next give a word-for-word translation of the Chinese :—

(1) T'eng prince high tower overlook river shore
(2) Gird jewel sound bell stop song dance
(3) Picture roof-tree morning fly south coast cloud
(4) Crimson blind evening roll west hill rain
(5) Quiet cloud deep-water shadow day far far
(6) Thing change star move how-many time autumn
(7) Tower interior emperor son now where is
(8) Balustrade outside long river vain of-itself flow.

The following translation into intelligible English will help to show the elliptical character of Chinese poetry :—

(1) The high palace of Prince T'eng looks down upon river and shore ;
(2) No more, in cars with jewels decked and tinkling bells, the courtiers come for song and dance.
(3) Around the painted roofs fly at morn the clouds from the southern coast ;

(4) The crimson blinds, rolled up at eve, reveal the rain on the western hill;

(5) And far away appear the quiet clouds and darkling pools.

(6) Things change, time passes, and how many years are gone?

(7) And the prince of this palace, where is he now?

(8) The long river beyond the balustrade flows on alone and unchanged.

Chinese poetry has, it will be seen, the conciseness of a skeleton telegram; but in elasticity and pregnancy of meaning, in disregard of time and, indeed, in contempt of grammar, no telegram, skeleton or other, can come up to it.

The tea-ceremony is, perhaps, the strictest and most complicated of all the ceremonies with which the cultured Japanese used to surround himself. The ceremony, when carried out in fun, is very intricate; but it may be briefly described as follows:— First, the guests who arrive on the appointed day are shown into the waiting-room and when they are all assembled, they are conducted into the tea-room. This room should properly be a building by itself, and the commonest size is nine feet square, that is, one of four mats and a half, the half-mat being in the centre. The maximum number of guests is five, four of whom sit in a row and the fifth at right angles to the rest. The host faces the row; he brings in the tea-utensils and sets them in order. The guests are first regaled with a slight repast; and when it is over, they are requested to retire into the waiting-room, while the host puts away the trays and plates and sweeps the room. They are then called in again. A small quantity of powdered tea is put into the tea-bowl which is used on these occasions, and hot water is poured into it and stirred with a bamboo-whisk until it is quite frothy. The bowl is handed to the guest at the head of the row; he takes three sips and a half, the fourth sip being called half a sip as it is much slighter than the first three, and after wiping the brim carefully, he passes it on to his neighbour, who also sips and hands the bowl to the third guest, and so on to the fifth guest, who returns it empty to

TEA-MAKING.

the host. After this loving-cup, the host stirs a bowl for each of his guests, that is, he makes tea in the bowl for the first guest, who drains it in three sips and a half and returns it to the host, who then washes it and makes a fresh bowl of tea for the second guest, and so on until the last guest is served. As this process takes a long time on account of the formalities which have to be observed in making, serving, and drinking the beverage, sometimes two bowls are used so that while one guest is drinking and admiring a bowl, the host can be making the other for the next. The tea in the loving-cup is stronger than that in the others.

The bare procedure is simple ; but the complexity lies in the hard and fast rules to be observed in the arrangement of the room, and respecting the utensils to be used, the manner in which they should be handled in making tea, the way in which the tea should be drunk, the number and style of bows and salutations to be made in offering, receiving, and returning the bowls, and also in the instructions as to when and how the bowls and other articles in the room are to be taken up and admired, and the manner of expressing such admiration and of replying thereto. The formalities are as strict as court ceremony and are often irksome to the beginner who is nervous and afraid of exposing himself at every step.

The description above given refers to the formal process as practised by one of the schools of the ceremony, which can be followed only in a family which can afford to build a separate tea-room for the purpose. But the ceremony need not always be so exacting. The general principles, such as the making, offering, and drinking of powdered tea and the courtesies accompanying it, are now taught in most girls' schools, because the knowledge of the ceremony certainly adds to their grace and imparts to them that quiet, stately bearing which characterises the Japanese lady of culture. Indeed, this calm, sedate gracefulness is the result of the study of the tea-ceremony and is assuredly a more valuable acquisition than the knowledge of the formalities themselves.

Flower arrangement is an art which plays an important part in the decoration of a room ; for the *kakemono* which hangs in the alcove of the parlour loses half its attraction unless there is before it on the dais a vase of flowers to match. The alcove is the part of the room which draws first notice upon entrance, and the flowers share with the *kakemono* the earliest attention of the newcomer.

The idea underlying the art is that flowers should not be thrown anyhow in a bundle into a vase, but that due consideration should be given to their artistic arrangement. The flowers should even in a vase be arranged as they might appear in nature. It is not always, it is true, as they actually appear in the open air ; but they are arranged as they might look if aided by art under certain conditions, for the flowers in the vase always have a degree of symmetry which is but rarely found in nature. Their form is often artificial, but not opposed to nature, just as dwarfed trees are stunted by art but have perfectly natural shapes. The rules regarding the position of the branches in a vase are certainly conventional, insisting as they do upon balance and symmetry of form, but they do not go beyond the bounds of possibility. The only objection, in fact, that might be brought against them is that there is always present the danger of taking for normal forms what are seen in nature perhaps but once in a million.   But of the gracefulness of the arrangement there can be no two opinions.

Although we speak of flower arrangement, the art is not confined to flowers, but extends also to the treatment of trees and shrubs without flowers.   Among the trees, the branches of which are, when in flower, put into vases, are the plum, camellia, cherry,

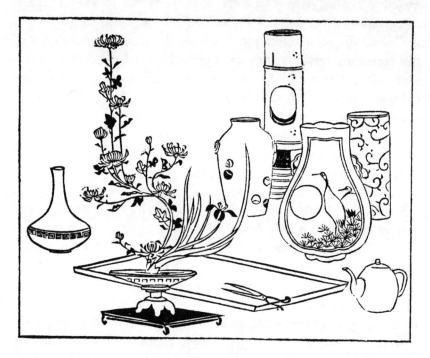

FLOWER-VASES.

peach, rose, azalea, Japan quince, and wistaria, while the herbaceous flowers are innumerable and include such different plants as the pot marigold, corchorus, peony, bleeding-heart, iris, anemone, primrose, red-bud, sweet flag, hydrangea, clematis, safflower, corn-poppy, common mallow, day lily, cockscomb, globe amaranth, chrysanthemum, narcissus, lady's slipper, and Cape jasmine.   Branches of trees noted for their foliage are also put into vases, such as the magnolia, yulan, pine, and similar evergreens; and others bearing fruit are in no less favour, like the loquat, plum, nandina, and pomegranate. In short, the art is practised with most trees and shrubs, cultivated or wild.

The principle of the arrangement in its simplest form, which deals with three stalks or branches, is that the middle stalk or branch, which is the longest, shall rise perpendicularly, or nearly so, and of the remaining two one shall branch off horizontally to one side and the other slant upward on the other side of the central stalk or branch. More stalks or branches may be taken, but their positions are only amplifications of the two lateral ones. The central piece being always single and amplifications being of equal number on both sides, there is invariably an odd number of stalks or branches. The manner of amplification or the position of the secondary stalks varies with the different schools of flower arrangement. The only condition they all insist upon is that the stalks or branches shall be in a way balanced on either side, but shall not show perfect symmetry which is never to be found in nature.

As stalks which completely satisfy the conditions required for their artistic arrangement cannot be readily procured, it becomes necessary to bend and twist them into the requisite shape. They must be so bent and twisted as not to snap, crush the fibres, or display splits, but to conceal the artificial alteration of their structure. While the arrangement of the stalks and flowers calls for taste and judgment, their manipulation demands no less dexterity in carrying out the design formed ; and it needs considerable practice to be able to bend the soft stalk of the orchid and the tough branch of the plum with equal ease and neatness.

Next in importance to the arrangement of the flowers is the manner of making them draw water. To this end various devices are used, of which the commonest is to burn the bottom-end of the stalk ; this end, on being then dipped into the vase, sucks up water which is thereupon circulated into the rest of the stalk. The hardwood of a tree branch is often crushed at the end to facilitate its permeation by water. Some plants are put into hot water ; others are covered with mud or nicotine at the end ; and others again are dipped in a strong infusion of tea and Japan pepper. Salt is sprinkled over bamboo to keep off insects, and with the same object tobacco powder is thrown on some plants.

The shape of the vase is also of importance and has to be taken into consideration with the *kakemono* exhibited. They are of various shapes. The commonest are of china, tall, round, and slightly bulging in the middle. Sometimes they are more slender, and sometimes no more than deep dishes, square or round. If they are to be hung up by a chain, as in a tea-room, they are shaped like a boat or a water-bucket; or if they are to be hooked on a peg, they are made of china or bamboo. The pedestal for the vase is also of diverse shapes. It may be a flat piece of wood or china, or have legs, one at each of the four corners or one at either side flattened out.

Another art is the making of what are called " tray-landscapes." For this an elliptical tray, whose diameters are about a foot and a

A TRAY-LANDSCAPE.

foot and a half, is taken, and on it landscapes and sea-views are drawn with pebbles for rocks and sand of various fineness for the ground. Such a landscape forms an ornament for the parlour.

The only Japanese musical instrument taught in girls' schools is the *koto*, a kind of zither. As the *koto* is the most adaptable of all Japanese instruments to western music, it is more readily learnt than others at schools where the piano and the violin are also taught. There are several kinds of *koto*, the number of strings on them ranging from one to twenty-five; but the one exclusively used at schools has thirteen strings. It has a hollow convex body,

THE KOTO.

six feet five inches long and ten inches wide at one end and half an inch narrower at the other, and stands on legs three and a half inches high. The strings are tied at equal distances at the head or broader end and gathered at the other; they are supported each by its own bridge, the position of which varies with the pitch required. Small ivory nails are put on the tips of the fingers for striking the strings.

But extensively as the *koto* is practised by school-girls and ladies of position, the national musical instrument is the *samisen*, a Japanese variant of the old European rebec which was introduced into the country by the Portuguese in the sixteenth century. In the old days it was considered vulgar to play the *samisen*, which consequently lay long in obloquy and was only to be found among the merchant and lower classes. But now, though the prejudice against it is still strong among old-fashioned people, it is in greater favour than the *koto*. It is played everywhere, at home, in story-tellers' halls and theatres, and at every tea-house party.

In its common form the *samisen* has a belly, four inches thick and covered with skin, which has convex sides, seven and nearly eight inches respectively, and has attached to it a neck twenty-five inches long with a tail-piece of six inches. There are three pegs in the tail-piece for the three strings of the instrument, which are carried over the neck and tied at the further end of the belly where a small movable bridge keeps them from touching the face of the belly. The belly rests side-wise on the right knee of the player, whose right hand strikes the strings with an ivory plectrum, while the fingers of the left hand support the neck and stop the strings. The top-string is the thickest and has the lowest notes, while the third string is the finest and has the highest notes. The *samisen* just described is known as the slender-necked *samisen* ; the other kind, which is of larger dimensions, with thicker strings and is played with a heavier plectrum, is only used in singing *gidayu,* or ballad-dramas.

On the scale of the *samisen* there is still a great diversity of opinion, musical authorities being unable to agree as to the exact nature of the notes it emits. Its scale is certainly different to that of any European instrument ; but, roughly-speaking, its range is about three octaves, the notes of which are put at thirty-six, comprising what would in European music be sharps and flats. The ranges of the two kinds of *samisen* naturally differ, the smaller giving higher notes than the other.

The *samisen* is early taught. Girls of seven or thereabouts are made to learn it while their fingers are still very pliant. But the lessons are hard to learn as the tunes have to be committed to memory, for there are no scores to refer to. There is no popular method of notation ; the marks which are sometimes to be seen in song-books are too few to be of use to any but skilled musicians. The lighter *samisen* does not require much exertion to play ; women can thrum it for hours on end ; and they make slight indentations on the nails of the middle and ring fingers of the left hand for catching the strings when those fingers are moved up and down the neck to stop them. But with the heavier kind the indentations are deeper, and the constant friction of the strings hardens the finger-tips and often breaks the nails, while still worse is the condition of the right hand which holds the plectrum. The plectrum, the striking end of which is flat as in the one for the slender-necked *samisen*, is heavily leaded and weighs from twelve ounces to a pound when used by professionals ; and the handle, which is square, is held between the ring and little fingers for

THE SAMISEN.

leverage and worked with the thumb and the forefinger. At first the pressure of the corners upon the second joint of the little finger is very painful ; but the skin becomes in time indurated and insensible to pain. It requires both strength and dexterity to strike the thick, hard-drawn strings with such a heavy plectrum.

The peculiar scale on which it is based has prevented Japanese music from being appreciated by foreigners. That it is crude is undeniable ; indeed, no other Japanese art has been left so undeveloped. In most other arts we have stamped our national individuality upon what we borrowed from others ; but in music we can hardly say that there is anything characteristically Japanese about the slow tunes of the thirteen-stringed *koto* or the quicker jangle of the three-stringed *samisen*. They have of course changed in our hands from their original forms ; but the alteration is not something that we can attribute to our national genius as we should in the case of our pictorial, glyptic, or ceramic art. Moreover, music has never, like the other arts, had munificent patrons. We read often enough of a great daimyo or lord in the old days surrounding himself with famed painters, sculptors, makers of lacquered ware or swords, but never of one taking under his protection a musician of note. What musicians enjoyed his favour were those employed for the performance of music at sacred rites ; and none won the daimyo's patronage by the charm or power of his music. No encouragement was then held out to music ; and even the musicians whose names are known to posterity earned their living, precarious at best, by catering to the general public.

Samisen-music cannot in truth be said to appeal emotionally even to those Japanese who enjoy it. They admire a *samisen*-player for his execution, for the lightness and rapidity of his touch and the rich resonance of the strings under it ; but of the expression, the emotional quality of music, neither he nor his audience know anything and probably care as little. And it must be admitted that the *samisen* can never charm and enthrall us like the deep-sounding cathedral organ ; and its want of volume deprives it of any power to make a cumulative impression upon us. In short, our *samisen*-music is mainly a matter of dexterity, with a modicum of taste and judgment. We do not look to it to sway our passions, —to move us to tears or laughter, to stir up in us anger, awe, pity, or wonder, or to fire us into bursts of patriotic enthusiasm.

CHAPTER XX.

PUBLIC AMUSEMENTS.

Pleasures—*Nō*-performance—Playgoing—The theatre—Japanese dramas—*Gidayu*-plays—Actors—A new school of actors—Actresses—Wrestling—Wrestlers—The wrestling-booth—The wrestler's apparel—The Ekoin matches—The umpire—The rules of the ring—The match-days—The story-tellers' hall—Entertainment at the hall.

WE Japanese do not take our pleasures sadly ; for when upon pleasure bent, we give ourselves to it heart and soul and forget for the nonce the cares and troubles that may at other times weigh upon our minds. And foreign observers, from seeing us in our hours of relaxation, taunted us, at least until our war with Russia showed us in another light, with frivolity and pronounced us a nation incapable of taking things seriously. Nothing could have been further from the truth than to suppose that we lead a butterfly existence, for we are as a nation serious, indeed, if anything, too serious. The *abandon* with which we throw ourselves into the gaieties of the moment is attributable rather to the rarity of our opportunities. Our women, in particular, have very little leisure, and if they wander with childish delight in avenues of cherry-blossoms or sit with quiet content on the verandah under the harvest-moon, it is because they are glad to snatch a few hours of innocent enjoyment from their round of almost ceaseless household work. The simplicity of our pleasures is but the natural outcome of the simplicity of our lives ; and if we have not the comforts and conveniences of European homes, neither do we suffer from the feverish stress and strain of European social life.

Of the various forms of public entertainment in Japan, the oldest and peculiarly Japanese is the *nō*-dance. It is a posture-dance performed to the accompaniment of flutes and drums, while a ballad is sung at the same time to explain the movements. It

A *NO*-DANCE.

was developed from the ancient religious dances and first came into vogue in the sixteenth century. The ballad, which is known as *utai*, is written in a mixture of the Chinese and old-Japanese styles and cannot be readily comprehended by those who are not versed in these styles. The dance is slow and stately, though sometimes there are quick movements in it ; it is performed by men with masks and in robes which were worn in ancient times ; the actors on the stage at a time are few ; and the stage itself has, except in rare cases, little setting. It is not, therefore, everybody that can appreciate a *no*-performance ; indeed, the fact that it is caviare to the general and its superiority in point of refinement to the common dances of the people have won for it great popularity among the upper and middle classes ; and the performances are largely attended. Many people also practise singing the *utai ;* it has the advantage over other ballads, when it is unaccompanied by a dance, of being sung without any musical instrument. The *utai* ballads are comparatively short, and in a single performance several of them are sung and danced.

The same *no*-dance is seldom repeated in a run. The programme is changed every day, because popular as the *no* is in a sense, its patrons are yet too few to justify a run of the same dance. For a larger public we must turn to the drama. The play is in Japan as in other countries the most popular public amusement ; but in few other lands is playgoing such an elaborate diversion as it is with us. In the old days the theatre opened early in the morning and did not close until nearly midnight ; but some twenty years ago the police authorities limited the length of a performance to eight hours, and now it lasts from six to nine hours. In some theatres the doors open at four in the afternoon and close at ten or eleven ; this allows a professional man to hurry to the theatre as soon as his office-hours are over and witness a performance in half an hour or so from its commencement ; but other houses open at twelve or one and close at nine or ten. Playgoing was in the old times a whole day's work, and women would prepare for it days beforehand and often lie awake the preceding night so as not to be late for the opening hour. They took their meals at the tea-houses,

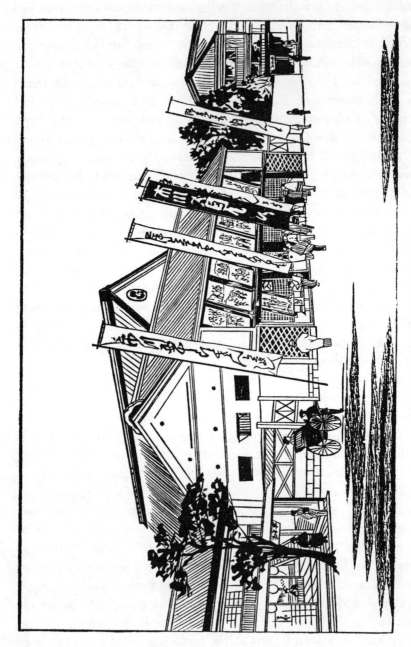

THE ENTRANCE OF A THEATRE.

which are even now attached to the theatres, especially the larger ones. Through these tea-houses people book their seats in the theatre; and they go there first to divest themselves of unnecessary paraphernalia before entering the play-house and are thence provided with meals and refreshments which they take while looking at the performance. It is therefore to the interest of these tea-houses that the performance should be going on at meal-time. Those who cannot afford to visit a tea-house go direct to the theatre and are similarly looked after, except in the case of those in the cheapest seats, by attendants detailed for the purpose. In fact, eating and drinking is inseparable from playgoing in Japan. People eat and drink while looking at a performance; some even cannot enjoy it unless they are regaled at the same time with *sake*. Playgoing is, in short, an expensive pastime in Japan.

The theatre is a large oblong building. Over the great entrance hangs a row of wooden-framed pictures representing the scenes played; the side-entrances lead to the gallery. In front of the stage as one enters the theatre is the pit, which is partitioned into small compartments capable of holding four or five persons

THE STAGE AND ENTRANCE-PASSAGE,

squatting. On either side are two stories of boxes and facing the stage across the pit is the gallery on the second or third story, which is mostly patronised by playgoers who, being unable to pay for the whole performance, come to see one or two of the best acts. From the sides of the stage two entrance-passages run through the pit towards the entrance. Actors walk under the passages to the entrance end and coming out into a box, make their appearance on the entrance-passage. These passages are very convenient as they give a larger room to the stage and impart a sense of distance when it is not expedient to crowd too suddenly on the stage. The stage is screened off from the auditorium by a drawn curtain in the larger theatres and by a drop-curtain in some of the smaller. When a popular actor is playing or some special piece is performing, curtains are presented by the patrons of the actor or the theatre ; and in such a case several curtains are drawn one after another between the acts across the stage for the admiration of the audience. Another peculiarity of the Japanese stage is the revolving-stage. A scene is set upon the front half of a turn-table which is flush with the rest of the stage floor ; and while that scene is being acted, the carpenters are putting up the next in the rear half; and when the first scene is over, the table revolves and brings the second to view, and so the play is continued without interruption. Yet another peculiarity is the presence on the stage of black-veiled men in clothes of the same colour. They are known as " blackamoors " and supposed to be invisible. At the commencement of a run, they stand or sit behind the actors and prompt them ; they remove from the stage any article that has ceased to be of use or pull away the dead in a fight if they are found to be in the way, or push a cushion to an actor when he is about to sit down. They are of great use, though it is hard to acquiesce in the fiction of their invisibility. The stage music is played usually on one side of the stage ; but when a *gidayu* is required, its performers are seated on a high perch to the left of the stage.

Only in rare cases is the day's performance taken up by a single play. The usual course is to have two plays, the first being of an historical character or concerned with disturbances in a dai-

THE REVOLVING-STAGE.

myo's family, and the second being a domestic play. For the Japanese drama is divided into three classes, the first being the historical drama, which deals with the times of war, most frequently in the twelfth, fourteenth, and sixteenth centuries, that is, the periods of the feuds which led to the establishment of the Shogunate, of the insurrections which resulted in the temporary rule of the country by two lines of Emperors, and of the ascendancy of the Taiko and Tokugawa Iyeyasu; the second treats of what are known as disturbances in noble families, the most common cause of which was the struggle for succession between the rightful heir and an illegitimate child of a daimyo; and lastly, the domestic drama depicts scenes in the lives of the common people, the favourite heroes and heroines of which were in the old days chivalrous gamblers, magnanimous robbers, and self-sacrificing courtesans. Of late, however, the domestic drama has greatly extended its scope, for now it presents pictures of modern life in reputable society. Then, two plays are acted in a performance, and there is not unfrequently a middle piece or an after-piece, or both, and such a piece presents a bright and gay scene with dancing in it. Thus, a performance is made to suit all tastes. This rule of two plays is not always adhered to; it is frequently disregarded by the new school of actors, who give only one play with an after-piece. We give a gay after-piece to relieve the strain of witnessing a serious and often tragic play, a curious contrast to the European *lever de rideau* which allows the playgoer to dine without hurry.

Plays are again divided into two classes according to their form. One is the ordinary prose drama; and the other is the *gidayu*, a kind of musical or ballad drama. The latter was brought into vogue two centuries ago by Gidayu, a singer, who gave his name to this form of drama. It was originally sung at puppet-shows; but as the librettos were written by Chikamatsu Monzaemon, the greatest of Japanese dramatists, they are highly valued as literature. The standard set by Chikamatsu was kept up by his immediate successors; but no *gidayu* of note has appeared since the third quarter of the eighteenth century. In Osaka, where Gidayu lived and sang, puppet-shows still draw large houses ; and no *gidayu*-singer of the present day is considered a regular professional unless he has gone through the mill at the Bunrakuza, the great puppet-theatre of Osaka. In Tokyo *gidayu* puppet-shows do not enjoy much favour ; *gidayu* are in the capital sung at the story-tellers' hall or performed on the stage. The *gidayu* contains the ordinary prose dialogue ; the singing part describes the feelings and movements of the puppets. But these explanations which do very well in a puppet-show, are too lengthy on the stage ; while the singing is going on, the acting is apt to become wooden, and the interest in the play is saved from flagging only by the beauty of the language and the skill of the singer.

There has of late been a great change in the histrionic art in Japan. Until about twenty years ago, the theatrical profession was mostly hereditary, and such as did not come of a theatrical family en'ered the stage as pupils of some well-known actor. None could practically become an actor without the countenance of the whole profession ; and if a pupil showed extraordinary talent, he was not unfrequently made his master's successor. For great histrionic names are handed down from generation to generation ; thus, the late Ichikawa Danjuro, the greatest actor of Japan since the Restoration, was the ninth of his name, and his rival, Onoye Kikugoro, was the fifth. The third great actor at the time was Sadanji, a pupil of the fourth Kodanji; the present head of the Actors' Guild is Shikan the Sixth ; and the most promising actor of the day is Uzaemon the Thirteenth. Not one of these names has been invariably handed down from father to son ; but'it is vested in the family, whose consent is necessary for its assumption by a pupil.

Some twenty years ago, a new school of actors sprang into being ; they were called student-actors as they came mostly from the student class. They formed companies and gave performances by themselves. At first they were looked upon with disdain by the professionals ; but they soon became popular and, not being fettered like the latter by the traditions of their profession, they were more natural in their acting and had freer scope. It was during the war with China and immediately after that their strong points came into prominence ; for when they acted scenes from that war, their representations were absolutely free from the conventionalities of the old school, and it was acknowledged that in the modern realistic drama the new school was decidedly superior to the old. In course of time the former began to learn the tricks of the trade as practised by the other, while the younger actors of the old school threw off the trammels of tradition in plays of contemporary life, so that there is now far less difference between the two schools. And in some theatres actors of both schools play together.

In most theatres actors take female parts as well as male. Many actors have made their mark in female rôles, and such characters are often specialised, some actors excelling in depiction of ladies of rank and others in representing women of the people and of the *demi-monde*. There are also actresses in Tokyo, but they seldom perform with actors ; for the instances which have hitherto occurred of such performances were not very successful. One theatre in Tokyo is occupied entirely by women, who play male parts as well as those of their own sex. The best actress of the day is Kumehachi, who has few peers in her line even among actors ; but it cannot be said that actresses as a whole enjoy high favour in Japan.

Another public amusement which vies with the stage in popularity is wrestling. Though there are often wrestling bouts in different parts of the city, the great matches to which all lovers of the art look forward every year are those which take place in January and May in the temple-grounds of Ekoin on the south side of the River Sumida ; for as they decide the combatants' position in the profession, they are fought in grim earnest.

There are some five hundred wrestlers in the Tokyo Wrestlers' Guild, which comprises all the professionals of the city. In the wrestlers' list they are divided into two sets, east and west. In each set there are some score of wrestlers of the first grade, and there are corresponding grades in both sets down to the lowest. When wrestlers of the first grade retire through age or disease from the active list, so to speak, they become, unless they leave the guild altogether and take up other callings, elders of the guild,

A WRESTLING-MATCH.

The elders are partners in the getting up of the Ekoin matches ; they also take in pupils, for no one can become a professional wrestler except under the ægis of an elder. For the young wrestler this is convenient, because he is always under the protection of his elder and naturally profits if, when he goes touring in the provinces, he is in the company of a wrestler of a higher grade from the same elder. When a wrestler is without a peer, he becomes what may be called the invincible champion. There have been less than a score of such champions since the first of them took that title two and a half centuries ago ; but at present there are two invincible champions at the same time.

Wrestling takes place in an arena of sand bounded by a ring, some twenty feet in diameter, formed of empty rice-bags and covered by a four-pillared wooden roof. It is surrounded by tiers of seats for the spectators. At the foot of each of these pillars sits an elder watching the match and acting as referee in case of dispute. At two opposite pillars are a bucket of water, a basket of salt, and a bundle of paper-slips, the salt to purify the body for the contest which may end fatally and the slips for wiping the hands.

The wrestler appears in the arena without clothing. He has over his loin-cloth a wide, wadded cotton-belt adorned with twine tassels when he wrestles ; but if he is a first-grade wrestler, he makes a formal appearance in the arena with others of the same grade before they commence their bouts, when he wears in addition an apron of heavy material richly enbroidered with his professional name or some other distinguishing mark stitched in gold.

The Ekoin matches last for ten days, or rather for ten fine days. Until lately, the booth was merely covered with matting or canvas, and as the rain leaked in, the matches could not be held on wet days. As, moreover, men are sent round the city with drums to announce the matches, the day preceding the match-day had also to be fine or at least to give reasonable hopes of fine weather on the following day, so that one fair day during a spell of rain was of no use. A run of matches might therefore last for twenty days or more. And all the time the elders had to feed the wrestlers to

THE CHAMPION'S APPEARANCE IN THE RING.

keep them together, and so, long-continued rainy weather might swallow up the profits of the run, especially as the Japanese wrestlers with their huge paunches are hearty eaters. A permanent building for wrestling matches has, however, been erected at Ekoin; it was opened in June, 1909. It is the largest building of the kind in Japan and holds more than ten thousand spectators. The great hall will, in spite of the heavy initial cost, pay in the long run as there will be no need to put up a booth each time and matches can be held irrespectively of the weather.

The matches commence with those of the lowest grade, and the best bouts take place late in the afternoon. Before each bout a summoner appears in the arena and calls out the names of the two combatants, who, as they are already waiting outside the ring, immediately make their appearance, and the umpire formally announces their names. They drink a cup of water and purify themselves with a pinch of salt. They crouch opposite each other and, at a word from the umpire, grapple with each other. It often happens that one of them is not ready for the grip, and they separate; once more they rise and drink water and return to their former positions. Some wrestlers repeat this until the spectators are tired out. But when they do tussle, the struggle does not take long; and if they remain long in each other's grip without coming to a conclusion, the umpire separates them and lets them refresh themselves with water before they resume the bout. The umpire then puts them exactly in the same position as they were before. It is remarkable with what accuracy he makes them resume their former position; he can tell at a glance their exact posture at each moment of the bout; and he does not make the least error in the bend of their bodies or the touch of their hands. Such an eye naturally requires long training; and the umpire has, like the wrestler, to rise from the lowest rung of his profession. At first he presides over the bouts of the wrestlers of the lowest grade; and as he acquires skill and experience, he rises to a higher grade until finally he umpires the matches of the foremost wrestlers. His decision is seldom disputed; and in the rare cases when it is called in question, he appeals to the elders sitting at the four pillars.

The rules of the ring are very strict. If a wrestler falls, touches the ground with a knee, a hand, or any part of the body other than the soles of his feet, or steps on the rice-bags of the ring, he is declared defeated. The ways in which he can cope

THE ENTRANCE OF A STORY-TELLERS' HALL.

with his adversary were originally put at forty-eight; but they were subsequently increased to twice, and later still to four times, that number. These original forty-eight throws were divided into four classes of twelve each, namely, the butting with the head, grappling with the hands, twisting with the hips, and tripping with the feet. From these were developed all the later methods.

During the first days of the matches the wrestlers of the first grade are paired with those whose positions on the other side do not correspond to their own; and then the matches become gradually more equal until on the ninth day those of the same position on both sides are pitted against each other. It is the most exciting day of the whole series; but on the tenth and last day those of the highest grade seldom appear and the interest in the matches flags as a matter of course.

These great matches, occurring as they do only twice a year, throw the whole city into a fever of excitement, and while they are on, one hears of nothing else. In the booth the enthusiasm is very great, and it rises to such a pitch when a clever throw takes place or a favourite distinguishes himself, that the spectators throw into the arena their overcoats, tobacco-pouches, or whatever else come handy as marks of their approval to the victor. They afterwards send presents in money and recover their property.

Thus, playgoing is expensive and takes up the best part of a day, while the wrestling-matches which arouse universal interest occur but twice a year, other matches being mostly of local interest only. Neither of these amusements can serve to while away a few hours of idleness or relaxation ; to those who wish to spend an evening pleasantly and at little expense, the story-tellers' hall is always open. It stands conspicuously in a street ; for over a wide entrance, the walls of which are studded with numerous pegs for suspending the clogs and sandals of its patrons, hangs a large square lantern announcing on its face the names of the principal performers, while the name of the hall is inscribed at a side-end. The hall itself is a great matted room with a platform at the furthest end. The spectators squat promiscuously on the mats and watch the performances or listen to the tales of the story-teller on the platform which is about four feet high and can be seen from all parts of the room. The hall opens at six or half-past ; but it only begins to fill an hour later and closes at about ten o'clock.

Entertainments of various kinds are given at the story-tellers' halls. In some the story-tellers proper appear ; half a dozen or more come upon the platform in succession, winding up with the chief story-teller of the evening. Those of the better grade tell serious stories, complete at a sitting or continued through the whole run of the company which is fifteen evenings, for they change twice a month. Most of the others, however, tell short stories, humorous and ending often in a word-play ; their object is merely to raise a laugh among their audience. There are also story-tellers of a different kind, whose speciality is tales of war and stories of men famed in Japanese history ; but as they talk seriously and not in the light

A STORY-TELLER ON THE PLATFORM.

vein of their more humorous *confrères*, they are not so popular as the latter. It is not, however, always the story-tellers who occupy the platform. In the course of the evening there may be music and singing by professionals or conjuring tricks. There are also several halls opened exclusively for the singing of *gidayu*; and though for their proper singing a deep, strong voice is really requisite, female singers are far more numerous than male in Tokyo. In the capital it is not as in Osaka, the home of *gidayu*-singing, for a young and pretty girl-singer finds greater favour than a male singer of skill and experience. In one evening half a dozen such singers perform, the last being the head of the troupe.

In these halls some of the stories told are far from edifying; but from others the lower classes become acquainted with the lives of the noted men of their country. The proletariat in Japan are probably more intimate with the history of their country than those of other lands. Such history may not always be authentic; but of the famous names in that history, warriors, statesmen, priests, and scholars, they hear from the more serious entertainers at the halls; and the *gidayu* has also an educative influence, for it inculcates unceasingly the duty of loyalty and filial piety and never tires of dwelling upon the nobleness of self-sacrifice.

CHAPTER XXI.

FEASTS AND FESTIVITIES.

Festivities in the old days—The New Year's Day—The New Year's dreams—
January—February—The Feast of Dolls—The Equinoctial day—Plum-blossoms—Cherry-
blossoms—The flower season—Peach-blossoms—Tree-peonies and wistarias—The Feast
of Flags—The Fête of the Yasukuni Shrine—Other fêtes—The Feasts of Tanabata and
Lanterns—The river season—Moon-viewing—The Seven Herbs of Autumn—October—
The Emperor's Birthday—Chrysanthemums and maple-leaves—The end of the year.

THERE are feasts and festivities galore in Tokyo. In the old
times the feast-days marked in the calendar were far more
numerous than they are now. In those days, while the
daimyo and his retainers travelled pretty often between Yedo and
their native province, the citizens seldom left town ; it was a red-
letter day with them when they set out on a pilgrimage to the great
shrine of Ise or on a trip to Kyoto ; and even these persons formed
a very small minority. The high roads were infested by robbers ;
and it was only with their lives in their hands that humble citizens
could go on a long journey. Being, then, confined in the town, its
inhabitants naturally took what pleasures they could in it and availed
themselves of every festivity to give themselves up to enjoyment.
The festivals of the tutelary deities were, for instance, celebrated
with great pomp ; on annual feast-days the time-honoured customs
were religiously observed ; and the flowers of the season were
admired and made occasions for general hilarity, for they served to
break the monotony of a purely urban life. But the great facilities
of transportation which have been introduced since the Restoration
have in these days diminished the interest of the better classes in
their city. The well-to-do men, who formerly considered it a
luxury to possess a villa on the outskirts of Tokyo, are now not
content unless they keep one at Kamakura or beyond for spending
the week-end in and another a hundred miles or more from the city

for their summer retreat. Kamakura and Enoshima, which are only thirty miles away from Tokyo, were in the old days so distant that they would not think of visiting them unless they intended to spend a few days there ; but now school-children are taken to those places on a day's excursion.   The ease with which men can leave the city has made them but lukewarm supporters of the institutions which gave the town its periodical gaiety ; for they no longer take an active part in the local festivities or pride themselves upon the fine show their ward might make on such occasions.   Even the flowers for which Tokyo is noted they go to look at in the country ; and the festivals of the tutelary deities have lost their former splendour, and their most prominent feature, the procession-cars, cannot now be built on the grand scale of the old days, for unless they can be bent low, they cannot parade the streets without snapping the innumerable electric wires which disfigure the thoroughfares of the metropolis.   Of the five great feasts which were held every year in former times, two are no longer celebrated in Tokyo, the Feast of Tanabata on the seventh day of the seventh month of the lunar calendar and the Feast of the Chrysanthemum on the ninth day of the ninth month, the remaining three being the New Year's Day on the first day of the first month, the Feast of Dolls on the third day of the third month, and that of Flags on the fifth day of the fifth month.

Still there remain many occasions on which the Tokyo cit may take his pleasure at home and abroad.   The first of these, the New Year's Day, presents the gayest appearance everywhere and is a day of general rejoicing.   On either side of the gate or front door at every house stands a large pine branch supported by an unstripped bamboo-pole or two, and overhead flies the national flag.   On the cross-beam of the gate or over the porch hangs a coil of sacred rope, to which are attached a piece of fern, a lobster, a bit of *konbu (laminaria)*, and an orange.   Indoors too, a piece of rope with a frond of fern is suspended in different rooms.   In the morning when the family gather for breakfast, a set of three wooden goblets are brought on· a stand, and the members of the household wish one another a happy New Year and drink spiced *mirin* with one of the goblets in the order of their position in the family ; and instead of the usual boiled rice, they eat cakes of pounded rice roasted and boiled in a soup of greens. This drinking of *mirin* and eating of rice-cakes is repeated on the two mornings following. On the New Year's Day people go out to present the New Year's greetings to their friends and relatives. This custom is now less observed than former-ly ; for in these days they greet one another by post, and millions of postcards pass through the Tokyo post offices in the beginning of the year. On the New Year's Day larger shops are closed, as well as offices, public and private. The streets are gay with the New Year's decorations and with people going to and fro for the New Year's greetings ; while in streets of shops and small houses young men and women and children may be seen playing at battledore and shuttlecock in the open road to the great obstruction of the thoroughfare, the fun of the game being that those who miss a shuttlecock have their faces smeared with Indian ink or white paint.

THE TREASURE-SHIP.

On the second, larger shops send out the first loads of goods for the year in hand-carts. These carts are adorned with flags bearing the names of the firms, and the shops pride themselves

THE NEW YEAR'S DECORATIONS.

upon the number of such loads they can send out on this day. In the evening hawkers come with pictures of a treasure-ship with the seven deities of fortune on board ; over the picture is written an ode of thirty-one syllables which is remarkable for being a palindrome. It runs thus :—

Na ka ki yo no to o no ne fu ri no mi na me za me na mi no ri fu ne no o to no yo ki ka na.

It will be seen that if the syllables are taken each as one sound, the ode is same when read backward. It may be translated : " They have all awakened from the long night's sleep ; and how pleasant is the sound as the ship rides the waves ! " These slips are eagerly purchased as they are supposed, if put under the pillow on this night, to give lucky dreams. The luckiest dream of all is, according to common superstition, that of Mount Fuji, next to which is a dream of a hawk, and the third that of an egg-plant.

On the fourth of January, the government offices are formally opened for the year, and other public and private offices follow suit. On the sixth the fire-brigades of Tokyo assemble in a public place and give acrobatic performances on fire-ladders to show their agility. This day closes the New Year's festivities, and the decorations are removed. On the eighth, the Emperor reviews the troops in the morning ; and on the same day most schools reopen after the New Year's holidays. The sixteenth is the holiday for apprentices and servants, who go home to their parents or spend the day at the theatres or other places of amusement. The sixth of January opens what is called the period of lesser cold and the twentieth is the first day of the period of greater cold. For a fortnight from the latter date many male votaries, especially of the artisan class, run thinly-clad at night to worship at their favourite shrines as such enthusiasm will, it is believed, make them proficient in their callings ; they ring a bell as they run. Some go to a well and pour cold water over themselves at midnight to be purified by that means from the sins of the world. Children go out before daybreak to practise their lessons, boys to read or fence and girls to sing or play the *samisen*. The shrines to which the first visit of the year should be paid are too numerous for mention.

On the second or third of February ends the period of greater cold, and with it nominally the winter season. In the evening peas are parched and thrown about in every room with the cry, " Fortune within, " and then they are flung outdoors with the shout, " Demons without. " This is to purify the house for the new spring season ; and the members of the family eat each a number of these peas, which is one in excess of the years of their age. The eleventh is one of the three great national holidays ; it is the anniversary of the coronation of Emperor Jimmu, the founder of the Japanese Imperial line, the other two being the New Year's Day and the Emperor's Birthday. There are six ordinary national holidays, namely, the anniversary of the death of Emperor Komei, the father of the present Emperor (January 30th), the Feast of the Vernal Equinox (March 21st or 22nd), when offerings are made to the Imperial ancestors on the equinoctial day, the anniversary of the death of Emperor Jimmu (April 3rd), the Feast of the Autumnal Equinox (September 23rd or 24th), the Feast of the New Season's rice which is offered at the great Shrine of Ise (October 17th), and the Feast of the New Rice which is offered to the other deities and eaten for the first time in the Imperial Palace (November 23rd).

On the third of March falls the Feast of Dolls. Towards the end of February, the dolls are brought out and tiers of shelves put up, usually against a wall of the parlour. On the highest shelf sit the Emperor and Empress, with a screen at the back and overhead a roof adorned with curtains. Below them sit the Court ladies, while lower still are the five Court musicians and two armed guards. These are the regulation dolls, and to them may be added any others. Then food is set before the Emperor and Empress on two miniature trays ; and all sorts of lilliputian household goods, such as chests of drawers, toilet stands, and kitchen utensils, are ranged on the lower tiers. Also white *sake*, which is *sake* barm dissolved in *mirin*, is offered to the dolls and drunk as well by the family. These dolls are displayed in every family where there is a daughter, and the feast is looked forward to by its female members, who invite their girl-friends to come and see the array of dolls. They are put away on the sixth or seventh.

THE FEAST OF DOLLS.

The equinoctial day is the middle of a week known as *higan*, or yonder shore, which is so called because prayers are said during the week for the souls of those on yonder shore, that is, in Nirvana. During the week dumplings and rice-cakes coated with bean-jam or sweetened bean-powder are offered to the dead and also sent as presents to friends and relatives. The family tombs are visited; and old-fashioned people worship in succession at the six great temples dedicated to Amitabha in the environs of the city, which entails a journey of some fifteen miles. Many old men and women visit different shrines on the equinoctial day as they have been told that if they pass through seven stone *torii* or shrine-gates on that day, they will not suffer pain when the time comes for them to quit this world.

In the latter part of this month the plum-trees are in full bloom. Though camellias are in flower earlier in the year, the plum-blossoms are the first of all the flowers to attract crowds of admirers. As plum-trees blossom sometimes while it still snows, the plum-tree blooming under a weight of snow is emblematic of faithfulness in adversity. The plum-blossom is not so popular as the cherry-blossom; and yet it is the subject of more odes and poems than the other. It possesses the grace and refinement which is lacking in the luxuriant clusters of cherry-blossoms. Its quiet hue, the delicacy of its fragrance, and the sense of loneliness it seems to impart appeal to the literary and poetical-minded, who go to a plum-garden with gourds of *sake* and drink under the branches to which they hang slips of paper with odes written on them in praise of the blossom. It is also associated in our poetry with the Japan bush-warbler, the most prized of our singing-birds, whose clear abrupt notes certainly sound pleasant on cold, crisp mornings of early spring. Though there are many plum-gardens in Tokyo, the most noted is that on the east side of the River Sumida, where stands an aged tree, known as the Plum-tree of the Couchant Dragon from the fancied resemblance of its gnarled trunk to the sleeping form of that fabulous animal.

At the end of March bloom the early flowers of the cherry called the *higan*-cherry; but it is in the first half of the following month that the real cherry season is in full swing. The birthday of Sakyamuni, the founder of Buddhism, is celebrated on the eighth of April, when an infusion of the *hydrangea thunbergii* is poured over a small statue of the Buddha and the liquid is sold in small

CHERRY-FLOWERS AT MUKOJIMA.

green-bamboo tubes to the votaries. It is said to be an effective charm against the breeding of maggots in summer. This ceremony of the washing of the Buddha, as it is called, is soon forgotten in the universal merriment of the cherry-flower season. The lovers of the plum-blossom may dwell upon the superior grace and delicacy of their favourite, but the darling of the nation is the cherry-flower; the former has been lauded by many a poet, but the latter is considered to be peculiarly Japanese, for no other land can boast the magnificent clusters without a leaf to break their continuity, which look in the distance like a bank of pale clouds, and when they fall, the scattering petals come down as lightly as flakes of snow. When we speak simply of *the* flower, or of the flower-time, flower-view, or flower-season, we allude invariably to the cherry-flower. The high esteem in which the cherry-blossom has always been held in Japan is exemplified in the saying, " Among men the samurai, among flowers the cherry, " which was, in the days of military ascendancy, the highest praise that could be bestowed. Again, how closely the flower is identified with the country, may be seen from the famous ode of Motoori, which runs; " Should a stranger ask what is the spirit of Japan, to him I would show the wild-cherry blossoms glinting in the morning sun. " That spirit is delicate and tarnished by dishonour as readily as the flower is scattered by the wind. The cherry-flowers bloom but for a few days; and that fact gives the motive to a celebrated *haiku,* or verse of seventeen syllables, which may be lamely translated :—

Ah, this world of ours!
But three days are gone; and where
Are the cherry-flowers?

The lightness and allusiveness of the original bring home the evanescence of life even more vividly than the snows of yester-year.

The earliest to attract crowds of pleasure-seekers is Uyeno Park, where along the walk and among other trees stand many aged cherry-trees. As the national museum and the zoological gardens are also in the park, the season attracts hosts of school-children who bring their luncheons and spend the whole day there. But it is the south-east bank of the River Sumida on the outskirts of the city, to which gather the largest throngs of sight-seers. Here an avenue of cherry-trees stretches for some miles, and men and women, as they pass under, are fairly intoxicated with the sight of the numberless clusters of cherry-blossoms. Many repair to it in parties, often in clothes of a uniform pattern and sometimes in comical guise. Next comes Asuka Hill, a few miles behind Uyeno, and then Koganei on a road west of the city, and lastly, the River Arakawa, on the north, noted for its cherry-blossoms of other colours than the usual pale pink. In the city there are many smaller spots where the blossoms may be seen to advantage.

About the same time as the cherry-flowers the peach also is in bloom; but it fails to attract many sight-seers. Towards the close of April, we have the azalea, which flowers for about a fortnight; it has not the delicate tint of the cherry-flower, and its deep red is apt to pall on the beholder. Besides, as it blooms when people are tired with gazing at the cherry-blossoms, its votaries are comparatively few, and somehow it does not arouse the enthusiasm that the national flower excites.

Late in April flower the tree-peonies; their magnificent blossoms command admiration. They are specially cultivated and need a great deal of tending; they are not, therefore, like the plum and cherry trees, often to be seen in public places, and are commonly displayed in private gardens and nurseries. The tree-peonies are not indigenous to Japan, but were originally introduced from China; and much as we admire these fine flowers, they do not appeal to us like the cherry-blossoms. A little later, the wistarias hang down their long clusters of purple flowers; they are best seen at the shrine of Tenmangu, not far from the plum-garden of the Couchant Dragon, where their pendulous racemes look doubly beautiful as they are reflected in the pond over which they hang.

The fifth of May is the Feast of Flags, which is for boys what the Feast of Dolls is for girls. On this day little flags are set up in a room, together with figures of men famous in history for their strength and valour. Outdoors a gigantic carp made of paper or cloth is tied to the top of a high pole, where it flutters when it is

THE FEAST OF FLAGS.

filled with wind ; the carp is emblematic of strength as it can swim up a rapid current.

On the fifth, sixth, and seventh of May is held the great semi-annual fête of the Yasukuni Shrine, which is dedicated to the spirits of the officers and men of the army and navy and others who died fighting for their country. Aides-de-camp are sent from the Imperial Court to make offerings at the shrine. Here firework displays and wrestling-matches take place and booths of all kinds are opened during the fête. The compound is crowded by the relatives of the dead, especially of those who fell in the Russian war, as well as the general public. The other semi-annual fête is held on the same days six months later.

Early in June the irises and sweet-flags flower ; there are gardens in Tokyo where these flowers are specially cultivated and shown to the public. June is also the month for the annual fêtes of many local deities. There are nearly fifty shrines where annual fêtes are

THE FÊTE OF SANNO.

held in Tokyo ; and the greatest of these are the Sanno and Kanda Myojin, whose fêtes were until lately among the famous sights of the city.   The fête of the Sanno takes place on the fifteenth of June, while that of the Kanda Myojin is celebrated on the same day three months later.

On the seventh of July took place the Feast of Tanabata, which is now seldom observed in Tokyo.   On this night, according to the legend, the only one in the whole year when the Weaver (the star Vega) can meet her lover the Cow-herd (the star Altair) on the other side of the Heavenly River, as the Milky Way is called, magpies come and spread their wings across the river to bring the lovers together.   And this meeting is celebrated with various offerings.   The sixteenth of the month is, like the same day in January, the holiday for apprentices and servants.   About this time, midsummer presents are exchanged between friends and relatives ; but the most important occurrence in the middle of the month is the Feast of Lanterns.   On the thirteenth, preparations are made for welcoming the spirits of the dead.   The family tomb is visited and washed, while at home the shrine is decorated with festoons of vermicelli, to which are attached ears of Italian millet and *panicum frumentaceum*, dried persimmons, and the fruit of the *torreya nucifera*, and the lower part of the shrine is enclosed with a little fence of cryptomeria.   In the evening, hemp-reeds are burnt in an earthen pan in front of the porch to receive the spirits who are then believed to enter the dwelling.   On the fourteenth, offerings are made at the shrine and a priest is often called in to recite prayers.   On the evening of the fifteenth when the spirits conclude their visit, the hemp-reeds are again burnt to speed them ; people light their pipes at the fire and smoke as a charm against diseases of the mouth and step over the embers to secure themselves against all ailments in the lower parts of the body.

About the end of July or beginning of August, the opening of the boating season on the River Sumida is celebrated with a grand display of fireworks, which is attended by large crowds from all parts of the city, while the tea-houses around are full of guests.   In August the morning-glory is in full bloom, and people repair at

THE FEAST OF LANTERNS.

dawn to Iriya in the north of Tokyo to look at the flowers for which
it is noted as the buds untwist into open blossoms, and pass on their
way home by Shinobazu Pond, close to Uyeno Park, and watch
the lotus-flowers burst open with a loud report.

On the twenty-sixth day of the seventh month of the old lunar
calendar, which falls ordinarily on some day late in August or early
in September, people climb up a hill at night or go to the water-side
to see the moon rise ; for it is considered lucky to catch a glimpse
of the three images of Amitabha which are said to be visible for an
instant before the moon comes into sight.   On the fifteenth of the
eighth month when the moon is always full, offerings of fifteen dumplings, soy beans, and persimmons are set before the moon and odes
composed in praise of the beautiful satellite.   Indeed, the eighth
month is poetically called the " month of the moon-view."

On the ninth day of the ninth month was observed in the old
days the Feast of the Chrysanthemum, when a party was held in
the Imperial Palace for looking at the flower and partaking of an
infusion of chrysanthemums in *sake ;* but this custom has died out,
and the Imperial chrysanthemum party is now given in the latter
part of November.   On the thirteenth of the same lunar month
occurs the last of the three moon-viewing festivals, when offerings
similar to those on the fifteenth of the preceding month are made,
the only difference being that the number of dumplings is thirteen
instead of fifteen.   People go out at this time to look at the Seven
Herbs of Autumn, the principal of which is the *lespedeza bicolor*
with its pretty little red flowers ; the other six are the *miscanthus
sinensis, pueraria thunbergiana, dianthus superbus, patrinia
scabiosæfolia, eupatorium chinense,* and *platycodon grandiflorum.*
The autumnal equinox is celebrated in the same manner as the
vernal.

The greatest event in October is the commemoration of the
death of Nichiren, the founder of the Buddhist sect of that name,
who died in 1282 at the temple of Honmonji, a few miles south-
west of Tokyo.   On the evening of the twelfth, the votaries leave
Tokyo in parties chanting prayers and beating flat drums ; and they
sit up all night in the temple or, if they cannot get lodging

OFFERINGS TO THE FULL MOON.

anywhere, lie down in the extensive temple-grounds. On the thirteenth, the anniversary of Nichiren's death, mass is held in great state in the temple. Even those who do not profess the Nichiren doctrines visit the temple to look at the crowds gathered there. The only other religious celebration of the kind that can compare with it is the commemoration of the death of Shinran, the founder of the Shin sect, which takes place on the twenty-eighth of November in the two great temples of Honganji in Tokyo.

On the seventeenth of October, the newly-harvested rice is offered at the great Shrine of the Sun-Goddess in the province of Ise ; and in a country where rice is the most important food, such an occasion is naturally celebrated as a national holiday. On the twentieth, the fête of Daikoku and Ebisu, the two gods of fortune, is celebrated in many merchants' houses with a great feast to which friends and relatives are invited.

The third of November is the Emperor's birthday. His Majesty reviews the troops early in the morning and holds a banquet at noon, to which the Imperial Princes, high government officials, and the foreign ambassadors and ministers are invited. A salute of a hundred and eight guns is fired in the bay ; and in the evening the minister for foreign affairs gives a ball to high officials, the diplomatic corps, and other persons of rank and position, Japanese and foreign. In this month the chrysanthemums are in full bloom ; at Dangozaka, not far from Uyeno Park, are exhibited scenes from well-known plays or representations of passing events, in which the figures are clothed with chrysanthemum flowers of various colours. They attract large crowds ; but the finest flowers are to be seen in the palace-grounds at Akasaka, where the Imperial chrysanthemum party is given, and at the mansions of noblemen and men of wealth. This month is also noted for the maple-leaves, which, when they become crimson, are highly admired ; and many people make pilgrimages to the banks of the Takinogawa, a few miles north of Uyeno Park, where they are to be seen in great profusion.

In December people are too busy with the year-end settlement of accounts and preparations for the New Year to indulge in festivities, though there are not a few easy-going men who get up towards the close of the month what are called dinners for forgetting the passing year. From the middle of the month, fairs are held in different parts of the city for the sale of articles required for the New Year's decorations and battledores and other things for the New Year's amusements. Towards the end of the month, year-end visits are paid among friends and relatives ; the New Year's decorations are put up ; and everywhere preparations are made for the New Year's festivities. At midnight of the last day, the temple-bell sounds a hundred and eight strokes to announce the passing of the old year.

CHAPTER XXII.

SPORTS AND GAMES.

Hunting—Horse-racing—Fishing—Outdoor games—Billiards—*Sugoroku*—*Iroha* cards—Ode cards—*Ken*—Japanese chess—The moves—Use of prisoners—The game of *go*—Its principle—Camps—Counting—"Flower-cards"—Players—How to play—Claims for hands—Claims for combinations made—Reckoning.

FIELD sports cannot be said to thrive in Japan. Fox-hunting, as practised in England, is unknown; indeed, hunting on a grand scale seldom takes place. Every year a large number of shooting licenses are issued; but reckless shooting has made game so scarce in the neighbourhood of Tokyo that any one in search of good sport must go a considerable distance from town. Game preserves are also very few in number, for there is scarcely one man of means in Tokyo who keeps such grounds. Nearly all the small birds are protected.

Horse-racing came into vogue soon after the Russian war. Many horse-race companies were formed; they throve as they sold pari-mutuel tickets on which they took a commission. The races became enormously popular; and people who knew nothing of horses or racing rushed in crowds to the races to buy these tickets. The thing became barefaced gambling, and so great was the scandal caused by these races that the sale of pari-mutuel tickets was prohibited, with the result that the races were entirely deserted and the shares of these companies fell from ten times their face-value to almost *nil*. Remedial measures were tried, but without success. These races had at first been encouraged by the authorities as it was believed that they would help to improve the breed of horses in Japan; but there was little prospect of that object being achieved, for the frequenters of the race-courses did not appear to take much interest in horse-racing beyond the opportunities it gave for gambling.

Fishing has many votaries. Boats put off from Shinagawa for

fishing in the Bay of Tokyo, especially in summer and autumn ; the
fish are caught either with nets or with rod and line.   Anglers may

CORMORANT-FISHING.

be seen at all seasons on the banks of the little rivers and canals
which traverse the city ; but their catch is quite insignificant.   The
most interesting method of catching fish is, perhaps, cormorant-fish-

ing in the Tamagawa, a river which runs a few miles west of Tokyo, where cormorants are, as in the River Nagara in Gifu Prefecture, which is celebrated for this form of fishing, employed to catch the *plecoglossus altivelis*, which abounds in the river. The bird has a tight ring around its crop, and when it has dived into the water and swallowed enough fish, the ring is pulled up and the bird is made to disgorge them. Another curious sight is the angling for the

ANGLING-STOOLS.

sillago. This fish is keen-sighted and very active, and takes fright and darts away as soon as it sees a boat rocking on the water. As, however, it is to be found in comparatively shallow water, a gigantic stool is set on a shoal, and the angler sits on it and patiently waits for the fish to take the bait. A boat remains not far off for emergencies, as when the angler, in his eagerness, loses his balance and goes bodily after the sillago. On a calm day, several of these stools are to be seen off the beach at Shinagawa.

Of the outdoor games which have been introduced in recent years from abroad, the oldest is, perhaps, lawn-tennis, which is still extensively played, although it must now yield in popularity to baseball. A Japanese baseball team crossed the ocean some time ago to play on the Pacific Coast of the United States, though not with very brilliant results, while similar teams have come from Hawaii and the Pacific States to challenge the Japanese college teams. Boat-racing is also very popular ; and races are held annually on the River Sumida by the Imperial University of Tokyo and other educational institutions in April when the cherry-trees are in bloom on the river-bank. Football is played to some extent, and hockey has been tried with little success, while cricket is seldom played.

Of the European indoor games, the one which has found most favour in Japan is undoubtedly billiards, at which many Japanese have attained considerable skill. Ping-pong enjoyed a temporary vogue, but has now become as obsolete as diabolo, the craze for which reached Japan not long after it arose in Europe.

We may now pass on to the principal games which are played in Japan. *Sugoroku* is a game played on a board by two persons. It is similar to backgammon, with the difference that the grand object of *sugoroku* is to get all one's men into the enemy's territory. There are twelve men on each side and twenty-four points to move to, and two dice are thrown alternately as in backgammon. It is a very ancient game which is hardly ever played nowadays ; and what

SUGOROKU

is now known as *sugoroku* was originally called the *dochu sugoroku* or travelling *sugoroku*.   The earliest of its kind is a large sheet on which the views of the fifty-three postal stations on the highway from Yedo to Kyoto are given in order in as many squares.   The starting-point is Yedo in one corner of the sheet, from which the squares are ranged along the edges until one of them touches the Yedo square, and then they are continued along the inner edges of the first squares, and still another set is formed along the edges of these second squares, until Kyoto is reached in the centre of the sheet.   Each player has a slip of paper with his name or mark inscribed on it ; it is put with the others in the Yedo square.   He throws a die in turn and moves forward according to the number turned up ; and the one who reaches Kyoto first is the winner.   As there are fifty-three squares, the minimum number of throws of the die is nine ; but the game may become complicated if, as is usually the case, the die must in the last throw turn up the exact number required for reaching the goal.   Thus, if five is turned up when only two is needed to reach Kyoto, the player is made to go back three squares from the goal and await his turn for the next throw.   Again, when a player comes to a certain square, he may be made to forfeit a turn or go back a number of squares.   When these rules are introduced, the game is very much prolonged. Hence, later forms of *sugoroku* have a smaller number of squares ; indeed, if, further, the place to move to is named in every square for every number turned up, a very few squares will suffice ; and some *sugoroku* have no more than a dozen squares and yet an exciting game may be played on them.

Sugoroku is played in the long winter evenings, and especially during the first days of the New Year.   Among other New Year's games may be mentioned the cards known as the *Iroha* and *uta* cards.   *Iroha*, being the first three characters of the Japanese syllabary or alphabet, is the name given to the whole syllabary ; and the *iroha* cards are so called because they have inscribed on them each a proverbial saying beginning with a different character of the syllabary.   There are forty-seven characters in the Japanese syllabary, and another card is added to make the number even and divisible. Besides the pack of forty-eight cards with the proverbs, there is another of the same number of cards with pictures corresponding to these proverbs; these latter have also marked in the corner the first character of the proverbs they illustrate to facilitate identification. Thus, if the card in the first pack has the proverb, *inu mo arukeba bō ni ataru* (A dog, by walking, may come upon a stick, a saying which is now taken to mean that by wandering about, one may meet with good fortune), the corresponding card in the other pack has a picture of a dog knocking against a stick and

IROHA AND ODE CARDS.

the character *i* in the corner. The card of the second character of the syllabary has the proverb, *ron yori shōko* (Proof is better than argument), and the third has *hana yori dango* (Better a dumpling than a flower, that is, use is better than ornament), and so on. The illustrations in the second pack are often fanciful, as they cannot but be when the proverbs do not refer to concrete objects. Thus, the illustration to the second proverb above given has an angry man with one hand on his sword and holding in the other the straw

PLAYING ODE-CARDS.

figure which the jealous wife used in the old days to nail to a tree at dead of night when she invoked curses upon her rival. The man is apparently showing his wife in spite of her protestations the straw image she has been using against his mistress. The game is played sometimes by spreading all the pictures in the middle and the players sitting around them. One person reads out the proverbs in any order he pleases, and the corresponding pictures are seized and put away. The player who has taken the largest number of cards in this way is the winner. The game, however, is more frequently played in the following manner :—The cards are dealt evenly among the players who spread them out exposed before them. When a proverb is read out, a player takes out the corresponding picture if he has it, and if not, he looks over the other players' hands and seizes the card as soon as he sees it. He takes it and gives one of his own exposed cards to the player from whose hand he has taken it. A slow-witted person's hand is always full, while a sharp player clears his quickly ; and the one who has first got rid of his hand is the winner. As the cards are often pounced upon at the same time by several players, the game is an exciting one, and not a few come out of it with their hands scratched and bleeding. Friends and relatives of both sexes join in these games in winter evenings, and some of them, it is said, consider it the best part of the game that they can touch or squeeze the hands of the players of the opposite sex by pretending to seize the same cards. For this reason, a strict paterfamilias not unfrequently forbids his household to play the game with those who are not its members.

The *uta* or ode cards are in two sets of a hundred each. There is a famous collection of a hundred odes composed by as many poets, which used in former days to be learnt by heart. These odes are used for the ode-cards. An ode, as has been explained in a former chapter, is made up of two couplets of five and seven syllables each, closing with a line of seven syllables. For the purposes of the cards, the odes are divided into two parts, the first comprising the first three lines, that is, the lines of five, seven, and five syllables, and the second the last two lines of seven syllables.

The cards in one set give each the whole ode with the name and picture of the poet, while in those of the other set appears generally the second part, and rarely the first part, of the ode. Thus, in the first set the first ode of the hundred runs :—

Tenji Tenno	*Aki no ta no*	*Kariho no iwo no*
	Toma wo arami	
	Waga koromode wa	*Tsuyu ni*
	nuretsutsu.	
(Emperor Tenji	Decayed is the rush-thatch of the watch-shed in the autumn rice-field, And the sleeves of the robe are becoming wet with dew).	

And the card of the second set has the lines *Waga koromode wa Tsuyu ni nuretsu.* The game is played in the same mannner as the *iroha* cards ; and the scramble for the cards is more exciting as the players do not always wait till the whole ode is read out.

There is a curious diversion called the game of *ken,* or fists, which, its name notwithstanding, has nothing to do with pugilism. The principle of the game is that there are three positions of the hands or fingers, each one of which beats one and is beaten by the other, of the remaining two. The game is played with one or two hands. That played with both hands is called the fox-*ken* ; its three positions are the putting of the open hands with the palms outward close to the temples in imitation of the fox, the stretching out of the right arm with the hand closed while the left hand is brought to the breast, which represents the huntsman with a gun, and the placing of both hands on the knees to show the staid manners of the village headman. The fox may bewitch the headman as that animal is popularly believed to possess magical powers, but may be killed by the huntsman, who, however, must not shoot the headman ; thus, the fox beats the headman, who beats the huntsman, who, in his turn, beats the fox. The game is played by two persons, who must move their hands with uniform rapidity, for the game is spoilt if either side moves more quickly or slowly than the other. It is a favourite game at convivial parties, especially if one of the parties is a geisha, though it is not so popular now as it used to be. The person who beats the other three times running is declared the winner, and the defeated party has, as forfeit, to drink a cup of *sake*. The stone-*ken* is played with one hand; in this the closed hand represents a stone, the open hand a piece of paper, and two fingers or a finger and the thumb spread out a pair of scissors; the stone may be wrapped in the paper, but is proof against the scissors, which may, however, cut the paper. This *ken* is played

THE GAME OF *KEN.*

less often as a game than for deciding in a case where one would toss a coin in England, for tossing up is unknown in Japan.

The Japanese indoor games we have above described are played mostly by children and young men and women, with the exception of the fox-*ken*, which is almost confined to convivial parties. The great serious games for grown-up people in the evenings, or in the daytime for that matter, are chess, *go*, and "flower-cards."

Shōgi, or Japanese chess, is played on a board with nine

squares a side, or altogether eighty-one squares.   There are twenty
men on each side.   The nine men on the end-row are the king in
the middle, with *kinsho* (gold general), *ginsho* (silver general), *keima*
(knight), and *kyosha* (kind of rook) on either side ; on the second
row the men are *hisha* (rook proper) and *kakko* (bishop) on the
second square from the right and left ends respectively ; and the
third row is filled with pawns.   The pieces are all of the same form ;
they have each a base with two converging sides surmounted by
two others which make an obtuse angle at the apex, and are thicker
at the base than at the top so that they can readily stand, though
they are always laid flat.   The name of each piece is written on the
upper surface.   The largest of these men is the king, next to which
are the pieces on the second row, followed by the men on the end-
row, while the smallest are the pawns.

The king can move one square in any direction ; the *kinsho*
has the same moves except to the diagonals behind ; and the *ginsho*
moves one square forward and diagonally in the four directions ;
and the *keima* and the *kyosha* have, one the forward moves only of
the knight and the other the forward move only of the rook.   The
hisha and the *kakko* have the same moves as the rook and the
bishop respectively. The pawns move one square forward and take
the hostile pieces in front and not diagonally.   When the pieces
enter the enemy's territory, that is, within the furthest three rows,
they are not queened as there are no queens in *shōgi*, they acquire
the moves of *kinsho*.   In that case they forfeit their own moves,
with the exception of the *hisha* and *kakko*, which retain them.
When the pieces are thus changed in character, they are turned
the reverse side up.

The capture of the men and checking of the king are the same
as in European chess ; but stalemate is unknown, for the reason that
we can make use of any pieces of our adversary that we may have
taken, and if our king is in danger, we can readily defend him by
putting in the field some of our prisoners.   This causes no inconvenience as there is no distinction of colour between the hostile
pieces ; their side is shown by the direction of the pointed ends of
the pieces.   The enemy's pieces may be brought into requisition in

his own territory; but they must move at least one square forward before they can be converted into *kinsho*.

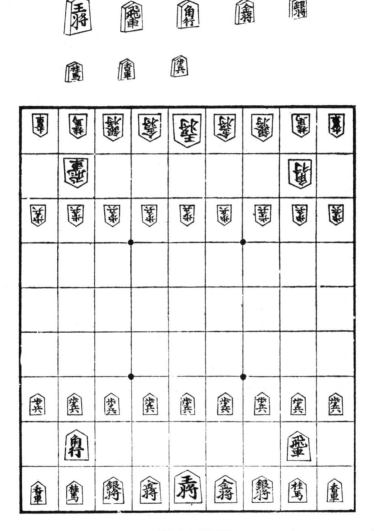

JAPANESE CHESS.

Shogi is universally played; but it is more especially the favourite game of the lower classes. Among the better classes, *go* is in greater vogue; it is much affected by retired old gentlemen, officials, school-teachers, and others of the professions. It is certainly more difficult and probably more scientific than the other.

Go is played on a thick square board with heavy legs. The surface is marked with nineteen parallel lines crossed by as many similar lines, making the total number of points of intersection three hundred and sixty-one. The game is played on these points, and not in the squares formed by the parallel lines ; and like *shôgi*, two persons take part in it. Either side has a box of round, flattish pebbles small enough to be placed without overlapping on consecutive points. They are distinguished by colour ; and the black is always given to the poorer player who opens the game, while the other takes the white.

The object of the game is to take as many as possible of the enemy's stones by surrounding them with one's own. A stone once

THE GAME OF *GO*.

put on a point is immovable unless it is surrounded and taken off the board ; it cannot move from one point to another. This siege of the enemy's stone lies in cutting it off along the lines passing through the point it occupies. The siege is successful in its simplest form when a single stone is surrounded on the four adjacent points on the two lines intersecting at its point. There is no way of breaking the square formed by these four stones, for the only way in which relief can be brought to a threatened stone is to make it a part of a chain which cannot be completely surrounded by the enemy. When a stone is thus surrounded on all sides, it becomes a prisoner and is taken off the board. A stone at a corner of the board is imprisoned by two stones as there are no other adjacent points, and one on the edge by three stones. In a word, a stone cannot act diagonally, but must always work along a line. In practice, of course, it is usually a group of stones, rather than single stones, that find themselves prisoners, as the siege operations are more difficult to detect when carried out on a large scale.

If it was only to surround the enemy and capture his stones, the game would be comparatively simple. It is complicated by the formation of vacant enclosures, within which if the enemy ventures, he must infallibly be captured. The object is to make these enclosures as large as possible, and since such camps, as they are called, would narrow the enemy's field of operations, he does his best to break the cordon by intruding a chain of stones before it is completed. Hence, there are four operations going on at the same time : we must break up the enemy's attempted cordon and surround his stones, and prevent his surrounding our stones and form our own cordons. This formation of camps, though really nothing more than a defensive measure, is in fact more important and difficult than the capture of the enemy's stones ; and the issue of the game depends generally more upon the size of these cordons than upon the number of prisoners actually taken.

Though the game should theoretically be continued till the board is completely filled with stones, it is seldom pursued to that extent; for where there is a great inequality of skill, the issue can be seen long before the finish and the game given up, or where camps have been formed, the vacant spaces need not be filled in. In most cases, therefore, plenty of stones remain in hand. When the game is finished, the number of points enclosed by the camps, if any, is counted and reckoned as so many stones gained ; and the difference between it and the number of prisoners in the enemy's hands is one's net gain or loss according as the former is greater or less than the latter. And the one with the larger net gain is naturally the winner.

Neither *shogi* nor *go* is a lively game. The latter, especially, calls for patience and hard thinking ; it may take hours or even days to conclude a single game. Besides. it does not lend itself to betting. The great gambling game is that of the cards known as " flower-cards," which is rapidly played and depends more upon chance than upon skill.

The pack is made up of forty-eight cards, about an inch by an inch and a half, which are in twelve sets, each set representing a month of the year. The first set has a picture of the pine-tree, which, being the principal part of the New Year's outdoor decorations, symbolises the first month. It is followed in order by the plum-tree, cherry-tree, wistaria, sweet-flag, tree-peony, and lespedeza, which flower in the second, third, fourth, fifth, sixth, and seventh months respectively. The eighth month is represented by the eularia, the ninth by the chrysanthemum, the tenth by the maple-tree, the eleventh by the willow-tree, and the last by the paulownia. It may be stated in passing that these months follow the old lunar calendar and are therefore some weeks later than the corresponding months of the solar calendar. All the cards are not of the same value. The highest, which is twenty points, is assigned to the pine-tree with a crane in the middle and a red sun above, the cherry-tree in bloom with a curtain underneath for a picnic party, the eularia under the full harvest moon, the willow under which a great scholar is learning perseverance from a frog which succeeds after many hours' vain attempts in reaching a branch, and the paulownia with the phœnix flying over it. Ten points each are given to nine cards, namely, the plum-tree with the bush-warbler, the wistaria with the cuckoo, the sweet-flag beside a plank path, the tree-peony with butterflies, the lespedeza with the wild boar, the eularia with wild ducks, the chrysanthemum with a wooden cup for the chrysanthemum-*sake*, the maple-tree with the stag, and the willow-tree with the swallow. Five points are the value of the cards with a *tanzaku*, a long strip of paper for an ode ; there are ten

"FLOWER-CARDS."

of them, that is, all the sets except the eularia and paulownia. The remaining twenty-four cards are worth only a point each. Thus, five cards at twenty points, nine at ten points, ten at five, and twenty-four at a point each, make the total value of the pack two hundred and sixty-four points.

The game is played by three persons. As many as six may join in it and the cards be dealt to them ; but three of them must throw up their hands. First, the dealer declares whether he will play or not and is followed in order by the rest. If any players remain after three have declared their intention to play, such persons may quietly give up play or, if their hands are good, they may insist upon being bought out. The player who has a free choice and elects not to play, has to pay a forfeit, from which those forced to retire are exempted. The players may be reduced to two, and sometimes only to one, in which case he is declared the winner.

The cards are first dealt out seven to each player and six others are turned up on the table. The players who retire return their cards, which are shuffled into the pile of undealt cards. When it has been settled who are to play, the dealer, or if he does not play, the one nearest to him looks at his hand to see if he has one of the same suit as any of the open cards ; if he has, he takes the latter with his card and put the two aside ; but if he has none to match or thinks it disadvantageous to take a card, he throws down a card which has no match on the table. Next, he takes the top card of the pile and opens it ; if it matches with any of the open cards on the table, he takes the pair and puts them aside : but if it does not match, he throws it down exposed among the open cards. The others follow in the same manner. As the number of cards in the three hands is twenty-one and six are open on the table, the undealt cards also number twenty-one ; and as every player matches or throws down a card in his hand and opens one of the pile, the last card of the last player is played when the last of the pile is turned up. The players then reckon the total value of the cards in their possession ; and according as that value is more or less than eighty-eight, which is one-third of the value of the whole pack, the difference between the two represents their gain or loss. The winner of the largest number also gets the forfeits paid by the retired players.

This is the simplest form of the game. It is usually complicated by claims allowed for certain combinations found in the hands dealt. Thus, if three of the seven cards are of the same suit, the holder can claim a forfeit of one and a half dozen points from each of the other two ; the forfeit becomes two dozen points for two or more *tanzaku* cards among plain ones, three dozens for a plain hand with only one card of a higher value, four dozens for three pairs of suits or a complete hand of plain cards, six dozens for two sets of three cards of the same suit, and so on to the highest which is twenty dozens for four cards of one suit and three of another.

Then again, if certain sets of cards are won in the course of a game, that game is closed and the value for such sets is claimed from each of the other two. Thus, six dozen points are allowed for the three purple-*tanzaku* cards of the chrysanthemum, tree-peony, and maple, or the three red-*tanzaku* cards of the pine, plum, and cherry trees, and ten dozens for the four twenty-point cards of the pine, cherry, eularia, and paulownia, and twelve dozens if that of the willow is added to them.

These payments for combinations make the game very exciting. Twelve games, to match with the months of the year, make a rubber, at the end of which the reckoning is made. For counting purposes two sets of counters are distributed, one of the value of one point each and the other of a dozen points. First, counters to the amount of ten dozen points are allotted to each player ; but of this amount three or four dozens are pooled to be given to the highest winner of the rubber, and so that lucky person really gets far more than his actual winnings. When a player has gone through his first lot of counters, he borrows more from the bank. At the end of a rubber when the settlement is made, the payment, if the game is played for money, is made at so much per point ; and even though the unit may be of a small value, the total account often comes to a respectable sum.

MORE ABOUT KPI BOOKS

If you would like further information about books available from
KPI please write to

> The Marketing Department
> KPI Limited
> Routledge & Kegan Paul Plc
> 14 Leicester Square
> London WC2H 7PH

In the USA write to

> The Marketing Department
> KPI Limited
> Routledge & Kegan Paul
> 9 Park Street
> Boston
> Mass 02108

In Australia write to

> The Marketing Department
> KPI Limited
> Routledge & Kegan Paul
> c/o Methuen Law Book Company
> 44 Waterloo Road
> North Ryde, NSW 2113
> Australia

KPI